JUSTIFIED ANGER

JENNIFER COLNE

Paperback: 978-1-964744-50-6
eBook: 978-1-964744-51-3
Library of Congress Control Number: 2024914173

Ordering Information:

Prime Seven Media
518 Landmann St.
Tomah City, WI 54660

Printed in the United States of America

TABLE OF CONTENTS

ACKNOWLEDGEMENTS

F irst, I would like to thank my Mum who has been my rock through everything including helping me to write this book. She has listened and given me advice and when needed; constructive criticism, sometimes in the early hours of the morning. You have also had similar feelings of anger, frustration, and helplessness. However, your kindness and generosity has shown throughout the turmoil and devastation we have encountered through our lifetime.

Without the support and encouragement from my youngest daughter this book would never have been written.

Thank you for allowing me to share your innermost thoughts and feelings. You are an inspiration which can help to influence others who may experience a similar situation. This horrendous journey you have had to endure has made you the person you are today. I am so proud of the way you have overcome all the heartache and disappointment and turned something so negative into something positive.

Thank you to others who have contributed to this book and shared their sensitive stories. My daughter's Psychotherapist and a good friend thank you for your patience, expertise and guiding my daughter towards the light and bestowing her with the confidence to achieve her goals.

Thank you to all my friends for giving me the encouragement and your valued input in this revised copy of Justified Anger.

Our thanks goes to the Solicitor for believing in us. We will forever be in your debt and never forget how you fought our case and found the Professor who listened and helped my daughter in her hour of need.

Last, but certainly not least, to a very dear friend for your loving and helpful support you provided at those distressing times, thank you.

PREFACE

The front cover depicts the context of the whole story. Pieces of the diary are the inner child's feelings and emotions of Emma the adult.

Emma used her non dominant hand to communicate with her inner child. The inner child is her younger self.

I learned how the wounded inner child cannot develop emotionally and witnessed through personal experience how painful and distressing it was to acknowledge that.

When a child is abused; physically, mentally or sexually and feels abandoned, the pain he/she felt then, is always there but has been camouflaged by the false personality of the human as they grow into an adult.

The inner child remains rooted in the subconscious, meaning it is mostly hidden from the conscious mind. If the young life of a child has been damaged from an early age, he/she has the ability to bury the feelings and emotions with the hurt and pain the child suffered at the time. The inner child needs to be healed and nurtured to find peace.

The adult then becomes the person he/she is meant to be.

CHAPTER 1

Katherine Year 2001

"Mum, lock all your doors!"

"Hi Katherine," before I could say anything else the phone went dead. Recently, my daughter had been experiencing irrational behaviour, that phone call had disturbed my psyche. It was hard to get those particular words out of my head; about an hour later I decided to contact

Katherine's primary nurse on the mental health ward at our local hospital, believing she was in a safe environment I had not responded to the earlier phone call.

After asking for her in person, Nurse Williams answered the phone,

"Hello Mrs. Colne, can I help you?"

"Yes, Katherine rang earlier I am a bit worried about what she said." After repeating what Katherine had told me; the nurse explained, "She is in her room, to put your mind at rest I will check on her, and ring you back."

It was twenty minutes later when the phone rang, at first I was expecting a positive response; until I heard the Nurse's tone of voice.

"Mrs. Colne I don't want to alarm you; but your daughter seems to be missing."

"What! Have you looked everywhere? Oh my God, where is she? she has been saying all sorts of weird things lately, she spoke of killing herself; she has already cut herself with a razor blade, find her, please find her." Nurse Williams sensed my fear.

"Mrs. Colne we are doing everything we can. If she makes contact, please let us know? Try not to worry we will find her, she has probably gone to the shop in the hospital with one of the other patients, we will let you know as soon as we hear something."

For quite a while there was no response, my irrational thoughts were doing somersaults; the motorway was just around the corner from the hospital, I imagined Katherine stood on the edge of the motorway bridge looking down watching the traffic speeding beneath her; one step and it could all be over. Shivering at the thought, terrified of my imagination; she is only twenty-four years old; with her whole life in front of her. Not being able to wait any longer I rang the hospital, a nursing assistant answered.

"Have they found her yet?" Shouting, as the poor individual on the other end of the phone had no idea of what I was talking about.

"My daughter has been missing for ages and I want to know what is happening I am going out of my mind."

The young assistant replied, "Please wait while I find a staff nurse to speak to you."

It seemed such a long while before Nurse Williams came to the phone.

"Mrs. Colne we are still in the process of looking for your daughter; we will let you know as soon as we find her."

She tried to convince me that Katherine would be fine. I knew something was wrong, feeling helpless, unable to do anything. Trying to get on with my housework, lunchtime came and went I could not face any food; just waiting to hear the phone ring.

I had spoken to my husband to let him know the situation, he was looking after his mum, he did offer to come home but I told him I would let him know as soon as the nurse rings me.

Not long after, the phone rang.

"Mrs. Colne?"

"Yes,"

"Katherine is having a lie down in her room, we have just given her some PRN. (Extra medication to the prescribed dose). I think it would be better for her if you visit tomorrow as she will be quite sedated for the rest of the day."

I had so many questions to ask, *Is she alright? Where has she been?* relieved with the news that she was safe I told Nurse Williams to give Katherine my love and that I will see her tomorrow. I immediately rang her father with the news.

It took me ages to find a parking place, time was moving on and I could not wait to see Katherine and find out what had happened the day before.

Finally I managed to squeeze my husband's Cortina Estate into the only space available. It was just a short walk from the car park.

I walked through the double doors and followed the sign for the Mental Health Ward.

This was different from the day before yesterday when Katherine was moved from A&E, (Accident & Emergency) she had seen the Psychiatric Consultant who was on duty at that time, I had explained about her bouts of depression, her self-harm and having suicidal thoughts.

He suggested Katherine stay in hospital for a short while as a voluntary patient until they have assessed her.

A nurse had taken us down to the ward by the lift I did not take any notice of where we were and how we got there. She had asked me to sit in the waiting area while they got Katherine settled.

There were comfortable chairs, and all kinds of information attached to the walls mostly about mental health. Deciding to position myself opposite the door into the ward I had hoped I could see what was happening. Unfortunately a young nurse pulled it to before making her way towards the Picu Ward (Psychiatric Intensive Care Unit).

Twenty minutes had passed when the nurse came out and said I could go and see her, but I would have to leave soon. She showed me to my daughter's room.

Katherine looked so uncomfortable in her surroundings. I did not want to leave her there in such a dismal environment; the pale green walls gave the room a cold feeling. The single bed with a yellow blanket covered the crisp white sheets and one pillow, she always had two at home. She let me unpack her small holdall. There was little room for any personal belongings, trying to make it homely I placed a teddy which she had treasured for years on the chest of drawers at the side of her bed. Luckily, she had her personal stereo, thank goodness she had music to listen to. There was a knock on the door, the nurse entered and said,

"Mrs. Colne I am sorry but I have to ask you to leave the Doctor is coming onto the ward." I put my arms around Katherine, but there was little response. She was lethargic, she managed a slight smile when I kissed her gently on the cheek; in a quiet voice I whispered,

"I will see you tomorrow."

Wait for the lift or walk down two flights of stairs, I took the latter. There were no pictures or paintings on the dull magnolia walls which would have helped to distinguish the cold, eerie feeling as I descended, tiptoed to avoid the echoing sound of my footsteps from my stiletto heels against the solid concrete steps; to my relief I reached the bottom, turned left, and opened a door into a darkened corridor, there was no one about; yet it was visiting time. Imagining there would be plenty of people around at that time waiting to visit their loved ones or friends of the patients. Not even Doctors or Nurses were to be seen.

When I reached my destination, I popped my finger on the bell below the small unbreakable glass window and waited for someone to appear. Eventually, after I had pressed the button countless times a lady dressed in a formal uniform came to take my particulars.

"Name please?" she said in a very abrupt manner, as if I had interrupted her coffee break.

"Ok, you can push the door."

Just as I was entering the room, a young girl made a dash to get through the gap before the door closed; fortunately, a man in uniform managed to stop her, it all happened within a split second. I completely ignored the situation, continuing to take notice of the directions towards the female ward. There were all kinds of peculiar sounds, some were wailing, others were shouting and screaming, turning a corner I could see a young lady being restrained by three staff. Then I heard the words.

"Get off me! Let me go home!" *That was Katherine's voice!* Immediately I ran towards them, just as I was catching up to her a nurse shouted my name.

"Mrs. Colne I need to speak to you please come in here for a moment," I turned back and reluctantly stepped into an office.

"What on earth is going on?" Demanding some explanation,

"Katherine is experiencing a great deal of emotional pain; she is very confused."

"Can you help her?" I asked despairingly.

"Yes, after the doctor has been to see her, we can sedate her, we are just waiting for him to come on to the ward."

I began to question the nurse after she had introduced herself as Nurse Williams, Katherine's Primary Nurse.

"What happened yesterday, where did you find her?"

Nurse Williams became more empathic,

"Please sit down," she politely showed me a seat.

"This is going to be distressing for you, by being a voluntary patient Katherine was allowed to come and go as she pleases, we did not have a right to detain her; she had left the building.

Another nurse and I found her about a mile away from the hospital." She hesitated, not knowing how to explain the rest of the situation. She leaned towards me and softly put her hand on mine and explained,

"Katherine was on her way home," I interrupted,

"What! Walking! It's such a long way." The nurse continued,

"She was confused, she told us she was going home to Kill her Family."

I was stunned, feeling physically sick after realising what Katherine was planning.

"My daughter wanted to kill us! It doesn't make sense."

I had tears in my eyes; the nurse passed me the box of tissues conveniently placed on the table next to me.

"Would you like a cup of tea?" Nodding politely as I was wiping my nose.

Nurse Williams left the office to find an assistant to make me a drink, I desperately wanted to see Katherine; I explained to the nurse when she returned,

"I need to see her".

"Maybe tomorrow afternoon, she is having some quiet time in the Picu Ward."

Ten minutes later I was walking back down the corridor, I do not know how I made my way out of the hospital, from what I had just heard I was in a state of shock.

How can I tell her dad? How can I tell anybody? I thought, *what is happening to our daughter? This is not like Katherine, she is usually fun-loving, happy, and content with her teaching job; she is fantastic with young children, so patient and*

understanding, with such a wonderful personality; then I remembered those last words she spoke to me.

"Mum, lock all your doors!"

So that was why Katherine rang; she was trying to protect us from herself.

Months later Katherine was no better and mentally deteriorating. The Consultant had already put her on a Section Two to assess her mental state. She was also on a ten-minute observation level; which meant she could not leave the ward and monitored on a regular basis.

Attending all the weekly ward rounds was not easy as Katherine was quite uncooperative. The Consultant had spoken about a Section Three if Katherine did not show any improvement.

Before the next ward round my husband and I received a letter to attend as Katherine's next of kin.

Katherine, an approved Social Worker, Katherine's General Practitioner, the Psychiatric Consultant, and the Ward Manager were all there waiting for our arrival.

When all the paperwork was completed and the relevant forms had been signed Section Three was explained to Katherine, her father and me. Although Katherine could not understand what was being said as she was so sedated she just agreed to everything.

We were able to spend a little time with her provided an escort accompanied us.

We went into the small garden adjacent to the room and sat on the wooden bench holding her hands, she was oblivious to what was happening.

Ten minutes later Katherine was escorted to the Picu ward where she would be staying for at least the next six months. My husband had said his goodbyes to Katherine, while I followed behind with her belongings.

We were entering what the nurse referred to as the 'bubble' which had three doors, one leading to the Picu Ward, one which can be entered from the outside when I come to visit and the one, we had just come from. The Nurse opened the first door with a key that was attached to a whole set of keys from a chain clipped to the nurse's belt. She then turned and proceeded to lock the door from which we had just entered.

We were all locked in the bubble which felt quite claustrophobic; then the nurse pressed a buzzer, someone came to look through a small pane of unbreakable glass. The nurse smiled as if to show that all was safe and secure.

This tall male nurse unlocked the door to the Picu Ward and we all entered, he quickly shut the door behind us and locked it, he too was carrying a large bunch of keys also attached to his person. We were shown into a large room, it was so quiet, the first thing that took me by surprise and completely unexpected were the bars against the windows which made one feel like a captive in a huge prison cell. The windows were long and let a great deal of light in; when they were opened, the tiny gap allowed a small amount of much needed fresh air into the room, it was the only thing that represented reality from the world outside. They each had metal shutters at the side which were closed and securely locked at night. I noticed a couple of nurses standing around and two female patients were sat in the middle of which I presume was the communal area. The television was turned on; one of the patients was staring at the screen, while the other was reading a magazine chosen from the stack piled neatly on the coffee table situated in front of six comfortable armchairs.

It was inviting and peaceful until I heard the rattle of keys; a nurse was unlocking a door into the small kitchen where a male patient was asking for a drink, only the staff were allowed to enter, the patients had to stand and wait outside the door for whatever they requested, drinks, crisps, biscuits etc. To the right of the kitchen was a large round table where male and female patients sat together to eat meals. Two staff looked after mealtimes; one would take a trolley down to the acute ward's kitchen with a menu from which the patients had chosen. The other nurse put plastic cups of juice on a trolley, plastic cutlery, and unbreakable plates ready for when the nurse returned with the hot or cold meals including deserts of their choice.

Everything was safe and secure as some of the patients on the Picu ward can present irrational behaviour, they can also be unpredictable and impulsively throw things. Nothing is available that can be a danger, even the staples in the magazines are removed as any sharp item can become an instrument for self-harm. All the furniture is bolted to the floor, including the television which is secured to the wall.

If any patient becomes aggressive and difficult to handle there is a small room which the staff call seclusion, it has a huge mattress where a patient can chill out and take their time to come down from a manic state, this is provided for the safety of the patient, other service users and the staff.

Katherine's room was basic, with just a single bed, clean white linen and a duvet, a fitted wardrobe and two cupboards under a melamine surface with a small sink. All her toiletries had to be locked away. At first

I could not understand this but when I realised these people are really disturbed and can have intrusive thoughts.

The safety is paramount in the Picu ward, and everything has got to be taken into consideration.

The things we take for granted can be a wonderful treat for the inpatients on the Picu ward. All their personal belongings are forbidden in the lounge area, such as personal stereos and mobile phones which can only be used with permission from the staff in their own rooms. There is a smoke room but there must be a member of staff present (hard work if you do not smoke it is like an opium den as there is no window to let the fumes out).

"Another ten minutes Mrs. Colne." I nodded reluctantly, I did not want to leave Katherine in this place, but I knew it was the best thing for her, and that I would see her tomorrow.

CHAPTER 2

Emma Year 2001

I t was 7pm on a dark cold January evening when there was a knock at the door, I thought; *who can this be?* I was just sitting down to watch my favourite soap on TV. I opened the door to find a stout middle-aged gentleman; he looked very official wearing a suit under his large mohair overcoat and carrying a briefcase. After introducing himself as a court official and showing his I.D. I enquired,

"Can I help you?" he asked if Emma Colne lives here? I replied,

"No, but she is here at the moment." I invited him into my home and showed him into the lounge. Emma had already heard her name mentioned and immediately stood up and walked towards this stranger. He opened his briefcase and took out a very formal looking piece of paper which he handed over to Emma. After scanning the page, a few words came to her attention she read them out loud.

"Be in Beddington County Court for 10.30am," she began to cry,

"Mum he can't do this to me, I can't believe that Carl is taking me to court for the temporary residence of Jodie and Zak."

The gentleman apologised and said in so many words,

"I am sorry I had to deliver this document in person." He was very thoughtful as he gave Emma his best wishes and made his way towards the door, I thanked him and showed him out.

I went back into the lounge where Emma was sitting on the sofa reading the formal notice word for word and re- reading it in case she had misunderstood anything.

With tears in her eyes she looked up at me and said,

"Mum what am I going to do?" Immediately I had to show a positive attitude and began to organize everything.

"Tomorrow we will find you a family solicitor," I tried to sound convincing by saying,

"Don't worry you're their Mum, there's no way any judge will take your children off you."

All the time I was terrified as Carl had got the children and that he had already stopped

Emma from seeing them. He was using Emma's mental health against her. The stress was proving too much for Emma and she began to have a panic attack, I thought. ***How dare he do this to my daughter; she needs compassion not emotional attacks.***

The following day I searched through directory enquiries and found a firm in the city. I dialled the number; a young voice answered the phone and I asked if I could speak to one of their family solicitors. I made an appointment for 10.30 the next morning.

Emma and I crossed the road from the bus station, it was 10.15 we had enough of time to look for Clifton & Singer Solicitors. It was all very strange as I had never had any dealings with solicitors before except for business reasons. We soon found our destination after following the directions the lady had given to me when I made the appointment. I opened the door and began to climb a narrow staircase leading to three doors, someone was just exiting one I enquired,

"Excuse me is this Clifton and Singer?" he replied,

"Yes," We both entered after the kind gentleman held open the door for us. I thanked him and we walked towards the reception desk. We were told in a very pleasant manner to take a seat.

"Mrs. Jenkins won't be long," the young assistant offered us tea or coffee, we both thanked the lady and politely declined the offer.

Approximately five minutes passed, a tall lady with shoulder length blonde hair came to greet us, we followed her into her office where a large table was cluttered with papers and files of all sizes. We were invited to sit down, and Mrs. Jenkins asked,

"How can I help you?" I spoke, as Emma by that time was getting quite agitated. After I had given Mrs. Jenkins a brief description as to why we needed her help she enquired?

"Why does your boy-friend feel he has a right to take you to court for the temporary residence of your children?"

I was then put into a difficult position; I felt I had to explain all about Emma and Katherine's situation and how it had affected both girls. I described it in brief as I was not there for that reason, I needed to sort out this court appearance as soon as possible, but Mrs. Jenkins had other ideas. She asked,

"Have you heard of Criminal Injuries Compensation?" Frowning, I shook my head and said,

"No," She immediately began to explain what it was. I was getting quite impatient and not listening properly to what she was saying, my main concern was to stop Carl from being able to take Emma's children away from her.

She soon put my mind at ease by explaining about this barrister who is excellent in cases like this and would look after Emma; Mrs. Jenkins excused herself whilst she made a few phone calls.

Leaving Emma and I alone frightened and apprehensive, I tried to make Emma feel positive about the situation as I had heard of this Barrister from a friend who I had rang the night before asking for advice.

She had worked for Social Services and mentioned this Barrister's name and that all the Social Workers who came up against him in court were terrified knowing that he won most of his cases.

Approximately ten minutes later Mrs. Jenkins returned with a slight smile on her lips.

"Well, we have got Geoffrey Barracks he is brilliant." *Thank God,* I thought to myself that name was just what I was hoping for. She then told us where and what time to meet him. Just as we were making our way to the door and thanking her for her help, she asked us to go into another office and complete two criminal injuries application forms.

Katherine was at the time still on the acute Ward, so I applied on her behalf and Emma answered questions that were being directed at her from a lady on the other side of the desk, they were not easy questions in fact they specified very personal and emotional ones.

This went on for some time. I had to write down what Katherine had told me; it was difficult to find the right words without showing too much emotion.

I was so pleased when we were escorted to the front door, shaking hands, and thanking the lady.

It had been a long day and an emotional one I just wanted to get home and I could see on Emma's face, she felt the same.

Court House

Emma and I arrived at 10.15am we were not due to see Geoffrey Barracks till 10.30am.

As we went through the automatic doors with the words 'Entrance' above, there were two court officials in uniform; I could see they both had radios strapped to their belts, I would not have been surprised if they were carrying a firearm. They looked and sounded serious when they told me to put my handbag on the conveyer belt enabling them to check the contents before proceeding any further. Then Emma walked towards this female also dressed in a similar uniform to her colleagues, in an abrupt manner she was told to stretch her legs and arms so that she could frisk her looking for any kind of object that could be used as a weapon. It was my turn, Emma watched me as I tried to smile and let her know everything was just protocol.

I understand the process for safety reasons, but it is so undignified, someone's hand moving across your person. I was thankful when that was over and we were shown up a long staircase, through double doors into a large room.

A uniformed gentleman escorted us to a desk at the far end where we had to sign in, then we were asked to sit and wait for Emma's Barrister to arrive. There were not many vacant seats left, looking round the room in the far corner we noticed two seats available. Immediately Emma made her way towards them in case someone else had the same idea.

I am not one to judge or stereotype but some of the people were a bit rough looking, bald heavyweight men with tattoos; young mums with kids that were out of control jumping on the red plush furniture. I muttered to Emma,

"Keep your head down, don't look or stare at them."

Barristers were coming and going with arms full of files, many of them were pulling small suitcases around with them, if I were not in that room, I would imagine I was in an airport lounge. I observed as people were being escorted into rooms which lead off from the large waiting room where we sat.

"Miss Emma Colne," the voice came from a loudspeaker,

"Thank goodness that's us," Emma frowned at me as if to say, **be quiet mum!**

We stood up and a lady directed us to one of the rooms, I was so relieved when we shut the soundproof door on all the comings and goings that were happening on the other side. We could now collect our thoughts until the Barrister and Emma's solicitor arrived.

We only had a few minutes to wait and when all the introductions were made Geoffrey began to talk, he was a tall very sophisticated man with an air of professional confidence, he was dressed in a well cut dark grey suit with a white shirt and a matching tie.

"Has your boyfriend ever hit you?" I was quite startled with such a question,

"Yes," Emma replied,

"He throws things at me, he once threw a knife at me and it landed in the baby's carrycot, luckily it didn't hit Jodie. He chased after me with a carving knife; I locked myself in the shower waiting for him to calm down." While Geoffrey was taking a few notes I looked at Emma, this was all news to me, she had never told me what she was experiencing with Carl.

She carried on saying,

"He went to punch me in the face I ducked and his fist caught the edge of the large mirror which was hanging on the wall above the electric fire, it fell to the floor shattering into hundreds of pieces."

I recollected, *the huge empty space above the fireplace that was in the flat soon after they first moved in together.*

Emma was remembering other times,

"He hit me across my face, I ended up with a couple of bruises around my eye, my mum rang saying she was coming round, but I managed to put her off, I didn't want her to see my face. I was frightened of his temper a couple of days after being discharged from hospital after my caesarean section with Jodie I asked him to do some washing for me I was not able to do much housework, after all he had taken time off work to help me. He said he would look after the baby while I did the cleaning and make the meals.

I was so angry and upset after explaining that I was in pain, I picked up Jodie and began to slowly walk up the metal circular staircase to our bedroom, he came after me grabbing at my dressing gown, luckily, he pulled on the belt which came away from the tabs, I was still quite big from being pregnant so I could not fasten it very well.

I quickly reached the bedroom door shut it behind me and pushed against it with Jodie in my arms trying to stop him from getting in, I was frightened of what he might do."

Geoffrey was nodding in an empathic sort of way.

"The next thing I want to tell you about is a bit perverted; he told me he imagined I was his best friend's girlfriend while he was making love to me. There was a time he physically threw me out of the house around 11pm at night, Jodie was about two months old.

I sat on the doorstep crying on and off for about three hours. I was freezing, I asked for my coat, but he ignored me and smiled standing at the window while he cuddled Jodie, then he pulled the curtain across; the light from my warm sitting room was gone.

I was left in darkness, I thought about walking the five hundred yards to the late-night garage, but I had no money. Eventually, I heard the key turn in the lock, and I let myself in."

I had no idea of all this abuse and how Carl had behaved towards my daughter, to think I accepted him and treated him as one of my own, I was so disgusted.

While Emma was finishing her statement with her Barrister, we caught eye contact and I could not hide my feelings, she could see that what she was saying was having an emotional effect on me.

"Domestic Violence, with emotional abuse," the Barrister said standing up, he gently patted Emma on the shoulder saying,

"Don't worry," smiling to my daughter,

"It shouldn't take long; I will get your children back for you."

Unfortunately, Carl's solicitor brought up Emma's mental health and after Emma's Barrister tried his best to change the judge's mind, it was ordered that Emma had to produce a Psychological Report for the court and that Carl would have the temporary residence of the children.

Emma was devastated.

The year was 1997 when Emma first met Carl. She had asked if she could bring this boy home to meet us and could he stay for dinner? I agreed as she seemed so happy that she had met someone who she really cared about.

After speaking to Carl, I found out he worked in a restaurant. I prompted him into talking about his future. I suppose I was being inquisitive as to where or if he had any prospects. I enquired about his qualifications, apparently he had left college before his course had finished as he wanted to earn some money. I smiled as I was dubious,

"So, where do you live?" enquiring with a frown on my face,

"I am renting a room at my friends." I then asked,

"Where are your parents?" he replied,

"They kicked me out," I did not like the sound of that, but I could not pry too much.

After a few months Carl started spending a lot of time at our house and gradually he left his friends and moved in with us. Seemingly, he lost his job. Approximately a month went by and Carl did not seem to be doing anything about looking for work, I suggested different opportunities from the local newspaper, I felt quite sorry for him as he spoke with little confidence. He asked if I could help him with his CV (Curriculum Vitae) history of his education and employment. My daughter was so infatuated with him I agreed, I also rang various companies enquiring if they had any vacancies. I bought Carl some smart clothes and he got himself a decent job with good prospects.

Approximately six months passed Emma and Carl spoke about getting a place of their own. I was frightened she may become pregnant as I thought she was too young and inexperienced; I was also worried as Emma was in remission of a pain she had suffered for so long.

Since the age of about fourteen years old the right side of her abdomen was sore to touch, it was so bad she had to spend most of her time on the sofa. Following many appointments with various general practitioners she was sent for tests.

The results all came back normal, but the pain was constant. After many months and plenty of pain killers prescribed by Emma's Doctor, the pain seemed to gradually ease off. Unfortunately, Emma had to have a lot of absences from school, which understandably had caused her to fall behind on her schoolwork.

Some days were better than others. Emma also experienced awful panic attacks, one time she had fallen backwards and hit her head on the corner of the wall and apparently knocked herself out. I tried desperately to bring her round I screamed at my son Liam to fetch our next-door neighbour Fiona, she was qualified as a first aider and an incredibly good friend. When Liam returned with her she asked me for a paper bag, I wondered what on earth she would need that for. Emma began to open her eyes but her whole body was shaking, Fiona had taken control and spoke very calmly to Emma and gently placed the paper bag over her mouth and nose, then coaxed Emma to breathe normally.

For a short while Emma was able to live a relatively normal life, she had gone back to school and managed to achieve average results in her G.C.S.E.'s. Her confidence was beginning to grow and she had started going out with her friends again, I honestly believed things were getting back to normal. Emma so much wanted to be a secretary since she was a child.

We had bought her a second-hand computer which she could only use as a word processor, but still she was happy with it, she would type letters over and over to increase her speed, and she was forever asking us to dictate paragraphs out of a book.

Although Emma had lost a lot of valuable education, she still managed to get a place at college to take the RSA course. (A qualification which would help towards her career) Approximately eighteen months later and two months before her eighteenth birthday Emma met Carl, she was a huge fan of a particular boy band and Carl reminded her of the lead singer, she was besotted from the start of her relationship.

They soon found a flat and just before Christmas they moved in together and yes, my worst fear was confirmed when they explained she was expecting a baby the following November.

Eventually I accepted the inevitable. Emma's pregnancy went well, although she did suffer in the beginning and was admitted to hospital for a few days.

Since that time my opinion of Carl completely changed; he had arrived at our house and we had about half an hour to spare before leaving to visit Emma. I asked if he fancied a coffee, I felt there was something on his mind he was very jittery, I enquired,

"What's wrong, is everything all right?" assuming he had heard from the hospital.

"I have to tell you something, I feel so guilty, I have been to see my ex-girlfriend and I slept with her, what should I do?"

I was disgusted with him, I calmly said,

"You are not coming visiting with me, I think you should be honest with Emma, when she comes home you have to tell her what you have done and if you don't, I will, now get out!"

I rang my mum asking if she would like to come visiting with me, I was livid at Carl and I just needed to offload, my mum was so good at listening to me moan.

We had to hide our feelings and allow Emma to think that everything was normal. She did enquire to the whereabouts of Carl, we just casually mentioned he had to work. Which thankfully she accepted.

A few days later Emma was discharged, Carl did tell her what he had done. She was so upset, she needed to get out of the flat; she told Carl she was going to the shop, which was just around the corner.

As she was walking down the short flight of stairs leading to the front door, Carl jumped off the edge of the landing to try and stop her from leaving him, he caught her; and she stumbled down the last three steps.

Terrified something may have happened to the baby she immediately rang the hospital and they both went together in the ambulance. Fortunately, there was no damage done to the baby. Apart from Emma suffering from a sore back, everything was alright.

When they returned home Carl apologised and expressed his undying love for Emma, because of Emma's love for Carl she forgave him, and they both put it behind them.

Carl also apologised to me; I could never completely trust him again.

Emma was close to full term, the last visit to the antenatal clinic; the doctor had suggested she should be prepared as she could go into labour at any time.

The same night Emma and Carl arrived at our house in a taxi, she was frightened as she felt something was happening. My husband had obtained his First Aid certificate and it gave him the confidence to do what he felt it he had to do.

To this day I will never forget what happened next.

After coming downstairs with the number for the maternity ward my husband met me at the lounge door,

"I have just put three fingers inside Emma, I can feel something,"

I was too involved with Emma, worried as it was her first baby, and she was in quite a lot of pain during her contractions. It was too late to say or do anything about what Steve had just told me, I felt absolutely disgusted. I never forgot those words, as if he had the qualification to do such a thing! Not sure whether he believed he had, or was he just trying to make me think he had some kind of authorisation from achieving his first aid badge

I immediately rang the maternity ward and after telling the Ward Sister of Emma's symptoms she suggested we bring her onto the delivery suite, she said,

"It sounds like she is in the first stages of labour."

Emma was in labour but unfortunately, she was not dilating. A doctor explained twenty-seven hours later that the baby was becoming distressed and they would have to do an emergency caesarean section.

I sat on the delivery suite while Carl went with Emma, Steve had stayed at home with Liam and Katherine. I constantly watched the clock on the wall, the time seemed to go so slow, I tried to read a magazine but my mind repeatedly thought about Emma and how much longer is it going to take, I paced the room, looked out of the window.

It was late and all the streetlights below were shining bright against the dark sky, an hour passed, a nurse came in and asked if I would like a drink, I politely accepted her offer, after about five minutes she returned with a large mug of tea and some biscuits.

She made some small conversation before she needed to attend another patient, as she was leaving she made a comment about them being terribly busy tonight and six babies had already been born.

At last, the double doors were pushed open, and two nurses wheeled Emma in on a delivery bed. Another nurse followed pushing a small cot with a little baby bound in a pink blanket. Carl had a big smile on his face as I looked over at them both, Emma was exhausted but happy and smiling.

"Mum do you want to dress her?" I was shaking with relief and excitement that everything was OK and that the baby was healthy.

She was so tiny, her little fingers were so delicate you could just see her fingernails, I was so careful as I dressed her warm little body with a disposable nappy, a vest which seemed to smother her, her little toes were lost in the feet in the pink Babygro.

She had to wear a hat for the first day or two. She was gorgeous. I was so proud and lucky to see her so soon after she was born. They named her Jodie.

My husband and I were so happy watching Jodie grow up. Every little stage in her first year was so incredible, gradually sitting up for the first time, crawling over the carpet, playing with her toys, and then taking her first steps, we were a big part of Jodie's life.

I was thrilled to be a grandma and I enjoyed babysitting especially when Jodie took a dislike to her main course and threw her dish directly at my face. I was covered in Lamb Hotpot!

We celebrated her first birthday by having a little party for all her family and friends, we invited Carl's family, but they declined.

Soon after, Emma was expecting another baby, unfortunately her second pregnancy was extremely uncomfortable.

She experienced everything, morning sickness, heartburn, and severe backache so when

Emma went into labour two weeks early; we were not surprised.

She had to have another caesarean section and gave birth to a beautiful little boy. He was so cute they named him Zak.

My mum had given them some money towards a deposit for a two-bedroom house. With Carl's minimum wage they could not afford a full mortgage. Fortunately at the time the local housing associations were letting home-owners part buy half of their properties and rent the other half which was much easier for Emma and Carl as Emma was not able to work.

Emma and Carl seemed happy. Unfortunately Emma became ill again, looking after a young baby and a two-year-old during the day and at night took its toll on Emma. We decided it would be better for Emma, Jodie, and Zak to stay with us through the day.

I made tea for them including Carl, then I took them all home. Emma stayed overnight with Carl, and we arranged for me to collect her and the children at 8.15am every morning so Carl could go to work.

Zak was four months old, it was just after Jodie's second birthday when Carl and Emma began to have some bad arguments and their relationship started to crumble.

Carl was going out at night and not returning till the early hours of the morning, tormenting Emma that he was having an affair. She did not know what to think or believe.

I also witnessed a couple of violent outbursts from Carl. Emma's stress levels reached a new high, her pain was becoming unbearable. Their relationship was deteriorating. Carl should have been supporting Emma with the children, she would have appreciated some help at bath time instead of him leaving her to go out and enjoy himself.

Soon after Christmas things went from bad to worse, I was caring for Emma on a permanent basis and collecting the children every morning.

Carl did not seem to want to see Emma anymore, he came back from work in a taxi which he had waiting for him while I got the children ready, then he took them home; without coming in to speak to Emma. The love he once had for Emma was now turning to hate.

I was finding it exhausting trying to look after Emma and her children, plus taking care of my own family, Liam, and my husband, making meals, and doing all the household chores. I always made sure that I visited Katherine every night.

I had asked Carl to take the Saturday off and help me with the children or if his parents could look after them for one day; he did not need to work six days a week, it was just an excuse not to have to be in Emma's company.

I was absolutely shattered; Emma was not sleeping well. There was only my mum who was kind enough to help me, unfortunately she too was feeling the strain.

So, when the following Friday came and things had not changed, I tried ringing Carl to let him know I would not be collecting the children the next morning. There was no answer to my calls, I had no way of contacting him, I tried ringing his parent's house but to no avail.

I knew he was being difficult and not wanting to support me with the children, so Saturday morning I deliberately left the children with Carl. He had plenty of opportunity to organize something so the children would be taken care of.

Carl did not contact me, I wondered how he had managed on Saturday, I felt awful letting him down, but I was exhausted and needed to sleep. We never heard anything from him.

The following day was a Sunday, my mum and I were going to visit Katherine in hospital, Emma asked us to drop her off at her home as she was feeling a little better and wanted to see Carl and her children.

Being a Sunday visiting time was extended so me and my mum stayed with Katherine a while longer.

When I returned home a couple of hours later I was surprised to see Emma, she had been crying, I asked,

"What's happened?" she came to me with tears in her eyes,

"It was horrible mum, he's thrown me out, he wouldn't talk to me, he threw all my clothes out of the bedroom window; I could hear Jodie crying for me.

I shouted through the letterbox to her, don't worry sweetheart I will see you soon, I didn't want her to see or hear that I was upset."

Little did we know a couple of days later, the court official would turn up at our house on that dark cold January evening.

CHAPTER 3

Jodie and Zak

Things went from bad to worse, especially for the two young children who were so innocent in this bitter conflict between their mother and father.

The Court Order stipulated Emma would see her children on a regular basis.

Over the next six months Carl was difficult in allowing Emma time to see her children. He had another girlfriend, Lesley; she had moved in and while Carl was working she looked after Jodie and Zak. They also had to call her Mummy.

The courts had allowed Emma overnight access on the understanding she had her own home. She was fortunate to be given a two-bedroom flat through a Housing Association, once again we had to find enough finances to furnish it.

One Saturday morning Carl brought the children to Emma's, I was there to witness Carl saying,

"Jodie and Zak are not your children anymore; they have got a new Mummy now."

For no reason Carl stopped the children's contact with Emma, she had to go back to court for the Judge to order Carl to abide by the residence order and allow Emma her visiting rights. Each time that happened Emma had to contact her solicitor which took time, then wait for a response from Carl's solicitor before any appointment in court could be made.

Emma looked so smart each time she had to make a court appearance; she wore a burgundy suit, a white blouse and black shoes with a two-inch heel, her make-up was just enough to hide how she was feeling on the inside. I was so proud of her determination to fight for her children, she said,

"Mum, I can do this, I love my children so much and I want them back and I will do everything it takes to get full custody or at least shared custody."

Emma had seen an independent psychiatrist who had been asked by the court to complete a report on his findings. Emma had a good response from that, she was clever at hiding her true feelings, after all, she had hidden them since she was a little girl.

There were numerous visits to the Cafcass Officer who worked in conjunction with the courts. Emma seemed to get on well with Mrs. Tellsing she was quite a well-built woman with a motherly kind of personality, lovely with the children, Jodie enjoyed her company and she liked playing with the toys that Mrs. Tellsing provided. There was also something for Zak to keep him occupied, she watched while Emma interacted with her children. She also did the same with Carl.

When she submitted her report it read,

I think shared custody would be a good option, but I feel the animosity between the two parties would not be beneficial towards the children, so I think considering Emma's mental health problems; Carl should have full residence and make an adequate order for Emma to see her children on a regular basis.

Emma was devastated and so was I, all my positive thinking was gone there was nothing left to fight for I felt so empty.

It was just a formality when Emma last visited the courtroom to be told that Carl was awarded full residence of her children.

Since Carl had won the battle over the children, he had a different girlfriend every couple of months.

His parents looked after the children; while he enjoyed himself, then he met and married Jackie, she adored Zak and brought him up as her own, but she could not accept Jodie, each time she told Zak she was his real mummy it angered Jodie, she retaliated by saying,

"You're not Zak's mummy and you're not my mummy."

Jackie reacted by using physical aggression and sending her to her room. Jodie told us of the abuse she had to suffer at the hands of her stepmother. We did get Social Services in once when Jodie showed us bruises and disclosed how it had happened. Apparently, Jackie pushed her off the top of the bunkbed. I was appalled at how the Social Services dealt with the matter, nothing was done after she had been transferred to the local hospital for a Paediatric Consultant to see her and he confirmed her bruises were compatible to what Jodie was saying.

When the children spent time with Emma, Jodie screamed and kicked when it was time to go home. She hated having to leave her mummy.

Unfortunately, Carl was deliberately difficult regarding Emma's access. He demanded that Emma should stay away from his and his wife's house, the one he shared with my daughter and the one my mum paid the deposit for. We furnished that house for them; as they had little money, so it hurts to know

Carl shares it all with someone else and he forbids Emma near it. My Mum and I felt it was extremely unfair as Emma was left with nothing. We could not claim anything as Carl had the residency of the children. The system let Emma down, whoever received the custody of the children got the house and all its furnishings including the kitchen appliances, washing machine, the suite, the double bed, bedding etc., of which most of it my Mum and I were still paying for.

Carl stipulated that I had to collect the children for Emma. There was a small car park close to Carl's house and away from sight, so we decided Emma would come as far as that and I would drop her off to wait for her children.

In the beginning Jodie asked,

"Where is Mummy?" I whispered,

"Don't worry you will see her soon." After fastening Zak safely in his baby seat and putting the seat belt around Jodie before we set off; I said,

"Say goodbye to Daddy." She waved, smiling as she was so excited knowing that she was going to see her mummy.

Seconds later we turned the corner and there was Emma waving with a huge smile on her face. As soon as Jodie saw her, she shouted,

"Mummy! Mummy!" and Zak was smiling too, his little legs were jumping, and his arms were reaching out, Emma jumped in the back seat and put her arms around both her children, they were so happy cuddling and laughing together.

Emma decided to make the short time she had with her children, fun, happy and memorable. She had prepared toys for them both, been shopping and bought Jodie her favourite food. Everything was perfect, there were no tears; Emma played with both of her children trying to incorporate the playtime with Zak as well as Jodie. When Zak had a short nap, Emma was able to devote all her time to Jodie; reading a story to her while she was sat on her lap, their arms were around each other all the time and Jodie's head was resting lovingly against her mummy's breast.

When Zak woke up Emma suggested to Jodie,

"Shall we bath Zak?"

Jodie's face lit up and shouted excitedly,

"Can I help?"

"Of course, you can," Emma replied.

Emma put the small baby bath she had bought onto the carpet and asked Jodie to get the towels, baby powder and a clean nappy.

Jodie was excited as she splashed the warm water over her little brother's tummy, while Emma was safely holding him, he was happy splashing with his small chubby legs.

"I am not allowed to do this at Daddy's."

Emma cleverly ignored that comment by changing the subject, asking Jodie to pass her the sponge.

Bath-time was over, and Jodie had helped powder Zak before Emma had put his nappy on. Zak's vest was not clean, so Emma decided to put a fresh one on, unfortunately she had to dress him in the clothes he had come in, a tee-shirt with breakfast marks on the front and a small pair of shorts.

Emma was conscious of the time moving fast, she felt she had to prepare Jodie that she would be going back to her Daddy's very soon.

"Let's put all your toys away and then you can play with them next time you come." Jodie reluctantly obeyed her mummy and picked up one of her dolls.

"Can I take Candy back to Daddy's with me?" Emma replied,

"Of course, you can, she can sleep with you in your bed."

"I don't have a bed; I sleep on the floor." Jodie exclaimed.

Emma was taken aback with this comment,

"What happened to your bed?"

"Mandy sleeps in it." Mandy is Jackie's eight-year-old daughter. Emma began to question Jodie in a very matter of fact way,

"So, who sleeps in your bedroom?"

Jodie replied,

"Mandy, Zak in his cot and I sleep in the middle of them on a cot mattress. Daddy said another bed won't fit in the bedroom."

Ten minutes later Emma was helping Jodie with her coat, Zak was ready to go. There were tears welling up in Jodie's eyes.

"I don't want to go, I want to stay with you mummy," Jodie said crying.

Emma tried hard not to show her feelings,

"I know you do sweetheart, and I would love you to stay, but Daddy is expecting you and Zak: he will be upset if you don't go back."

Jodie said through her sobs,

"Ok, but I am coming back to see you and Nana and Granddad soon."

Jodie and Zak were supposed to come for their tea one night during the week; Emma received a phone call from Carl an hour before they were due.

"Jodie's tired and Zak is starting with a cold, they will see you at the weekend." Before Emma could speak Carl had put the phone down.

Emma was so upset, as the excitement of seeing her children, turned to despair.

That week stretched to an eternity for Emma.

I had dropped her off at her designated spot while I went round the corner to collect her children.

I knocked on the door and waited, Jodie came to the lounge window and began to wave with a big smile on her face, I waved back, and Carl closed the curtain, he then came to the door,

"The children are not coming today, Jodie was upset last week so I don't think she should come, you and her Mum have been upsetting her."

I tried to convince Carl that Emma, or I had not said anything to upset her in fact we had encouraged Jodie to go back to her Daddy's.

Carl had interpreted Jodie's behaviour was due to her seeing her mummy. He was adamant that the children were not coming with me. I could hear Jodie in the background crying,

"I want to go and see my mummy."

I heard Jackie telling Jodie to stop crying, I tried so hard to persuade Carl that the children needed to see their mummy.

"Please Carl, they are getting upset, I can't leave here without them." There was a definite,

"No" from Carl's angry features and then he shut the door.

Emma was distraught when she saw the car was empty, she had been waiting on the car park for about twenty minutes.

"What's happened?"

She saw my face, I said,

"Get in and I will explain everything."

On the way home I told Emma how Carl had reacted when I went to collect the children.

"He can't do this, it's not fair; he is not thinking about Jodie and Zak."

I tried to console her, but her anger was boiling up inside her.

"I am going to ring him; I'll talk to him."

The conversation Emma had with Carl was heated and his thoughts were much the same,

"Can I speak to Jodie?" I heard her say to Carl,

"What! She is not there! Where is she?"

Then she slowly returned the phone to its place on the coffee table.

I looked at her with a worried look on my face,

"What's happened? Where is Jodie?" Emma replied in a sad tone of voice,

"I don't know Mum he won't tell me, if she is there, he won't let me speak to her."

Over the next week Emma tried countless times to contact Carl but each time the phone went dead.

Saturday morning came and we fully expected to be seeing the children, when I arrived at Carl's house all the curtains were closed and there did not seem to be anyone in. I knocked on the door and the window for about five minutes.

The first thing Emma did on the Monday morning was ring her solicitor, she learned that her solicitor was in court most of the time, so she had to make an appointment for the following day.

That Monday felt like an eternity, wondering if the solicitor can do anything to help Emma see her children.

She began to write things down so she would not forget anything. I watched in earnest as her mental health was beginning to deteriorate, I tried to keep her spirits up by being positive and saying,

"Don't worry your solicitor will sort things out you will soon see Jodie and Zak and maybe you might get more time added on to your court order."

We were so naive with the court system; Emma had already met Carl's uncle who was a solicitor and it seemed he had given Carl some professional guidance.

Emma asked me to accompany her to the solicitor the next day, unfortunately things were not as easy as

I had anticipated. Emma explained everything from the beginning and Carl's attitude towards her, the solicitor was sympathetic to Emma's case as she knew how she felt and how much she was trying to keep it together; she told Emma she would first write a letter to Carl's solicitor, asking for Emma's access to be reinstated, if he does not agree to these terms then we will have to go back to court.

We left the solicitors down hearted, Emma felt she was totally abandoned by the system.

"I can't believe this is happening Mum, I am their mother and he won't let me see my children." Then the tears came, Emma was not crying for herself but for her children, through the sobs she muttered.

"What will Jodie be thinking, what will they be saying to them? Zak needs me I must be there for him, he needs my love, my cuddles when he cries and Jodie her little face, she will think I have broken all my promises to her, how can I let them know I still love them? Oh God! I miss them so much."

All I could do was listen and put my arms around her, I had no words of comfort or positive thinking anymore, we were in no man's land, waiting.

Weeks went by, Emma was constantly ringing her solicitor; the answer was always the same,

"I'm sorry Miss Colne I am still waiting to hear from Mr. Tench's solicitor, I will let you know as soon as I hear anything."

Emma thanked the solicitor and put the phone down, apparently Carl's solicitor had tried to contact him, but he was not replying to any of his calls, it was hopeless; Emma had also been told by her solicitor not to go to Carl's house as it could be interpreted as harassment.

Eventually the phone rang, and it was Emma's solicitor.

"We are in court on Tuesday morning at 10.00am, be there for 9.30am I would like to go through a few things with you. Emma came off the phone with a big smile on her face,

"Yes, we are in court, and I can't wait to speak to the Judge."

Tuesday morning came and we arrived at 9.15am. Again, we were frisked, and our belongings checked as we went through the same procedures as before. We did not have to ask for any directions; we already knew from previous experience where to go.

Emma's solicitor arrived approximately five minutes later she wrote down some notes with Emma, she seemed positive and mentioned she was happy that this particular judge was seated on Emma's case.

We were due in court at 10.00am but Carl had not turned up and his solicitor was getting quite agitated.

"Colne Vs Tench," was shouted from behind the table at the far end of the room, we watched as Carl's solicitor approached the person at the table; I could not hear anything, but I presume he was explaining why we were not ready to proceed.

"Blackhurst Vs Tootal," was the next statement to come from the same person behind the table.

"Oh no; someone else has gone in our time slot," Emma whispered to me,

"I think he is doing this on purpose," she said as she looked at the clock on the wall in front of us.

"Twenty minutes past ten, I wonder if he is going to turn up," Emma said with an exasperated sigh. We were all sat waiting except Carl's solicitor he was pacing up and down looking towards the double doors.

At last Carl walked briskly through towards his solicitor who was looking at his watch and giving Carl a stern look,

"I'm sorry I missed the bus," Carl's solicitor escorted Carl into a small room where he could take some notes of Carl's requests.

Both the solicitors entered a room with the statements from the two parties and conversed to try and agree on something, apparently Carl was proposing to reduce the time Emma spent with her children. And Emma was hoping to increase her time and hopefully gain overnight at the weekend.

Eleven O' Clock and the names 'Colne Vs Tench,' were called, everybody stood up and Emma followed her solicitor, she had already asked if I could attend, we were ushered into a large room with an enormous, polished veneer table, the Judge was seated in the middle; on the opposite side Carl and his solicitor were sat on the left, Emma and her solicitor were on the right with me behind Emma.

The presiding Judge asked Carl's solicitor if his client had any good reason to stop contact with the children's mother.

"My client believes that the time spent with their mother is upsetting for the children, he thinks that maybe a couple of hours on a Saturday will be more beneficial."

The judge turned and looked to the right,

"Do you agree with this?" he directed this question towards Emma. This is her chance, what she has been waiting for, to speak her mind, but all she could say was,

"No, Your Honour."

"Do you think an overnight might help and maybe if Grandma can stay over at the same time." He looked at me and I nodded and smiled then I said,

"Thank you, Your Honour."

Carl was so angry he tried to interrupt the judge, but the judge ignored his rude comments towards Emma. He then turned to Carl.

"I expect from now on there will be better communication between yourself and the children's mother." Carl could not say anything else but,

"Yes, Your Honour."

Emma walked out of the Courtroom feeling ten feet tall, she had already asked Carl in front of the judge if she could collect her children later that day and have them for tea, he had to agree, so they arranged a convenient time.

Emma and I arrived at the house; I stayed in the car while she went to the door, after a few minutes he opened the door and said,

"They are not ready yet," he shut the door and locked it with a key from the inside, I think he must have been frightened that Emma might barge in.

Eventually Carl brought the children to the door, passed Zak to Emma as Jodie put her arms around her Mummy's waist squeezed and cried,

"Mummy, Mummy," it was lovely to see them all reunited.

Things went well for a couple of months it was Jodie's fourth birthday, we had all bought presents and Emma had arranged with Carl that she could have the children the day after her birthday.

Emma had made a cake and prepared a little party for Jodie, she spread her presents neatly in front of the television so she would see them as soon as she arrived.

We went to collect the children. Jackie had Zak in her arms in the lounge, we could see her through the window. Carl answered the door and told Emma the children were going out for the day with his parents.

Emma was so angry she told Carl.

"Arrangements were made a few weeks ago, it was Jodie's birthday yesterday and you said I could have them both the following day, we are having a party and she has got some presents to open."

"No, we are sticking to the court order, and you will see them on Saturday."

Emma was not ready for giving up the fight, she did not want to make a scene, but she tried her best to make Carl see he was not being fair to the children, especially Jodie.

Carl twisted her words as Emma said,

"Zak needs me I am his mother not Jackie, and Jodie knows she is coming today."

"You are just jealous; Jackie has got something that you have not; she has got three children." Then he shut the door.

There was nothing else Emma could do, again she heard Jodie crying for her, it seemed like she was upstairs.

Emma pushed open the letter box and shouted,

"I love you, see you soon."

Months passed, Christmas came and went; things were the same. Carl's attitude never changed he hardly stuck to the court order and Emma was lucky to see her children when Carl saw fit.

Emma had been fighting for her children and keeping her spirits up for so long and it was having effect on her mental health, she became depressed. We tried desperately to encourage her that life will get better, but with a criminal court case pending and all the family court appearances for the children, it was too much.

Emma had forced everything to the back of her mind and when the system let her down and she was defeated, combined with the humiliation; she gave in to the demons of her mind.

She began cutting her arm with a razor blade, we did not go to the hospital; I was able to clean the cuts with saline and antiseptic swabs which the doctors had given me on prescription. I bought some stere-strips which I used to stop the blood flow, then each time I bandaged her arm, it was always her left one.

Emma was also punching walls with her bare fist and the top of her right hand had swollen, I took her to Accident and Emergency where they did an x-ray, luckily there were no bones broken. It was difficult to explain to a doctor how she had done so much damage to herself.

Then the flashbacks happened.

It was surreal to witness what was happening to her body, she would be sat watching television, then for no apparent reason Emma's head began to go backwards and forwards at such a rate, it was as if she were in a car and the brakes were being pressed hard, one after another causing whiplash over and over.

I was so frightened that she might break her neck, I had to put cushions behind to relieve the impact of her head hitting the back of the wall.

This episode lasted for around a minute which seemed forever, and then Emma slowly opened her eyes and the movements stopped as quickly as they had begun.

Twenty minutes later the same flashback happened again with the same force only much stronger, the leather settee was being lifted off the ground while her head was moving at the rate of about sixty a minute.

Emma's mood began to deteriorate, she was self-harming more and more. There were no tears just so much pent-up anger in between the flashbacks.

The time came to seek professional help, the doctor was aware of Emma's behaviour; I rang and asked her if she could contact the Psychiatrist, meanwhile Emma tried to take her own life by overdosing on painkillers.

Again, I took her to Accident and Emergency at our local hospital and we waited for the on-call Psychiatrist to assess her.

Emma was now proving to be a risk to herself, she had to be admitted to another hospital quite a distance away as Katherine her sister was still an inpatient on their PICU ward. The hospital's policy did not allow any relations to be admitted onto any of the mental health wards at the same time.

Fortunately, there was a bed available in a private mental health hospital about twenty miles away from where we lived. The Trust arranged that she could be admitted there and that they would fund it.

We drove onto a private road, then we came to some gates which had an intercom, I pressed the buzzer and a voice answered requesting who we were? I answered with both our names.

"Hello Mrs. Colne, we have been expecting you."

The huge gates automatically opened. I followed the directions for the car park. The lawns were mowed with surrounding flower beds full of colourful varieties of blooms, paths leading to a conservatory.

There were a few people sat reading on the wooden garden furniture provided for the patients. We walked up to the large front door and pressed the button, the door opened, there was a lady smiling waiting to greet us, she wore no uniform but was smartly dressed.

She introduced herself as Anne, in a very pleasant manner she announced,

"Please leave your bags here I will get someone to fetch them up for you." She then turned to Emma.

"Would you like to see your room?" Emma replied,

"Yes please." She was not in the mood for any conversation, so the lady looked towards me.

"The doctor will be in later to see Emma," as she led the way through a bright hallway with wall-to-wall thick pile carpets, framed pictures with beautiful landscaped scenery hanging neatly on the pale cream walls. To the left was a staircase stretching towards the first floor, you could tell that the cleaners were very conscientious as the white spindled banister shined without a speck of dust. We walked along a corridor that was lit up from the sunshine coming through the windows, again with similar decor and plush carpets. A door to a small office was ajar and the lady knocked and explained to the nurses that Emma was here and she was taking her to her room.

It was a such a lovely surprise when the door opened; the large picture window with green patterned curtains draped alongside the softly peach patterned wallpaper, they matched the beautiful single bed quilt cover, there was a white basket chair in the far corner with a cushion made of the same material.

The pale pine wardrobe was fitted neatly next to a matching dressing table with a stool tucked underneath. There was a three-drawer chest situated at one side of the bed, adjacent to a door leading into an en-suite bathroom. Considerable in contrast to Katherine's room at the NHS hospital.

A week later Emma seemed settled into her new environment, she had been prescribed strong mental health medication and she was on one-to-one observations, which meant she always had a nurse with her.

Meanwhile I had been to see Carl and explained where Emma was, he agreed that I could collect the children every Saturday afternoon to visit their mum.

While both my daughters were safe in hospital, I began to reminisce the past and how and when it had all happened.

CHAPTER 4

Looking Back

I have wonderful memories of my own childhood; my older sister Petra and I were brought up in a seaside town; we all lived with our grandparents who owned a newsagent on the main street. Our parents helped Granddad to look after the shop while Nana cared for us. I remember seeing the big ships sailing past as I watched from Nana's first floor window of their flat above the shop. She told me stories of when she was a little girl and how she met my granddad. I remember the sugar butties she used to make for me. My Mum left Petra sat safely in her pram outside the door, although it was safe in those days she could still be seen from the shop. Apparently, people would speak to Petra as they entered; she was always a happy baby with curly dark brown hair and brown eyes, she chuckled when customers chatted to her.

There was always a friendly atmosphere. Most of the customer's knew us and spoke to us using first names. My granddad had a tall stool for which he used behind the counter, when it was quiet, he let me sit and play with the money in the wooden till. At christmas I remember seeing all the big toys hanging from the ceiling, prams, bikes, train sets, pedal cars and lots of beautiful dressed-up dolls in tall boxes. Unfortunately, my memories of the shop remained as a child as we moved to another seaside town. There; my mother's parents owned a small hotel, it catered for approximately twenty-six guests. My sister and I had to sleep on the very top floor which was known as the attic. There were two large double beds and lots of room to play. We had our meals on a big table in the living room, when we had finished breakfast, my Nana prepared all the meals; I will never forget the delicious aroma of homemade soup, a variety of joints roasting in the oven, along with pastries and cakes. They had a regular clientele who would return each year. In those days people hardly went abroad for their holidays.

Soon after when all the chores were done and my mum had some spare time she took us to the beach. There we saw my Granddad as he worked part time as an engine driver on the little train which transported families along the promenade.

Petra and I both attended the same primary school and fought each other's battles; she was supportive when my friends fell out with me and vice versa. As children we were so naive, I remember a gentleman spoke to me and my sister as we were walking home from school. We had to walk down this long winding road on the outskirts of the town, there were no houses except for a large old building set back from the road, which was used as a High School, he stopped as he was passing us by,

"If you count every hundred stems of wood in the hedge you will see fairies." After I had pestered her, Petra agreed.

"98...99...100." Excited we knelt and began to look for these colourful little creatures expecting to see them flying about. We searched for a while but never found any. The following day we met the same man, he enquired,

"Did you see any fairies?" We both replied,

"No." Then he mentioned,

"If you go down that little lane behind the school grounds there's a fairy glen."

Luckily, we declined his offer, as we did not want to be late home. Looking back, as children we were so vulnerable; at the time we really believed we would see fairies. Eventually, we left the seaside towns and moved more inland as my father was working for an insurance company. In our teenage years Petra was always studying, she went on to college and University; with her excellent results in business studies she landed a well-paid job with good prospects.

Whereas I was outgoing had loads of friends; in fact my social life was buzzing. I did not have the finances like the rest of my friends, so I decided to leave school earlier and get a job against my parent's wishes.

At sixteen I was working in an office as a junior clerk. Enjoying spending my well-earned wage packet at the end of the week.

Buying myself the latest fashionable clothes and dancing at the local nightclub, I looked older than I was after carefully applying make-up and my friend would do my hair, I wore classy mini-skirts, nice fancy tops and white or black boots that was the fashion at the time.

Since I was about fourteen years old, I had boyfriends, thought I was in love every time. Until I met Steve, he was good looking, three years older than me, he wore nice fashionable gear, and he could play the guitar.

Steve was so full of wonderful ideas of what he wanted to do with his life.

Months passed and we became a real loved up couple, I was still working but instead of socializing with my friends I spent every minute with Steve, I loved him so much.

One day we were picnicking in a field, there was only the sound of the nearby trees rustling from the warm breeze, the sky was so blue, and the sun was shining. Lying next to each other, having just shared a bottle of wine, we made love and spoke of our future together.

Six months after Steve and I met we were getting married I was seventeen and we were madly in love. We had a fantastic day I wore a gorgeous long white dress with a lace hood attached to a long lace train. Steve wore a grey suit, white shirt with a silver tie.

He had a lilac-coloured handkerchief showing out of his left breast pocket. The same colour of the bridesmaids, Petra my sister, my cousin Gillian and Steve's younger sister Anne.

Money was short so we did not have a honeymoon. I took a couple of days off work, we were fortunate to stay at my Grandparents house for a few months while they were staying in Spain, my grandmother had a chest complaint and my Granddad liked to take her to a warmer climate for six months of the year.

Before they were due to return home, we were lucky to find a two-bedroom flat with its own private entrance above a sweets and tobacconist in the centre of the village.

Over the next six months Steve changed towards me, his loving nature disappeared, I had to give all my miniskirts to his sister and wear his mum's clothes, I just wanted to please him, so I did everything he wanted including quitting my job. I had to look for another position closer to where we lived, I was not allowed to socialize with anybody from my new employment. If I was home late I had to explain why and where I had been. When it was a colleague's birthday, they asked me if I would like to celebrate with them by going for a lunchtime drink. I had to decline, as I was not permitted to leave the work premises until I had finished for the day.

Some days I was so sad with my life I confided in a good friend at work, she suggested I leave Steve as he clearly did not trust me. That night I had gathered enough courage to challenge him; I told him he could not love me as he did not trust me, he then told me to leave, as he started to pack my bags.

With hindsight I should have gone, but I loved him so much, I apologised and carried on pleasing him by not speaking to anyone about my marriage and his controlling behaviour.

Regarding our sex life he had fantasies of which I thought was normal, so I pleased him, in bed, the car, the woods, etc.

One minute I had to wear his mother's clothes covering my knees and never show any cleavage; the next he had me teasing men by opening the buttons on my blouse which he had chosen for me to wear, showing half my breast, wearing short skirts and bend over to show the top of my stockings and suspenders, usually it was when we were at a garage getting petrol, he chose the right moment when there would be men coming home from work. He liked to watch and when I got back in the car I had to explain the response I got from any man that noticed me, this always sexually excited Steve. Sometimes I made it up, to please him. If I got the chance to hide in the shop, I quickly fastened my buttons, I felt so embarrassed when I did not get the chance and Steve could see me through the window of the shop.

In bed while we were making love, I had to invent stories from the beginning of our foreplay. He never pleased me first or anytime through our love scene. The stories were always the same, I was being raped by someone, he would start me off with the scene and while he was inside me, I carried the story on. Gang rape did it for him, the more men the more sexually excited he became, if he was not ready to release his sperm, I had to make the story real where each man was hurting me and swearing, dirty filthy words. My sex life went on like that through our whole married life. I was accustomed to it.

Despite his controlling behaviour and sexual fantasies, I stayed with him.

Three years later Katherine was born we were delighted that our first child was a girl. We were so proud when she started to sit up without any support, then when she said her first word which of course was "Dada." It was also amazing to see her take her first step.

Being the first grandchild, she was spoilt by my husband's family.

A few months before Katherine was born we sadly lost Steve's Dad, he was a lovely man, when we told him he was going to be a grandad, he was over the moon.

Katherine helped Steve's mum through her loss, I took her to see her every day, at first it was my choice and then according to Steve it was my daily duty. When he came home from work he took Katherine again to see his mum. Anne, Steve's sister found it hard to accept the loss of her father, she was not coping very well.

I think he thought he was helping by doing things his dad would have done if he were there. I was also happy to support them for the next twelve months.

Then I was expecting our second child, my pregnancy went fine, except for trying to find clothes that fit me. I bought some material and made myself some skirts, I could not make myself look sexy anymore.

Emma was born, she was so cute and mischievous, as she grew older her personality took on an independent and innocent nature, she had a lovely sense of humour and she loved making people laugh, especially her father and his side of the family. I had passed my driving test when Katherine was a baby. Steve would not put me on the insurance to drive his car, so I did not get the chance to see my parents regularly.

After Petra and I had moved out of the family home, mum and dad decided to downsize and they found a little farmhouse with a smallholding. My dad took ill, it was so sad that he could not enjoy all his hard work at modernizing the farmhouse; they had put a conservatory on the back overlooking the garden and the orchard which he had been determined to finish. He was able to spend the rest of his days in the comfort of his own home.

Steve eventually put me on the car insurance so I could go and see my parents, sadly my father died later that year. I could not bear the thought of my mum being all alone in that farmhouse; so the children and I went to see her most weekends. She said,

"The children always brighten the place up with their laughter."

Katherine would be about five years old; Emma was around two years old when the landlord decided to put his shop premises up for sale, he gave us the first option to purchase the property and the business as a going concern.

My father had left me a substantial amount of money which we had put into a building society for the future. I had a chat with my mum, and she was happy for us to use it as a deposit to buy the property and the business.

We had decided Steve would keep his job and I will work in the shop. My friend collected Emma in a morning after dropping Katherine off at school with her daughter Haley. She also had a little boy the same age as Emma they played well together so she was pleased to look after her. I appreciated what Stella did for me, I tried to offer her more money as my child carer, but she was adamant; we had been friends for a while.

My life was busy working hard to make the business profitable. My husband was not a peoples' person and hated being behind the counter, so he would take on my role by bathing the children and preparing them for bed; when I had finished locking the shop up for the day, I went upstairs ready to read my children a story and put them to bed. It was a nice scene when I entered the lounge; Steve was brushing Emma's long mousey brown hair while she perched on his knee.

Katherine was sprawled out in front of the television watching a video that she had chosen from the videos in the shop, we rented them out on a nightly basis. Both children were pleased to see me, I felt awful I could not do the things a mother was supposed to do, at the time the business was so important. Steve had fallen out with his boss and impulsively given his notice in, not realizing the consequence of his actions when he had shouted,

"Stuff your job!" and then walked out.

I had to keep the money coming in.

A few years passed, Steve was organizing the books with the accountant and looking after the accounts, making sure the wholesalers were paid on time. I was constantly asking Steve for more stock to fill the shelves. By now the business was thriving.

We had invested in toys and party gifts. I had bought the shop fitters in to enable me to arrange a good display of boxes of chocolates of all shapes and sizes and we provided quality cards for all occasions.

The customers were delighted, they did not have to catch the bus into the city as we had an excellent standard of merchandise to choose from. We were the only shop in the village that provided this service.

Christmas and Easter were our busiest times. The business was doing well, I employed two part-time assistants to help so I could spend more time with the children. Steve bought a new car, and we purchased a static caravan close to the sea which enabled us to have a break from the shop every so often.

The last few years had been happy, the business was established, and things were running smoothly. On one of our short weekend breaks to the seaside, we were all walking along the promenade when Steve noticed a fortune teller, for a laugh he suggested I have a go.

I ducked under the dark maroon tasseled curtain which jingled as I passed through. It was rather dim, a gypsy like person sat behind a small round table she greeted me with a pleasant voice,

"Hello dearie, sit 'urself down." pointing to the stool provided. On the tapestry covered table there was a Crystal ball and a pack of Tarot cards these were expensive readings, Steve had only given me a small amount of money, so she read the palm of my hand and told me I have three children I said,

"No." She was adamant,

"There's definitely three here, have you had a miscarriage?"

I said,

"No." The little old lady announced that I was going to have another baby quite soon and it will be a boy.

She asked me if I was pregnant, I replied,

"No, I haven't got time to have any more children yet." She said,

"Sorry lovie, y'ur gon'na have to make time."

The fortune teller also told me a load of jargon about my future which I passed on to Steve, but I kept the information about the baby secret, as I did not really believe it myself. Two weeks later I missed my period, it did not bother me at the time as I was not always regular.

The following month when I missed again, those words from the gypsy came flooding back. I made an appointment to see the doctor. He confirmed that I was just over two months pregnant. I must have been expecting when I visited the gypsy. I was overjoyed at the thought and could not wait to tell Steve. I knew it was going to be a boy.

After my son Liam was born. My Mum's younger sister Kathy came over from Canada to stay with her for a while. She was so interesting telling us all about the Horse Shows she attends. She has a stall and sells all kinds of things to do with horses.

From brasses, cups with horse prints, pencils, rulers, plates, ornaments etc., the most profitable items were garments printed with horses of all different breeds. Kathy also took orders for Horse Farms; they wanted their Logos printed on their work wear. She was so busy with orders coming in, it was fortunate that my Uncle Dan was also interested in horses and he was there to help.

My Mum chose to move closer to us. She rented somewhere until the farmhouse could be sold. Kathy had talked her into moving before she left England, she did not want to leave her on her own.

My Uncle Dan was missing his wife and finding it hard to manage without her, so before Kathy left for Canada, she made sure my Mum was safely near me and my family.

Steve was so impressed with the idea of Screen printing, he suggested we could do the same as my Aunt Kathy but with aircraft and sell at air shows.

We purchased the correct machinery to enable us to accomplish our goals for the future. This gave Steve a positive outlook on life he was besotted with aircraft.

He began to book us in as traders at the air shows, we invested in a large coach which accommodated the whole family. All the seats were taken out except for six at the front.

We stored all the equipment in the luggage compartment under the coach, tables, awning, and the boxes of clothing printed with fantastic designs of aircraft, some with modern day airfare and some displaying the Great Britain war planes. American Bombers and 1st World War Biplanes.

Steve arranged for my sister-in-law Anne and her husband David to look after the shop for the weekend.

It was so exciting filling the coach with everything we needed, Katherine and I had been and bought a small kitchenette it consisted of a gas hob with three burners with room underneath to store a gas bottle. A small sink, some shelves around the side and a cupboard which enabled us to carry some food.

I was determined that we would all sleep comfortably and keep warm, so I stitched the two ends of a double quilt together for both girls, Liam our young son had his carrycot with plenty of blankets, he was not quite 12 months old, he was such a good baby, hardly ever cried and eat, 'Ha-ha! give him a large custard tart he would devour every crumb.

Our first show was about one hundred and fifty miles away. We wanted to be up and ready, so we left early morning around 2am, the children were half asleep when we transferred them from their warm beds into their sleeping bags which were equally as comfortable.

Steve drove while I navigated, he had already mapped out the route for me. It was a nice journey the roads were quiet except for the trucks making their way towards the docks. The sun was sneaking a peep from the depths of the horizon. We had timed it well; arriving at our destination around 5.30am. We were not the only ones who had the idea of getting there early. Vans, Buses, Lorries etc., were queuing up at the gates.

The sun had already risen but there was still early morning dew on the grass, rabbits were running around everywhere, I made sure Steve drove slowly as I did not want any rabbits squashed under the big wheels of our coach.

We came to a barrier where Steve had to show some paperwork to prove we were legitimate traders. A man dressed in uniform acted serious when he saluted a passer-by also dressed in uniform.

The red and white barrier lifted, we were escorted through to our place where we would park the coach and set up our stall.

The girls started to wake,

"Hi, we're here," I shouted excitedly,

"Look at all those planes lined up over there," pointing towards some Hawks, a couple of Harriers, a few of the old 2nd World War planes; Spitfires, Hurricanes, a Lancaster Bomber and there in the far corner of the airfield was the Vulcan Bomber.

The first thing I did was fill the kettle with some water we had brought with us and yes, the hob worked when I managed to connect the gas bottle, I made a good cup of tea for everyone. Liam was ready for his bottle of milk which I could also warm from the boiling water. I know it sounds silly being excited about such trivial things, but when something works, we were so pleased with the result.

Steve emptied the large storage compartment at the side of the coach, he stared at the instruction booklet as he began to put together the 12ft x 4ft stall.

When he had finished erecting all the steelwork and setting up the awning, it was my responsibility to arrange the merchandise so the passers-by would be attracted by the display. Approximately an hour later I stood at the front of our stall to view my presentation from a customer's outlook; I was pleased as I took notice of the red, white and blue array of sweatshirts hanging on coat hangers; showing off the colourful designs of aircraft that Steve had been painstakingly determined to catch most of their detail, he was a perfectionist when it came to drawing his designs;

Lightening's, The Battle of Britain Lancaster Bomber, Spitfire and Hurricane, Harriers, Hawkes, single Spitfires, all together we displayed approximately ten different designs.

Then the piece de resistance The Red Arrows, these are what brought the hundreds of thousands of people to air shows, we catered for most of the Red Arrow displays. Steve managed to get many of the detailed manoeuvres printed on our garments.

There were already quite a few stalls erected and people were busy arranging their merchandise.

I had arranged a teddy bear sat in the corner of the stall wearing a Red Arrows T-shirt in a 3-6 mths size, this brought people over to the stall fascinated that they could buy a T-shirt with such a popular design for a young baby.

Then I had to cater for all children's sizes, the adults including extra-large sizes. For an obese person that would not be disappointed I kept a few double extra-large sizes under the counter. Each

T-shirt was folded so the design could be seen from the front. Adult's and children's T-shirts were hung on coat hangers at the side of the awning showing off all the designs, hoping to keep my display in order and avoid people rummaging around like a jumble sale. When I was satisfied with my actions, I pulled the flap at the front of the awning and covered everything from view, then I returned to the coach, which was situated directly behind the stall. I began to prepare breakfast, cereal and scrambled eggs. After tiding up, washing the pots, changing Liam, and motivating the girls to get dressed. I was anxious to return to the stall. Steve had set up a highchair for Liam, Katherine wanted to stay and help me while Emma was excited about going with her dad to see the planes.

The coolness of the early morning dew had disappeared, the sun's rays were becoming stronger, and people were starting to walk along the corridor of 150-200 stalls.

At first people just walked over and looked at the stall, children were pointing and laughing at the teddy wearing the T- shirt.

Then the car parks began to fill up and crowds of people from all walks of life were coming to the stall, asking questions,

"Have you got that one in a small adult?" the person was pointing to a sweatshirt with the Red Arrows design and commenting how good it was.

I felt proud as I was folding it neatly into a carrier bag,

"Can I have these please?" a lady passed six different T-shirts over towards me, I managed to catch a glimpse of Katherine, she was also busy selling children's sizes of different designs, although she was only in her sixth year and preparing to go to high school, she was intelligent and very good with money, since we had bought the shop she had been fascinated with counting money also she was able to understand how to treat customers and if she had been given a twenty pound note she asked the customer politely to wait for me to serve him/her the change.

The expression on her face told me she was coping and happy to oblige each customer, she caught me looking at her we smiled at each other and carried on selling.

Liam was happy playing with his toys, Katherine and I never stopped, we were so busy right up to when the planes started their displays which was around 1.00pm.

Steve and Emma arrived back in time for me to feed Liam. Katherine rushed to a caravan where they were selling hotdogs, burgers etc., she came back laden with an armful of goodies, we were famished.

The afternoon was even busier and by the end of the day when most of the thousands of people had returned to their cars, we began to stack the few T-shirts and sweatshirts we had left and put them carefully back into the boxes for the next airshow.

When everyone had gone and there were just the traders left, Steve had put the stall away, Liam was asleep in his carrycot; I just sat outside the coach with a nice cup of tea quietly reminiscing the whole day and felt happy that everything had gone well.

That was our first airshow and every airshow we attended was just as busy, whatever the weather the crowds still turned up to see the displays of aircraft on the ground and in the sky, we made friends with many of the traders and sometimes organized barbecues after the crowds had gone.

We were now in our second year and each show was as good as the first. The designs were selling well, and we were taking plenty of orders.

Sometimes Steve booked two shows on the same weekend, miles apart. On these occasions I would drive our van with Katherine keeping me company and Liam in the back, while Emma sat at the front of the coach with her dad.

He had accompanied us to the first show which was always the bigger of the two, this one was Biggin Hill which spanned the full weekend. Steve did not want to miss out on the smaller show as he knew from experience that particular one would also be busy.

Katherine wanted to stay with me and Liam, whereas Emma always went with her dad, he told her he needed her to help him erect his small stall and fetch him drinks while he was busy selling.

They would leave late afternoon so they could set up and stay overnight on the airbase, I made sure they both had warm sleeping bags as they were sleeping in the van, when the night air draws in it gets colder.

I always thought Emma was happy to go with her dad, he made a big fuss over her saying how good she was; I think she enjoyed the attention.

When the next day was over and we had sold a huge majority of the stock, we had something to eat, put as much as we could into the coach and waited for Steve and Emma to return so he could take the stall down and drive the coach home.

We arrived home late, Anne and David had locked up and left the shop clean and tidy.

During the week they came to see us, it was not unexpected they were always popping in. Usually it was around tea- time, I was such a push over;

they knew I would invite them to stay. David was upstairs with the girls watching TV and keeping them occupied. Anne stayed and spoke to me while I put the chips on the stove and prepared salad and cold meat. Anne had been clothes shopping, she asked me my opinion when she pulled a black dress from a carrier bag with quite an expensive designer logo.

She held it up to her and I thought to myself how nice she would look in it with her short blonde hair, the dress had an off the shoulder look, so she was able to carry it off with her tall slim figure. Next, she took this box from the side of the table. She said,

"Don't tell David," As she showed me a beautiful pair of designer black open sandals. No wonder she was hiding them as she was not working at the time, she had been off sick for a while and David was a student Mental Health Nurse at the University in the city, so money was a bit tight.

Anne asked me if we were having problems with the shop as she noticed the stock was low saying,

"Customers were not happy. I had to disappoint them, they asked for goods that would normally be on sale, but I had to pretend that the delivery was late." I replied,

"Yes, I know, it doesn't look like Steve has paid the last invoice so they won't send the next delivery."

There was silence, nothing else was said. I turned to set the table.

I was not so sure of how many chips to put on David's plate as he was overweight in fact I would go as far as saying he was obese; he could carry it off as he too was tall, I guess around six foot three inches.

It was three years ago since Anne first introduced David to us, he was not what I expected and I never thought that Anne would be attracted to someone who did not care much about his appearance, the clothes he wore were not clean and he had an odour of sweat, when he smiled, I noticed his teeth could do with a good clean.

When Anne spoke about him, she explained she had felt sorry for him, he was a loner, and he did not have any friends. He was quiet with a gentle nature I thought!

Steve had many friends from his previous job. We met them and their wives at the local pub once or twice a week whilst Anne and David babysat for us.

At the time we had no reason not to trust David, with hindsight I should never have left my children with such a monster.

My girls seemed to get on well with him especially Emma, he gave her lots of attention more so than Katherine, she always sat on his knee when we all sat down to watch a family film together, she laughed when he tickled her.

When she was little he used to pick her up and hold her high so she could touch the ceiling; I cringed terrified that he might drop her as he balanced her on the palm of his large hand.

Anne must have sensed my fear and tried to convince me that she would be alright, she said,

"Don't worry, he won't hurt her."

Little did I know?

The following morning, I rang Petra she was always there for me when I was p...... off. My sister lived approximately thirty miles away from where Mum and Dad used to live, she was busy with her important job as a Marketing Assistant Manager for a large company which retailed upholstery covers. The head office was situated close to the centre of London and had various factory outlets which spread from the south of England as far up north to Edinburgh in Scotland.

Petra visited most of these on a regular basis she would have to travel a great deal; so it was understandable that she could not always support my mother when my dad was quite ill. Petra would call on us unexpectedly, I was always happy to see her, but I felt there was an atmosphere between her and my husband Steve.

I loved the time I spent with her, the kids certainly enjoyed her company as she took them shopping and bought them each a gift, she spoiled them because she could not see them on a regular basis.

It was nice to have a chat with her I felt I could confide in her, sometimes if Steve and I had argued it was nice to have someone to talk to, it was usually about Steve's drinking or his attitude towards me.

When Steve first refused to put me on the insurance this had angered Petra who drove a BMW company car, she was so independent with her high-class lifestyle, completely the opposite of mine.

When I blurted out all my pent-up anger to Petra she just said,

"Leave him," I explained that I loved him and would stay with him no matter what.

I used to get quite angry when Steve had not got enough money in the bank account to pay certain cheques. Instead of sharing the burden with me he would worry to the point of making himself ill with the stress; then he would ask me to get involved.

It was nearly always me who had to phone the bank and between the bank manager and myself we would decide which cheques to pay and which ones to send back. The bank manager was very patient and extremely helpful, but this did not stop me from feeling totally embarrassed as these phone calls became a daily duty.

I began to realize the money from the shop which was supposed to pay the bills was being used for something else.

While I was still managing the shop, Steve looked after the books and all the finances I was led to believe that there was enough profit out of both businesses to cover the expenses for the air shows.

We managed to keep things going for a while longer, it was so embarrassing to see my little shop losing its customers; there was very little stock left on the shelves, luckily I had the van so I was able to chase up to the wholesalers which was about three miles away, I took some of the takings with me, leaving Susie in charge while I managed to buy a few things to fill the shelves; the stock I bought was what we usually sold so it didn't stay long on the shelf.

Susie was a long and trusting friend she had been working for me in the shop for a couple of years, she knew things were bad, but she did not know how much.

Things went from bad to worse, the bank manager suggested we put the property and the business on the market before the bank foreclosed.

Neither of us were happy with the idea but it was the right thing to do. I felt so sorry when I had to tell Susie what was happening and that we would have to let her go. She was upset, but also understanding.

Within a short space of time, we managed to sell the shop and the property, but there was not much capital left as most of the proceeds went to the bank, including paying off the rest of the creditors.

Fortunately, my mum had moved into the village. Apparently my sister had conveyed to my mum that Steve and I were having problems, she felt she wanted to support me and the children.

Until we were able to support ourselves my mum suggested we all move in with her.

Meanwhile Steve had rented a unit on a small industrial estate just outside the village. The air shows were still doing well, and the finances enabled Steve to buy more machinery and stock up for the air shows which were only seasonal.

My mum was available to look after the children, Katherine helped as well. This gave me a chance to help Steve by canvassing schools, local businesses, leisure centres, etc., offering our services and our expertise as a printing business, also distributing leaflets in and around the city, as he needed extra finances to cover his overheads.

Steve seemed to be coping well and keeping busy and allowing me to believe his new venture was successful.

Months later, Christmas had been and gone we were kept busy printing for schools and local businesses in the city.

Steve had plenty of new aircraft designs for the sweatshirts and T shirts. He was rushed off his feet trying to print for the businesses, in addition to printing all the garments for the air shows. Bright colours of quality sweatshirts and T shirts were arriving weekly, we had shelves in one corner of the unit for different sizes to be stored ready for printing.

There was a huge six colour carousel which took up most of the room at the bottom close to the large sliding door which was handy when we had to completely wash off all the ink from each screen. We used smaller screens when we printed the same design for children as well as adults. It was all very chaotic.

The air show season had begun, we were geared up every week with all the printed garments, baseball caps, sports bags, etc.

When everything was on show with all the wonderful colours of garments printed with fantastic designs of aircraft, (Steve had excelled this year with his creativity, he had drawn aeroplanes with much more detail.) We stood back and said,

"Yes, it's all been worth it."

We had been travelling every weekend to the shows up and down the country, we were doing well, selling lots of stock, getting really good feedback from the quality and designs. Each time we visited an air show the children came with us, we made sure they were safe and comfortable sleeping in the coach.

Other times, I had followed in the van so that Steve could leave us to go on to another show not far away, he always took Emma with him.

We arrived home after a busy weekend. The following day I received a phone call from a stranger,

"Hello, are you Steve Colne's wife?" I replied,

"Yes, can I help you?"

"I have just entered your husband's unit and found him groaning under a large metal set of shelving, he asked me to ring you. I have already sent for an ambulance." I thanked the gentleman got my keys and dashed to the unit arriving at the same time as the emergency services.

Steve was taken to the hospital in the city where he was immediately seen by a doctor and in turn sent for an x-ray. I was informed as to what was happening as I could not leave my children and my Mum had gone to

London to meet some friends. I learned that Steve had broken some ribs and badly broken his leg which will need an operation; he would have to stay in hospital for quite some time.

I rang the hospital around 9.00am the following morning, I was told to ring back later when the doctors did their ward round about 10.00am so Steve should have been seen by then. A nurse answered the phone and passed me on to a doctor, she was nice and asked me to go and see her before I visit my husband.

I arrived half an hour before visiting time, wondering why the doctor wanted to see me. I knocked on her door,

"Come in," when I walked into the room there was a consultant sat down with papers on his lap, the doctor introduced herself and the gentleman as Mr. Grice.

"Please sit down Mrs. Colne," I did what I was asked, unsure of why I was there.

"Your husband has cracked three ribs of which one has punctured his lung. He has also suffered a tibia shaft fracture and the fibula is broken; he needs surgery.

We have repaired the lung which was vital before the Orthopaedic Surgeon can operate on the leg. He is on pain relief. I asked,

"Can I see him?"

Then Mr. Grice escorted me down in the lift to Intensive Care, a nurse met us in the corridor the Consultant introduced us, she then took me in to see my husband. I got such a shock he was unconscious, and all wired up to machines, I never expected to see that; I had not prepared myself for anything like this, I felt sick and dizzy I needed to sit down before I collapsed. The nurse made me a cup of tea and gently spoke to me, she could not give me any positive information. However, she was very empathic as she explained what will happen.

"He is in good hands, Mr. Grice is one of the best Consultants in this area, ring the ward whenever you want, someone will always be here to give you up-to-date information." I thanked her and slowly left the ward in a complete daze, how I managed to get home I do not know it was as if my body was on automatic.

The next day I rang the hospital to see how Steve was before I went to visit him.

"He's had a comfortable night."

Later that afternoon I stood with other relatives waiting outside to see their loved ones on the same ward. We made small conversation about the weather, everyone looked so sad and apprehensive of what to expect when they entered the ward.

Steve was lying with his eyes closed, he did not look comfortable as he was still wired up to the machines. I spoke to him hoping that he could hear me, I felt I was talking to myself, but I had to let him know I was there for him. I spoke for an hour, I told him what the children were doing and that they send their love, and he does not need to worry about the business.

I returned home and made various phone calls. I postponed all the orders until further notice, my only concern at that moment was whether Steve would ever be the same again.

One week later, ringing every day to see if there was any change; only to be told,

"No, I'm sorry, he's had a comfortable night".

He had got an infection, so they had put the operation back until he recovered.

Each morning I received the same negative response, until one day.

"Your husband is feeling better, and his temperature has gone down, the consultant would like to speak to you as soon as possible."

I could not believe what I was hearing, at last; I had never lost hope and I knew it was only a matter of time to hear something positive. I quickly got washed and dressed, dropped the children off at school then made my way up to the hospital. I phoned my mum after I had spoken to Mr. Grice.

"Yes, it is good news they want to operate soon."

A couple of days later, after I had been visiting regularly; I decided he had to have a business to come back to. One of our good friends Nicholas, offered to do the books and his son Andrew was pleased to lend a helping hand whilst waiting to go on to university, he had just finished college. Apparently, he was looking for a job for the summer holidays.

I explained to Nicholas that I could not afford to pay Andrew much as I did not know what the financial situation of the business was like.

He was kind when he said,

"Don't worry Audrey and I will sort that out, we just want him to do something with himself over the summer holidays; also, he will be helping you." This act of kindness made me feel extremely humble and I valued Nicholas and his family's friendship.

Several days later, Nicholas had been doing the books and Andrew was a brilliant help, we managed to get a few orders out, fortunately, I had helped Steve with the screens and the colour carousel, it took us a bit longer, but we managed between us.

The next morning before Nicholas went to work, he came to the unit, the worried look on his face made me question him,

"Is everything alright," I asked,

"No, Jenny the books are in a terrible state, there's a lot of money going out, much more than you have coming in. There's no receipts to show any bills have been paid, there's invoices dating back to last year." He explained all this before sitting down at the desk and opening the folder.

"I don't understand, we are doing well at the air shows surely he must be banking the takings. We've got plenty of work coming in from schools and businesses."

Then I started to think back, Steve rarely let me use the carousel and never let me have anything to do with the financial side of the business, all he wanted me to do was arrange to meet people after I had left a leaflet advertising our company.

"I will ring the bank manager, explain what has happened and see if he knows anything." I thanked Nicholas and he left for work.

Immediately, I rang the Bank Manager, luckily it was Mr. Lawson the same person that we had used when we had the shop.

"Hello, Mrs. Colne it's been a long time, how are you?"

I explained in short what had happened to Steve and how I needed to know the financial situation of the business, I mentioned I needed to buy stock to fulfil the rest of the outstanding orders.

"I am sorry, but without Steve's consent I am not allowed to tell you anything and I can't let you take any money from the account."

I was devastated when the Bank Manager explained this, I understood he was doing his job.

He had suggested that there must be some health insurance. Steve told me he was insured,

I remember his words,

"I am insured right down to a common cold." We had laughed at the time; not realizing how important it was.

I returned to the unit looked through Steve's papers and found the Insurance Company.

There was a name at the bottom of the letter, so I rang and asked to speak to him in person.

"Hello, this is Anthony Belthorn can I help you?"

I explained who I was, what had happened and how do I make a claim? He put me on hold for a short while until he had found Steve's details.

"I'm sorry Mrs. Colne but your husband has not paid any premiums for quite some time, we can't let you make a claim."

I got off the phone and thought, *what the hell is happening?*

The only thing to do was to get consent from Steve to let me use the bank account. I quickly wrote the words on a piece of writing paper all I needed was Steve's signature. That was easier said than done.

The Consultant told me they would be operating soon.

Every day I went to visit I took the letter with me. They were keeping him mildly sedated it was so difficult, he could speak a little and understood that I needed his signature to keep his business going. Eventually after the third day, with my help he slowly managed to sign the piece of paper. That same day I took it to Mr. Lawson, he explained everything. It appears that Steve had taken out a huge loan of £20,000 and was having to pay large monthly instalments back to the bank; that was not the only problem, there was no money in the account. The last two month's payments were unpaid, and this month's payment was due soon, we were looking at nearly £3000 and we had not got a penny.

The day came of Steve's operation I decided to go to the unit to keep my mind occupied. Andrew was printing some sweatshirts for a school, while Nicholas was with me as I was trying to explain what the bank manager had said.

I made us all a cup of coffee while we tried to come up with some ideas,

"You have got to do the shows and keep the money coming in." Nicholas said. Then there was a knock at the door, I thought it might be a rep they were always popping in for a coffee,

Steve was friendly with quite a few reps he used to say,

"Jenny you can go now I need to speak to Mike," he was a representative of a company that Steve had bought a lot of stock from.

Whenever reps turned up, I always went home. I probably spent a few hours a day at the unit, Steve always seemed so busy sat at his desk he did not want to make conversation and he was constantly on the phone.

I received such a shock when I opened the door to see a bailiff standing there. He had come to collect £1,200 owing for the rent of the unit. I told him I did not have that amount of money, and could he come back next week as my husband was on the operating table having a major operation as we speak. The bailiff agreed to return the following week.

I had had enough, I was so angry with Steve, although he was so ill, he should have told me how bad things were. I asked Nicholas if he would not mind taking Andrew home and that I will ring him tomorrow, I was going to lock up for the day.

At that moment in time, I never wanted to step foot in that unit again.

Thank God Steve's operation was a success. According to the consultant he had said,

"It will be another six weeks before we can think about Steve coming home."

Friends were rallying round to help to do the shows with me we managed to do a few but we were running out of stock, I rang the wholesale company where we buy the sweatshirts and T-shirts, but they would not let me have any more unless I paid them in full.

The air show season was slowly coming to an end we had sold most of the stock, what little money we made from the takings went towards the bank loan, I did everything I could to stop the bank from foreclosing.

The inevitable happened the Bank Manager's secretary rang and asked if I could make an appointment to see him.

It was 10.30am I sat waiting to be called in to see our Bank Manager, knowing exactly what he was going to say.

"If you advertise your business as a going concern, it will show some goodwill and that you are trying to find the money for the loan. This will give you a lot more time." I never expected this news, Mr. Lawson was trying his best to help us.

It was a lot harder than I thought telling Steve, I tried to explain if we do not listen to the bank manager and do what he suggested we will lose everything. He had only been discharged six weeks earlier and he was not in any fit state to decide what to do, I had not dared tell him how bad things were in case it made him ill. I had been told that little stress would be a big factor in his recovery. He said,

"Bullshit, I'll save my business."

Monday morning came he was going to walk to the unit after I had said he could not go it will make him ill. So I ended up driving him, when we arrived he told me to leave him I was not allowed to enter the unit.

He managed a few days before I got a phone call to come and pick him up, the manager of the company next door to Steve's unit told me he was concerned as he looked quite ill and breathless.

I picked him up and settled him back at home. The next day I went to the unit myself and while I was there, I received dozens of phone calls, Steve had been ringing all the creditors promising that they will get paid in full very soon and could he have some more stock. He had put orders in for lots of sweatshirts and T shirts. The manager had received a note on his desk about the order, I had to apologise and tell him the truth.

Months later the business was sold, and the proceeds went towards paying off the creditors. Unfortunately; my mother in-law's house was guarantor for the £20,000 bank loan. I did try to explain to her that if we put it on the market, she would salvage something; but she didn't believe me and so she lost her £70,000 house as the bank did forclose on the loan. Steve would not take the blame as he explained that it was my fault I ruined his business and lost his mum's house.

My husband never worked again; he would get upset if I mentioned that I wanted to look for a job. With hindsight I know now that I was being controlled and emotionally abused. If ever I answered back or did not agree with him, he would sulk and become quite ill, so to keep the peace and avoid Steve from getting upset I would bow down to his every need.

Over the years I seemed to grow a strength of assertiveness and got myself a little part time job at our local corner shop. Meeting people again helped to improve my self- respect and gain more confidence. My husband was drinking more and more, starting early in a morning with a couple of whiskeys before lunch and then carrying on through the day till bedtime.   The manageress mentioned one morning that my husband had been buying a quarter bottle of whiskey at least two or three times a day; I felt so embarrassed I explained it was for medicinal purposes.

The past ten years I had tried to support him, I took him to AA meetings from which I got a mouthful of abuse,

"I have not got a drink problem, I'm nothing like those people."

I think I stayed with him out of pity, because when I finally asked him to leave, I never looked back, I had no regrets in fact; I never missed him.

CHAPTER 5

Emma and Katherine Growing up

As the girls were growing up, I remember Steve and I going to a parents evening, we got a complete surprise, when Katherine's teacher commented on Katherine's behaviour and explained she would not concentrate, instead she was disrupting the rest of the class; apparently it had got so bad Katherine had been sent to the headmaster on several occasions.

Over the next couple of months, we tried to give her more attention and help her with her schoolwork, unfortunately Katherine did not settle down.

Steve and I received a letter from the school asking us to make an appointment with the headmaster. We did; the following day as we were concerned as to why he wanted to see us.

We both sat waiting outside his office, I felt like a child again waiting to be chastised.

Mr. Sprite was a tall gentleman, with an overpowering personality, his dark moustache matched his dark brown hair, and I would put him in his late forties. The look on his face made me feel quite uneasy as he introduced himself as the Headmaster of Little Beddington Primary School. I had already got the impression that Mr. Sprite did not accept us.

I remembered earlier that year, one Sunday morning when I had attended church, he had mentioned to the congregation that he did not agree with businesses being open on the Sabbath day; he had looked in my direction knowing that we had opened our shop to the public on a Sunday.

With an extremely sharp tone to his voice Mr. Sprite announced that Katherine would not be moving up into the top class with the rest of her friends but that she would benefit by staying another year in the same class. We were disgusted and outraged; we tried to persuade the headmaster to change his mind, but he was adamant with his decision.

I felt I had to do something so the following Monday morning I made an appointment to see the headmaster from another school a few miles from where we lived.

Katherine was so happy when we told her that she would still be going into the top class, but it will be at a different school. Emma also moved to the same school as Katherine, there she met her best friend Karen who has and still is standing by Emma; she is a wonderful and kind person, she has stuck by Emma for all of twenty-seven years, there is no grey areas about Karen, she says it how she sees it.

"Stuff the lot of them," she tells Emma when her family and friends give her a hard time.

Emma was quite an extrovert, completely the opposite to Katherine she was a home bird, she would say,

"If only I could be like Emma, she has so many friends even when she is ill, they are still there for her."

When Emma was feeling good there was no stopping her, she enjoyed life and loved being with her friends. She stayed over at a friend's house for a few weeks, she phoned every day to make sure it was ok. I allowed her to do what she wanted as I was happy to see her enjoying herself, she certainly made the most of it when she was not in pain.

To help Katherine from becoming too bored with her life; I took her to a horse sanctuary where they looked after and cared for horses and ponies that had been maltreated. Over the next six months she had shown a huge interest in the equine side of life.

She and Emma had joined a riding school, they both enjoyed hacking out together on some nice quiet country lanes. They loved grooming and they learned a lot towards looking after a pony.

On condition Katherine worked for the local newsagent by doing a paper round every morning, we let her have her own pony from the Sanctuary, we found a livery yard close by.

Katherine's confidence began to grow as she met some friends, unfortunately she would not do her paper round without me, nor would she go to the stables on her own, I would always have to accompany her; I did not mind as it got me out of bed early.

Six o' clock, I reached for the alarm, it was still very dark I went into Katherine's and Emma's bedroom she was already up and getting dressed, we sneaked quietly outside to the shed as we took our bikes and pedalled towards the stables which was about half a mile away. Katherine was so happy to see Brandy her pony, she led him outside after putting on his head collar. Then she would set to, mucking out the stable and putting fresh straw down and filling his hay net, also making sure he had fresh water. It was great to see Katherine looking so healthy, this pony had changed her life, given her a responsibility which she accomplished with pride and enthusiasm.

Emma and Katherine were close when they were young, they joined the youth club together. There was a time when Katherine was about fifteen and Emma would have been nearly thirteen when they had supposedly gone to the youth club, which was approximately half a mile away from our house. They had asked if they could stay out till ten thirty; after a little persuasion from me, their dad agreed ten thirty and no later.

Eleven o'clock came there was no sign of them I was getting quite worried. Steve said, "Right, I am going to look for them," I had to stay behind as our son was in bed. Steve came back half an hour later hoping that they would have come home, it was getting on for twelve o'clock and all we could do was to sit and wait.

Thank God, I thought as I heard them sneak in quietly, Steve went mad and told them both to get to bed. He had already been to the Youth Club it was all locked up. The next morning, they had to explain where they had been and why they were so late.

Apparently, they had stayed at the club for a short while until some of Emma's friends mentioned they were going to a party at the edge of a lake, which was deep in the large wood situated at the far end of the village. The wood spread for miles and at night it would be extremely hard to see anything. Emma and Katherine had been lucky to have found their way home, they admitted to me how scared they were, they did not need to be punished by being grounded; they had already learned their lesson.

Katherine and I went shopping in the city at the weekends I asked Emma if she would like to come but she always had better things to do. I just laughed and accepted it.

Saturday was usually a busy time most people had been paid from doing a full week's work, so they were spending their well-earned cash. Katherine and I loved window shopping and when we were exhausted, we found a nice little cafe where we would catch our breath with a cup of coffee and one of the special cream cakes which were home made on the premises. Later we resumed our shopping spree; I got the few things I went for and usually bought my three children something to wear. It was always enjoyable, Katherine seemed to like my company, whereas Emma preferred to be with her friends.

I felt I was close to Katherine we had a lot in common. I showed Emma in different ways how much I loved her; but she felt quite distant when I went to give her a hug.

I remember saying to my mother-in-law,

"Emma shies away when I try to show her any affection, she doesn't seem to want me to cuddle her anymore, I suppose it's because she is getting older." She replied with a hurtful comment,

"Oh, I can."

Unfortunately for Emma her time with her friends became short-lived, the pain in the lower part of her abdomen was beginning to interrupt her lifestyle. The doctor was getting quite concerned and sent her to the local hospital for more tests which all came back normal. Over the past twelve months it was uncanny what was happening to Emma, during the week she experienced the pain but towards the weekend she seemed a little better.

I would have thought she was scamming, but I saw how much pain she was going through and so I understood. Thinking she was trying her best to overcome it; we allowed her to visit her friends at the weekends. She persevered with the pain, however at times her friends had to bring her home.

After having to endure the pain more frequently, Emma was referred to a Gynaecologist who arranged for her to have a laparoscopy which was so uncomfortable for he; I commented on how brave she was, she never showed any emotion, and hardly ever cried.

I stayed with her while the anaesthetist gave her an injection to put her to sleep, she looked so peaceful when she had reached number four that was when I was told to leave and that I could see her in recovery after the operation.

Again, the results were clear, which was a huge relief, but also worrying,

What was causing this pain?

Over the years she had tried her best at school and college; although her absences contributed to her not achieving the results she would like to have received.

She had met Carl whom she had fallen madly in love with; they had moved in together and had Jodie.

Before Emma separated from Carl, she had asked him to go to the shop for some aspirin; whilst Carl was away, she took an overdose of painkillers, luckily out of the blue my cousin Michael had called round and realized something was wrong.

He immediately got her into the car and fetched her to our house, Carl had stayed at home to look after Jodie who was now almost three months old.

I opened the door to see this ashen faced, gaunt fragile looking person on my doorstep, who I had only seen a few days earlier, she nearly collapsed in my arms fortunately Michael was holding her.

"Emma, what on earth has happened to you?" She broke down as she told me she had taken some tablets, more than she should. I asked,

"How many?"

She was sobbing while she said,

"Mum I didn't want to kill myself; I just couldn't take anymore." Later, she got the all-clear from the hospital.

The next day she told Carl that she was leaving him. Emma was finding it difficult to cope with her own emotions, looking after a young baby and putting up with Carl's unsympathetic behaviour. He was also treating her very badly both physically and mentally. She and Jodie moved in with us.

Emma started having some real peculiar dreams, we later found out that these were flashbacks from her past.

Katherine also experienced similar flashbacks, she would wake up in the middle of the night gasping for breath, she found it difficult to go back to sleep; so, she would switch on her television. She then claimed she could see horrible things on the screen.

One late evening after we had all had dinner, Steve was in a foul mood and he started shouting at Emma, she turned on him, they were both shouting at each other, then she brought up his drinking, saying something as she was heading towards the door. Emma had been gone for about ten minutes, I went upstairs to see if she was alright, there was no sign of her in the bedroom she shared with Katherine and Jodie was fast asleep in her cot.

I opened the bathroom door, and she was sat on the toilet seat viciously cutting at her wrists luckily, she was using a safety razor.

Emma and I returned to the living room after I had cleaned her up, the cuts that she had managed to make were superficial and did not need any emergency intervention.

Her father and Katherine were oblivious to what had just happened upstairs. There was still a tense atmosphere between Emma and her father. Liam had come in from playing football he was in his second year at high school and had plenty of homework to keep him busy, so he had gone straight to his room.

The argument between Emma and her dad was still festering, until it came to a point, they started shouting at each other again, Katherine went upstairs to make sure Jodie was still asleep, Emma was about to follow when her dad stormed at her; slammed the door with his hand, then aggressively pinned her up against the door.

"Let go of her," I screamed, as a surge of energy went through my body I grabbed at his shoulders, told Emma to sit down on the settee and shouted at her dad to go upstairs. I then told Katherine and Liam not to come down.

Emma was sat in the corner; her arms were around her legs she was rocking to and fro like a little child, I said,

"Come on Emma, talk to me, what's wrong? What is going on? Why are you doing this to yourself? You have got a gorgeous little daughter upstairs who needs you." She replied,

"I don't know, I can't help it."

"I am frightened you might go too far; you have already taken an overdose now you are trying to cut your wrists; you are going to have to go into hospital." Then she said crying,

"I can't, I can't go to hospital,"

She seemed terrified when I mentioned that; I enquired,

"Why not."

"He works there,"

I was confused, I said,

"Who?"

"He's a psychiatric nurse, I'm not going to hospital."

It was hard to understand what she was trying to say, the only person I knew who worked in mental health was her Uncle David. I needed to know what she meant; so, I asked her,

"Is it Uncle David?"

She began to cry,

"Yes Mum, he abused me when I was little, he raped me Mum."

I held her close and after a couple of hours of talking and crying we quietly went to bed, I stayed in Emma's single bed all night with my arm around her while she eventually fell asleep. I could not get the thoughts out of my head, the words that Emma used the night before were still pungent in my mind. We needed to get the police.

She was terrified the next morning, I told her to stay in bed while I go down and explain things to her father.

He listened as I calmly told him what Emma had disclosed the night before, he did not respond the way I expected him to, he just sat there smoking his cigarette, never said anything. I said,

"We need to contact the police."

Then he told me to go and fetch Emma downstairs. I did.

I got such a shock when Emma walked through the lounge door with me following behind, her dad was standing in such a dominant position, with a stern look on his face.

Before I left the room and went upstairs as I was ordered, I was disgusted to hear the way he handled the situation regarding our daughter's disclosure.

For a while nothing was said about the subject.

I was totally disappointed with Katherine's response to her sister when I explained she had been abused by their uncle.

It was hard to understand her thinking when she would not empathize or show Emma some compassion, I said to her on more than one occasion,

"Emma needs your support, put your arms around her she needs a hug to show you care," but Katherine could not show any kind of empathy; actually, she was the complete opposite, it was as if she despised Emma for mentioning the abuse.

I did ask Katherine if she was alright, had anything happened to her as a child? It was a difficult subject; but I had to ask. She abruptly replied,

"No, I'm fine."

One evening I was putting the tea out on the table, when Emma explained she was uncomfortable sat on one of the hard pine chairs, I went into the next room to get a cushion, when I returned Emma was hunched up on the floor in the far corner of the room shaking.

Katherine was shouting,

"Mum! Mum! What's happening?"

I was in complete shock, gasped out loud,

"What on earth is going on, Emma are you alright?" she did not acknowledge me, it was as if she was somewhere else, and we did not exist. Eventually she seemed to come back to earth as that is the only way I can describe it. She began to explain,

"It felt like a knife was sticking inside me when I sat down on that chair, it took me back to another place, I wasn't here Mum! What's happening to me?"

Emma began to shake uncontrollably, all I could do was put my arms around her and spoke to her in calm, soothing voice,

"Sh.sh.sh, it's going to be alright" I rocked her in my arms like a baby.

"He was there, I saw him."

"Who? Where?"

"Just then Mum, I saw Uncle David."

"What do you mean?"

"He was stood there, and he was shouting at me, I was back in Aunty Anne's living room; I remember it was where they used to live, and I used to go and stay with them."

It was hard to understand what had just happened; nevertheless, I had just put the tea out, I was more concerned about them having something to eat than dwelling on what had just taken place. Liam was due home from school soon he had stayed for some football training as they had a match on the Saturday. I did not want him to see Emma like this. Steve had gone for a lie down; nowadays he spent most of the time upstairs after he had been drinking heavily during the day.

Emma started to experience all kinds of abnormal feelings such as anger so bad she felt she needed to smash her fist against a wall, she said,

"It stops the pain from getting worse," I interrupted,

"What pain?" she said,

"I can't explain it, I can't cry the only way I seem to be able to give myself some relief is to hurt myself.

At night-time when my husband had gone to bed Emma would talk to me.

"He used to give me drinks of Shandy and sweets, he told me I was his special little girl. When Aunty Anne went to bed, he sat me on his knee and put a film on, I remember it was always a cowboy film, Uncle David liked cowboy films.

When the music got louder, he jumped me up and down on his knee, it hurt and I started to cry, he told me to put my face straight; then when the music stopped, he threw me onto the floor and told me to get dressed.

I found it extremely difficult to accept what Emma was saying, I could not grasp it. I felt physically sick, I believed her, but to imagine their Uncle David my ex-brother-in-law doing something so despicable to my daughter, his niece, she would have been so young and innocent, so fragile, I wanted to kill him. He had hurt my little girl and I did not know! I could not help her I tried to envisage how she must have felt but it was too painful for me.

Over the next few weeks Emma confided in me at night when my husband had gone to bed. She needed to talk, and I listened to the horrible disgusting details of what that evil man had done to my young daughter. The only way I could cope with what I was hearing, was to imagine Emma was talking about some other little girl and not herself; if I had acknowledged that little person was my beautiful daughter then I know I would have broken down and collapsed in front of her, so I listened to the detailed memories every night. Emma said it helped to talk. She also said her memories were very hazy, she expressed by putting both her hands around her head and stating,

"There's more Mum! There's more! I can't remember it."

I explained to my husband about the conversations I had with Emma, he did not want to acknowledge it and when I tried to get him to listen; he replied,

"I am a man I know what and how a man thinks you don't have to tell me." This comment immediately shut me up, I should have known I could not expect any support from her dad.

He had been drinking more since Emma disclosed the abuse.

I became angry and spoke to him about getting the police involved, but I was stopped in my tracks as my husband mentioned that there were complications to this; the abuser had connections with an Irish paramilitary organization and that we would all end up in body bags if we went to the police. Steve took advantage of my innocence; I was so naive to believe my husband was in touch with Special Branch; seemingly, he had been given a list of wanted men from his sister who was the wife of the abuser.

I know it sounds so far-fetched, but I had no reason not to believe him. With hindsight I should have realized that my husband was completely against contacting the police; for reasons unknown to myself.

When he was supposedly on the phone to Special Branch, he told me it was all top secret, I could not be involved. I was so gullible, believing that he was trying to protect his family.

Over the next couple of months there was always a bottle of whiskey in the kitchen cupboard, he started drinking around 10.30am by 1.00pm he needed help to climb the stairs to have a lie down it was not easy as he was stumbling and swaying all over the place. It was such a relief when he had gone to bed. Every day was the same.

Time went on, Emma had gone into remission, the pain had gone, and she contacted Carl, she explained what had been happening over the last six months. They spoke at length, declared each other's feelings, and decided to make another go at their relationship. Emma and Jodie moved back in with Carl.

Ten months later Zak was born.

Emma and Katherine's relationship deteriorated, Katherine spent most of her time at work; she had managed to achieve her NNEB at college and got herself a good job in the local preschool. I noticed her mood had changed, her bubbly personality had disappeared and when she came home she spent most of her spare time in her room, her appetite had reduced I tried to get her to eat small portions, but she just refused to eat.

She had been invited to a party with some of the girls from work, she did not say what time she would be back, so I waited up for her. Hearing a taxi pull up outside, and screams and shouting I went to see what was happening, two of Katherine's friends were trying to get Katherine into the house she was pulling away and screaming,

"I'm going to kill myself; I want to die."

I immediately went to help them, I thought she must have had too much to drink I questioned her friends after we had managed to get Katherine to lie down on the sofa.

"How much has she had to drink?" their reply was,

"Hardly anything, she just started screaming and kicking the doors, banging the walls with her fists, we got her a taxi straight away."

I thanked her friends for their help and offered them a hot drink, but they politely refused and went home. I returned to the living room where I sat close to Katherine and put my arms around her, and she began to sob like a child.

"It's happened to me Mum, it's happened to me what Uncle David did to Emma he's done the same to me."

Although Katherine had disclosed that she had also been abused by the same man; my husband was still reluctant to go to the police, I wanted to, but did not dare go behind his back. He did not tell me what was going on with Special Branch, he just kept on saying watch for the daily newspapers.

In the next six months we managed to get Katherine some counselling, but she was going downhill fast, I took her to see our family doctor and explained everything to her, she gave Katherine some anti-depressant tablets.

In the meantime, Emma had started again with her anxieties, I really did not want them to get as bad as they had been before Zak was born; I did some research and found a Psychotherapist. I rang the number of a Mrs. Fieldsend-Jones. In short, I described the feelings that Emma was experiencing and how it had all transpired. She said she should be in hospital, I explained that she could not go to hospital as the abuser was a psychiatric nurse. She immediately understood and told me to go to the police, then she would be able to help us. I also mentioned about the concern regarding the abuser's connections with another source. She then gave me a phone number of a person that she thought might be able to advise me.

I was in such a dilemma, I casually mentioned to Steve that I had been in touch with a Mr. Colin Fletcher who was a solicitor.

"He has explained that we should go to the police and that we will not be in any danger from another source."

Steve had no choice but to agree with me, as I was adamant after speaking to Mrs. Fieldsend-Jones I had to do something to help our girls.

Steve decided to be the one to take Emma to the police station and make the complaint. A few days later a Detective Constable Tracy Williams came to take her to a specific venue where it was equipped with all the relevant instruments to make a full statement. Emma was so nervous but Tracy (she told us to call her by her Christian name) was lovely with her, she gently explained what it would be like and what was going to happen. Then she took Emma away after I had given her a big hug, there was still little response from her body contact.

The following day we received a phone call from Tracy,

"The CPS (Criminal Prosecution Service) feels they have enough evidence with Emma's statement alone to charge him, but they want to wait for Katherine's statement so they will have a good solid case."

I waited for Katherine to come home from work; then I asked her how she felt about giving a statement soon. She replied,

"I'm alright Mum, I can do this."

I rang Tracy and arranged for her to collect Katherine Thursday evening to give a statement. She was pleased that both girls were co-operating, as she knew from experience it was not easy for anyone to relive the trauma and remember all the gory details.

Friday afternoon we got a phone call off Tracy, she said,

"We're going to arrest him on Monday it will be around lunch time," I thanked her for letting us know.

Monday came I did not hear anything till 7.20pm. Steve had taken Liam and Katherine to the Badminton club. Emma was at home with Carl and her children. There was an almighty crash on my front door, as if someone had kicked it hard; I was terrified, my dog was barking and growling, luckily the curtains were closed as it was early November.

Then there was another thud, I had to let Steve know, so I crouched down took the phone and dialled the number of the leisure centre. Someone on the desk answered, I quickly said,

"Can I please speak to Mr. Colne he is in the Badminton club?" the man asked me to wait while he went to fetch him. Steve came to the phone,

"What's the matter?"

I blurted out what had just happened, he did not seem too bothered when he asked me,

"Are you alright now? It's probably kids messing about, I can't come home just yet."

I felt I had to be I was quite perturbed with his attitude, so I said,

"Yes." He put the phone down after he said,

"I will see you later."

I needed to know if it was David, it had felt very frightening, I rang Tracy, told her what had happened the night before and I enquired,

"What time did David leave the police station?" she replied,

"Around 6.30pm." my heart skipped a beat; it was close to the time when he would have arrived at our house after travelling from the police station in the city.

She was concerned and told me to contact her if anything else happened. I thanked her and put the phone down.

Days later David was charged with, 'Counts of rape, attempted rape and sexual assault.' He was then put on conditional bail.

Although it had been a good result for the police, we still had the next twelve months to get through before the trial.

Katherine became ill after making her statement and had to be admitted onto a mental health ward at our local hospital.

After fighting for her children in the courts and losing the battle Emma was also admitted onto a mental health ward.

CHAPTER 6

1ˢᵗ CICA Offer

E mma was into her third month as an inpatient at the private Mental Health Hospital. Her consultant was trying to find more funding from the Care Trust.

Katherine was still detained under the Mental Health Act at our local hospital, so there was no chance for Emma to be moved there. I was hoping and praying she could finish her treatment at the Priory.

I decided to prepare for the worse. I rang the solicitor who was dealing with the criminal injuries compensation, thinking, if there were monies owed to Emma, maybe we could use it to fund her stay a while longer; otherwise, she could be moved to a hospital out of the district.

The CICA application had been in the solicitor's hands for well over twelve months, various solicitors had been dealing with the case as the original person had left and they used a locum every so many months. They seemed very certain that the case may be completed soon.

Months later Emma returned home, she had improved a great deal and was coping with the feelings of needing to self- harm through using some of the techniques she had learned from the Priory. However, she was still experiencing flashbacks; fortunately, they were not as strong as they were.

One morning she received a letter from her solicitor explaining that the criminal injuries had offered an award, which I thought was a ridiculous amount and would not have funded a hospital admittance for a couple of months.

The solicitor had suggested that if Emma could produce more evidence, then there might be a chance of increasing the award by another £7,000.

These cases of historic sexual abuse are difficult to prove, as there is never any practical evidence.

I decided to contact Colin Fletcher the solicitor who I had spoken to nearly two years earlier; I do not know why but I had never forgotten his name, all I was told at the time that he specialized in cases for the criminal injuries.

"Hello, Mr. Fletcher, my name is Jennifer Colne, I don't know whether you will remember me; you helped me when I needed some very important advice." I went on to explain a little more,

"Yes, of course I recall our conversation, how are you and your daughters?" I told him what the CICA were offering, he spoke positive about Emma's case and mentioned about the psychological damage.

I relayed all this information to Emma, and we arranged a time to meet him.

We arrived at his offices in Nottingham. I pressed the button on the intercom and spoke to a pleasant female voice.

"We have an appointment with Mr. Colin Fletcher," she allowed the huge glass door to open, we entered and proceeded to walk towards the lift. Again, we walked through another glass door up to the reception desk where we had to sign a book, what time we arrived and who we were expecting to see.

We each sat on one of the brown leather armchairs in the waiting room I noticed in one corner a beautiful green plant stretching towards the ceiling. There was a large flat screen television on the wall, the channel was on the twenty-four- hour news. Piled neatly on the oak coffee table were the daily newspapers.

The lady from the reception desk asked us politely to follow her into an office which had a large, polished rosewood table surrounded with at least eight chairs.

We both moved towards the back and pulled out a matching seat which looked comfortable with burgundy, soft leather cushions.

Before the receptionist left us, she asked us if we would like a cup of tea or coffee, after the long journey we both replied,

"Yes please, coffee with two sugars."

A few minutes later she came back with a tray laden with a coffee percolator, milk jug and a matching sugar bowl and three cups and saucers plus an assortment of biscuits, she politely asked us to help ourselves, so we did. In the middle of the table there was a dish of sweets and pens engraved with the solicitor's company's name.

A couple of minutes later Colin Fletcher entered the room, first appearance was nothing like I expected, he walked with an air of authority, very professional when he spoke but he had a young boyish kind of face, not much taller than myself as I stood up to shake his hand across the table. It was lovely to meet him in person for the first time as this gentleman had been a huge influence in my life. I seemed to get the same impression that he was thinking the same, when he smiled and introduced himself,

"It is nice to meet you at last Mrs. Colne; can I call you Jennifer?"

I smiled back,

"I prefer Jenny if you don't mind."

"And I am Colin, and this must be Emma," he went to shake her hand.

With all the introductions out of the way, he proceeded to ask me,

"Have you appealed yet?"

"No, I wondered if you could help in that way, I really don't want to carry on using the same solicitors as I think they have been most inefficient." I gave him some good examples,

"They used the same statement from an independent Psychiatrist for both the family case and the CICA case," I continued as he listened with interest.

"The truth is Emma was fighting for the custody of her children so when she saw the psychiatrist, she was strong enough to push her anxieties to the back of her mind to complete the statement, which was good in the eyes of the family courts. However, the psychiatrist saw through Emma and did make a small comment to that affect."

Colin listened as I spoke for at least twenty minutes it was all coming out, he was so easy to talk to, then it was his turn.

"Yes, I will be glad to take on your case." He then went on to question me about many things, mainly regarding Emma and her NHS care. I was able to answer everything, with a positive attitude; then he said.

"There wasn't enough medical evidence supplied by the previous solicitor which would have proved permanent psychological damage." I had already read that small section at the back of the book of tariffs which the previous solicitor had given to me. I agreed with him and said,

"I had questioned the solicitor about it, but they didn't seem to listen, even when I rang them continuously explaining that Emma was in hospital suffering from flashbacks of her abuse, surely that proved psychological damage?" Colin nodded, then he asked Emma to sign some papers to save time later.

He was now graciously bringing the meeting to a close, he finished off saying,

"I will be in touch when I have all the information I need, till then don't worry."

I thanked him, shook his hand again and we left feeling extremely pleased with the outcome, even Emma had a smile on her face, knowing someone is listening to her plight.

It was a while before we heard from Colin, one morning his secretary Lucy rang me asking if Colin could make an appointment to come and see Emma and myself. I immediately said,

"Whenever it is convenient for him," so she looked in his diary, mentioned that he was available on the Friday morning of that week. We arranged it for 10.00am.

It was Tuesday when I had made the appointment, now it was Friday morning; both Emma and I were excited, I asked myself why was he making this long journey to see us? And apprehensive of what Colin was going to say.

I polished and hovered making sure Emma's flat was nice and clean. I had already boiled the kettle twice and had the coffee ready in the cup so I could make a drink as soon as Colin arrived, I did not want to miss anything he had to say. I got a phone call; he was on his way, but they had got caught up in some traffic.

Eventually he turned up. The driver sat and waited in the car while Colin attended his meeting with his clients. I offered to make his driver a drink, but Colin said,

"Thanks, he has a flask." I felt a bit uncomfortable leaving him in the car, but the sun was coming out and it was quite warm.

Colin sat down, I put his coffee down beside him on a small table, he took out a lot of papers for Emma to sign, the good news was he had heard from the

CICA they had accepted the appeal, and he was asking for an interim payment. I asked why, he announced with a smile on his face.

"I want Emma to see a private Psychiatrist who specializes in Post-Traumatic Stress Disorder, I have been in touch with Professor Gordon Andrews, and he is willing to see you next week."

Emma was still having her flashbacks, fortunately they were not as severe and as frequent as they had been, she had one in front of Colin when he came to see us, he had been very understanding while it was happening and had respectfully left me to help her.

Again, we had to travel quite a distance up north to see this private psychiatrist. I appreciated my friend Peter coming with us, he sat in the back, whilst Emma was in the passenger seat.   Each time Emma had a flashback, Peter was able to lean forward and apply smelling salts under her nose, and this soon brought her back to reality.

It was scary at first, I would just be having a conversation with her about anything, other than what was going on with the present subject; when her head started jolting backwards and forwards, I heard the loud thud each time it hit the back of the headrest, all I could do was carry on driving as we were on the motorway. Although we had placed pillows all around her and behind her head for safety, there was still a strong impact.

We arrived outside a converted stone cottage with a beautiful view of a park clad with huge oak trees.

I lifted the brass knocker and slowly banged it against the dark, oak panelled door, a small lady wearing a white apron greeted us and showed us into a room, I think it was meant to be a waiting room, but it was so fascinating; in the far corner was a polished walnut upright piano and some other musical instruments, we sat on the antique high-backed chairs situated around the room. The housekeeper offered to make us a cup of tea or coffee. We all accepted as we had not had time to stop. When we reached our destination; we had just a few minutes to spare before the appointment time.

Approximately five minutes later a small man with greying hair and a slight bald patch introduced himself as Professor Gordon Andrews, he shook our hands with a firm grip, then turned towards Emma with a smile.

"Would you like to follow me?"

She looked in my direction; I knew what she was thinking; frightened she may have another flashback without my presence. The professor seemed to understand and said,

"Don't worry if I need you, I will send for you, we are only next door." Then they were gone.

Emma was terrified of strangers, let alone being in the company of one by herself. She was finding it awfully hard to trust anyone and had been for a long time.

Half an hour later I looked at the grandfather clock which stood proudly on the opposite wall to the huge oak fireplace. Worried sick, that Emma might have another episode. Peter said to me,

"The professor will know what to do."

I had been told by Colin that the professor was expensive he charged by the hour, I picked up a country life magazine; but my mind was not functioning. Twenty minutes later, Emma and the professor entered the room, I looked at Emma to make sure she was alright, Gordon

Andrews sensed that I had been worried and put my mind at rest.

"Yes, she has had a flashback and I let her come out of it herself she was comfortable, please trust me when I say, I have seen these intensity flashbacks before."

I explained we use smelling salts when it is imperative we need to bring her out of it as soon as possible, I told him she experienced a few on the way to see him so we had to use them. I was quite surprised when he smiled and said,

"Good idea, whatever works for you."

He had spoken to Colin Fletcher and between them they had agreed that the professor would see Emma on a regular basis, he first wanted to give her a prescription of a cocktail of drugs including anti-psychotics and a strong anti- depressant which should benefit her intensity flashbacks, not to completely stop them; but to take the edge off them. Then he got out his diary and asked if we could come back in a month, in the meantime he would also make a report on his findings for the CICA case. He exclaimed it would be a positive report and not to worry.

"I have known Colin for a long time he is very good, he gets results."

On that note, I shook his hand and thanked him and so did Emma, then we left.

After the long journey back, we were exhausted and just wanted to relax as Emma had encountered quite a few flashbacks on the way home. Luckily, Peter was strong and able to support Emma's neck from injury while I carried on driving.

The prescribed medication was quite strong and took Emma a while to become accustomed to it. We had to cancel the next appointment with the Professor as she really was not well enough to make the journey.

He understood, and we made another appointment.

It was about six weeks since we first met Professor Gordon Andrews.

We received a report from Colin in the first-class post. The first page was an introduction of the Professor, his Curriculum Vitae held an extraordinary amount of information.

Degrees of Bachelor of Medicine and Bachelor of Surgery. A member of the Royal College of Psychiatrists, a member of the Expert Witness Institute, a visiting Professor worldwide etc., most of his employment history and all the awards he had achieved plus much more.

The report included a statement from me; and the statement from Emma which was particularly good to say she could not talk about things that had happened to her, she had put an excellent description in. The professor's conclusion was so true he had not missed anything; it was as if he had known Emma for years and seen for himself the trauma, the unhappiness, and the painful life she had experienced up to now from such a young age. He explained in detail the Post Traumatic Stress Disorder he had diagnosed, including Major depressive disorder, along with the Psychotic intensity flashbacks. That is the official clinical name for the involuntary movements Emma has suffered for so long.

Reading the report, I feel someone for the very first time had listened and heard Emma's cry for help, and Professor Andrews has taken the time to do something to help her. It has always been a complex disorder of symptoms; I now think maybe she might have a chance of experiencing a normal life, if all her symptoms can be controlled.

Colin had included a letter saying, he is pleased with the Professor's response and that it is an excellent report. It will be positive for the CICA.

I had not realized when we met Colin, he would have a great impact on our lives in such a positive way. I will forever be in his debt.

I was much more content now that we had found someone who understood what was happening to Emma; after seeing so many different Psychiatrists, Therapists, Doctors and Nurses' who were really baffled when they were confronted with Emma's Psychotic Intensity Flashbacks.

After Emma had been experiencing these flashbacks all day long, by night-time she needed some respite; we were both completely exhausted.

The first time I had phoned for an ambulance the paramedics were confused when I explained what the symptoms were. I tried to enlighten them.

They seemed to listen, but I could see they had not seen anything like it before. I told them Emma would be able to walk to the ambulance, once she has finished having a flashback; there was a window of time before the next one.

Emma was comfortable on the small bed in the ambulance; I had taken a thick, soft pillow with us to protect her head. The paramedics allowed me to travel next to her so long as I wore the seat belt provided.

We had been travelling by road, I do not think they realized the risk at first, so they steered clear of the motorway. Unfortunately, Emma had a bad flashback she went unconscious, then her head began to jilt aggressively backwards and forwards, this episode lasted for about a minute and half, meanwhile the paramedic was in control, she had banged on the front of the ambulance to STOP. She was trying desperately to take her pulse; but Emma's body began to twist into such a position that the paramedic had to quickly unfasten the belt, which was now being stretched to its fullest, her back curved to almost breaking point; I was so frightened that her spine would snap.

All the paramedics could do was wait until Emma came out of her comatose state. Eventually she was able to do the necessary checks.

Then she said to the driver,

"Step on it." I think she was frightened Emma might have another one, we were speeding towards the hospital with sirens and flashing blue lights; cars were moving over to one side to let us pass.

Within minutes we arrived at the hospital, I went to check Emma in at the reception desk, in the Accident and Emergency dept.

After I had given all the relevant details to the lady behind the counter, I was taken by a nurse to sit with Emma; she was still laid on the narrow bed from the ambulance waiting for an available cubicle. Unfortunately, Emma had another episode; luckily one of the paramedics stayed to help me as there were no nurses around.

Eventually a cubicle was free, Emma was transferred from the ambulance bed onto a much larger bed with steel sides which resembled a baby's cot.

Nurses came to do all the Orbs; I presume that meant, blood pressure, pulse, and her temperature. The paramedic had given Emma some gas and air in the ambulance to help her cope with the pain she was left with, after her flashback. While the nurse was with us Emma asked if she could have some; it would have made the pain that little bit more bearable.

"I'm sorry we can't give you anything until the doctor has seen you." The nurse went and pulled the long curtain across we were left alone.

About ten minutes later Emma began to have another episode of head movements, each time her head banged down on the pillow the bed shook, and the noise echoed from the steel frame. I was hoping a nurse would have heard the commotion and come to help; but that did not happen I had to deal with the situation on my own.

After I managed to calm Emma, I opened the curtain and looked around. Doctors were sat on high-backed stools looking at computer screens situated on a huge table which resembled an over large breakfast bar.

Nurses were walking about carrying out their duties. I tried to get some attention, expecting someone to have at least heard all the noise Emma had made; but it was as if nothing had happened.

I asked a nurse if I could get some water, she kindly showed me where the plastic cups were stacked, and which tap to use. I thanked her and returned to Emma's cubicle. I purposefully left the curtain open.

Approximately twenty minutes later Emma had another episode, extremely strong, with aggressive head movements.

After about a minute her head stopped and her spine began to bend backwards, I then had to shout for assistance as I could not hold her, she was completely unconscious; her body was twisting into another direction, her leg had got stuck between one of the bars that was meant to protect a person from falling out.

A nurse came in while I was still shouting, "Help! Someone, please help me!"

She was astonished to see Emma's mangled body twisting, her leg was pushing through the bars, I was frantic as I was holding her head, she had nearly turned full circle the nurse immediately came to my aid, she grabbed a blanket and lodged it between the bars and Emma's leg.

I explained to the nurse that Emma would be alright in a minute, I just needed help with her leg as I was still stopping her head from pushing through the bars on the opposite side.

Emma resumed normality just as the doctor appeared, I thanked the nurse before she left, and I then had to describe Emma's symptoms, which was so difficult you had to see it to believe it. The doctor listened with interest and prescribed a muscle relaxant drug which the nurse will give intravenously, it worked wonders.

Emma had a few more flashbacks but they had reduced in strength, and I could easily cope.

We could not leave till they had completely stopped, which was about a couple of hours later. That was the first of many trips to the hospital, most of the staff knew Emma by sight, they were nice, and they left me to cope, but always offered to help.

Some of the on-call psychiatrists had seen Emma on numerous occasions and immediately got a nurse to intravenously administer the appropriate medication; knowing that it would ease Emma's physical flashbacks and give her some relief.

Most of the times we visited the hospital for the same reason, we always had to be taken by ambulance, as it was too dangerous for me to drive without an escort to help Emma. The number of occasions I had to reiterate Emma's symptoms with so many different paramedics.

Sometimes the same one may turn up and he/she would explain to their colleague, which gave me a little respite, others could remember Emma's name and they were so compassionate with her.

There is also the odd one that is not as empathic and can be a little impatient, but overall, the Ambulance Service were excellent when it came to decorum and dealt with Emma in a very efficient and dignified manner.

CHAPTER 7

Emma meets Kevin

Emma's flashbacks had subsided for a short while and she decided to look for a job. There were several vacancies at the time; but there was one that appealed to Emma. It meant travelling, she was alright with that; she said,

"Mum, I feel so much better, I need to experience life and meet new people." I understood and she began to apply for the position of a data administration assistant at the main hospital in the city. She came to a few questions that were difficult to answer regarding mental health,

Have you any problems? She put 'Yes' she had to elaborate. Emma completed the application to the best of her ability and posted it to the correct address.

A week later she got a date for an interview, not expecting a positive response she was overjoyed at the prospect they wanted to see her. We went shopping and found a nice dark grey suit which was tailored to fit Emma's figure, unfortunately she had put on some weight while taking the increased amount of medication. We bought quite a few white blouses. Emma could not make up her mind, so we took them all. She also tried on some black patent shoes with a two-and-a-half-inch heel, which at first, she found it hard to walk in, but she soon got used to them, she was determined to get this job.

Two weeks later a letter came through the post, they must have been impressed with Emma as she read out loud the first couple of lines,

"We are pleased to accept you as one of our employees," she carried on further down the page.

"We would like you to attend an appointment at our Occupational Health Dept. on 9th July 10.30am."

They were willing to give Emma a chance, she had been completely truthful in the interview, she had all the relevant qualifications and the job rested entirely on the outcome of the Occupational Health Dept.

Emma was asked lots of questions about her mental health and she answered them truthfully. She had to do some physical tests and an aptitude test.

A couple of days later she received a date when she would be starting and that they were pleased with her performance, again she was ecstatic with the good news.

One night she had been out socializing with her new friends from work, when she met Kevin, he was seven years older than Emma and very understanding when she explained everything about herself and her mental health a week after they had started dating.

Kevin did not live far from the hospital, so it was easy for him to pick Emma up and take her back to his house, which he shared with his dad. Emma felt comfortable staying at Kevin's she was happy for the first time in a long time. Kevin's father Ronald and Emma got on so well together, he made her laugh with his great sense of humour. Emma needed that, although she had been through so much pain and personal suffering, she had never lost her sense of humour. Sometimes I wonder if that has helped her overcome such a lot of unhappiness in her lifetime.

She too brought some sunshine back into Kevin's Dad's life as he had recently lost his wife, Kevin's Mum to cancer; apparently, he and Kevin nursed her through to the end, which was devastating to watch her suffer, hoping and praying it would soon be over for her.

Ronald's face lit up; as Emma walked through the door with Kevin, she sat and had a banter with Ronald, while Kevin cooked supper for them all.

Kevin was good in the kitchen he could make some exotic meals as well as the conventional ones.

His Mum had taught him a lot; he had watched and learned with enthusiasm.

Emma's medication seemed to be working, she was blissfully happy and had been for nearly six months.

Unfortunately, she started feeling unwell again, Emma had to hand her notice in; she loved her job and everything it entailed, but this was different to what she had experienced before. She collapsed at work a couple of times, then at home. There was no warning she could be just walking from one room to another when she slumped to the floor for no reason. Sometimes she hurt herself if there was an object, like the coffee table in front of her. We were terrified of her going up and coming down the stairs. She has fallen back on me on more than one occasion luckily, I managed to support her and slowly I lowered her to the ground.

Each time this happened she seemed to be unconscious and after a few minutes she would open her eyes and wonder why she was lying down in such a weird position, whether it was at the bottom of the stairs, in the kitchen or even on the path as she was walking to the car. The doctor suggested Emma sees a neurologist; I could not wait for an appointment coming through the post. I decided to ring the hospital and ask to speak to a neurologist's secretary, I was quite surprised when the telephone receptionist asked if I could wait a minute while she puts me through. I explained why my daughter needed to see the consultant and asked if he accepted private patients?

"Yes," came the reply, I was so relieved I made an appointment straight away; providing I got a referral from Emma's doctor.

Immediately I rang the doctor's surgery, the receptionist told me there were no appointments left, I explained the urgency and reluctantly she put me through. Straight away Emma's doctor faxed the referral to the Consultant's secretary. Within a couple of days, the Consultant Neurologist saw Emma, she collapsed in front of him, when he was able; he did all the necessary tests to determine what may be causing these seizures. I was so worried thinking she had epilepsy, but he put my mind at rest when he explained he could not find anything wrong, and all the tests came back normal. His words were,

"These are non-epileptic symptoms."

The Consultant organised a CAT scan for Emma, through the NHS, just to make sure he had not missed anything and that a scan would confirm there was nothing seriously wrong with Emma's brain. Fortunately, the result of the CAT scan was clear.

Both Kevin and I were relieved, but also wondering what was causing Emma to collapse. Although she was experiencing these symptoms; Emma was not feeling any pain and so long as she had someone to support her everywhere, including the bathroom, as it had happened in there, which had been embarrassing for her. She had to lose all sense of dignity as her safety was much more important.

We made an appointment to see Professor Andrews. Kevin came with us to help with Emma and to meet the professor. We both explained what was happening to Emma; as she could not; she did not know. She was unconscious at the time to know anything. It was only when me or Kevin had prevented a major accident, did we tell her what had happened to her.

There were no medical signs; she was still taking her anti-psychotic medication and her antidepressant. We also told him the CAT scan was clear.

Professor Andrews spoke to Emma, Kevin, and me he explained what he thought may be happening to her. Not in any clinical terms, just easy enough for us to understand what he was saying.

"The emotional pain could be too much for her conscious mind to accept and it is your body's way of protecting itself by switching off, there is no need to worry as you," he looked in Emma's direction,

"Will always come round, just make sure you are in a safe environment."

Kevin was very understanding and wanted to support Emma through everything she had to contend with, including helping her with her children and protecting them from seeing anything when Emma collapsed.

Eventually the episodes of collapsing did reduce until they finally stopped, and we could all get back to normal.

Around that time, Kevin spoke to me about his feelings for Emma, how much he loved her and wanted to look after her, he then asked me for my permission to marry her. I was so happy for them; but before I agreed, which would have been so easy to do if Emma had not had so many problems. I had to be completely sure Kevin understood Emma's plight and that he would support and care for her when she needed him. From his next comment, I knew he was the right one for Emma and her children, after he had declared his undying love for her, I realised that he would totally honour his marriage vows, so I gladly gave him my blessing to marry my daughter.

Emma was so happy to accept Kevin's proposal, it gave everyone something to think about as they decided to get married that same year.

Coincidently she received a letter from Colin. The CICA had made an offer of an award.

I am pleased to tell you they are offering a substantial amount. He went on to say how much and when.

She was already under the Court of Protection; her deputy who was also employed by the same company in which Colin represented; will be looking after her well-being and all her finances.

Most of it was to be used for private treatment. There was also enough to purchase a house big enough for the children.

Emma and Kevin were happy together, Emma still had access of her two children at the weekends, and they loved their new house. Emma and Kevin decorated each of their bedrooms, Jodie's was all pale pink; typical of a little girl that was into princesses. Zak's was a complete contrast, blue with Thomas the Tank Engine and Yellow with Bob the Builder.

Choosing a venue which would correspond with the date for the church, proved to be a lot harder than we expected, luckily there had been a cancellation at a restaurant which catered for weddings, they had a beautiful, landscaped garden at the back with a river rippling gently in the background, everything fell into place. Then, there were the invitations to send out in plenty of time; not forgetting Emma's dress and the bridesmaids' regalia.

The day finally came I was so proud of Emma, she looked beautiful, she had chosen a Maid Marion type dress, low shoulders with little detail, just a few small pink flowers with pale green leaves embroidered along the top of the bodice which tapered down to a slim waist, the white silk material fell over a hooped underskirt that enabled the dress to spread out evenly down to the floor.

She decided not to wear a veil or a train; just a delicate tiara round her strawberry blonde hair which the hairdresser had put up in curls, with a small amount falling into ringlets just touching her shoulders. Her slender neck showed off the diamond cross, a little present from me, as I had never envisaged this day.

Jodie also looked gorgeous in her pale pink flowing bridesmaid dress, she was a smaller version of her mother, wearing a delicate tiara around her tiny head of beautiful curls, she carried a posy of pale colourful roses like her Mum's bouquet.

Zak led the procession very slowly and carefully holding a white silk cushion with two gold bands attached with cotton, (I was not taking any chances). He was so cute in a velvet burgundy shorts suit with a white fluffy shirt, the hairdresser had gently spiked his dark brown hair which made him look even more mischievous. Liam one of Kevin's ushers showed everyone to their seat, he was growing up and he looked so handsome.

Emma and her father walked gracefully down the aisle to a tune which was special to Emma and Kevin. There, standing before the Alter was Kevin looking extremely smart in his dark grey suit, white shirt, and a burgundy cravat. The smile on his face spoke for itself; when he saw his wife to be, Emma handed her bouquet to her chief bridesmaid Katherine and her dad passed Emma's hand over to Kevin.

The ceremony was blissful, everything went without a hitch, photographs were taken, speeches were made, one from Emma's Dad, another from Kevin's best man, a friend he had grown up with since his school days and letting a few secrets out about Kevin in his youth; we all learned quite a bit about Kevin that day which made him blush.

Later that evening everybody joined together outside clapping, joyous and waving the happy couple off for a week in Paris.

Fortunately, Emma was in remission for quite a while, they were delighted to find out that she was expecting a baby boy the following June. Her pregnancy went well except for a quite a bit of backache. When she told her children that they were having a baby brother they were so excited and could not wait for him to be born.

Again, Emma had to have a caesarean, the baby was a healthy 6lb 8oz. Carl had allowed us to take the children to the hospital to see their mother. Jodie's little face lit up when she saw her tiny baby brother. Zak was quiet, it was sad as he was smiling but he did not really understand that Darren (that is what they all decided to call him) was his little brother.

CHAPTER 8

Six Years Later

A month before Emma and Kevin's sixth anniversary a very dear friend had been fatally injured in a road accident, we all went to his funeral, as we were walking away from the graveside; my ex-husband put his hand on Emma's arm and led her away towards our car.

Emma was never the same after that day, she seemed to grow a hate towards her father, it came to a head when she rang him and screamed down the phone,

"I never want to see you again; you're not my father and you won't see my children."

Katherine and Liam found out and confronted Emma. It seems their father had told them that he had not been well for a while and that he would have to go to the hospital for some tests. This had been going on for about six months and when they questioned him about the results, he would not tell them anything. This attitude caused them to think the worse, they were really worried about him; therefore, this made them annoyed with Emma when they found out what Emma had said to their dad, they could not understand why? And Emma could not tell them, she was not ready to disclose anything about her father.

They were pushing her; Liam threatened,

"If anything happens to our dad, you will not be welcome at his funeral."

Hoping that statement might change Emma's way of thinking, they both got a shock, and so did I when she retaliated,

"Good! I wouldn't want to go; in fact, I'll dance on his grave when he's dead."

I noticed Emma was becoming more agitated as they were firing questions at her.

"What has he done to upset you like this?" Katherine shouted in a harsh tone.

Emma stood up and screamed.

"I'll tell you! I'll tell you!"

Then she ran out of the front door in her stocking feet; she raced up the avenue and round the corner out of view. I chased after her but before I could stop her, she punched a brick wall so hard with her fist; it bled and her knuckles disappeared, meanwhile Liam and Katherine had jumped in Katherine's car, Liam got out he was shocked to see what Emma had done to herself, I shouted,

"Leave her alone!" I think he knew I was serious, he got back in the car, and they drove off.

That was the beginning of the feud between my children; unfortunately, it gets much worse, when the community psychiatric nurse Miss Rylands intervenes.

Cindy was dancing in a local Theatre Production. Katherine had asked me how many tickets I would like, eagerly I had replied, "Six," I thought of my daughter Emma, her three children Jodie, Zak, and Darren, me, and my mum. This was before Emma had said anything about her dad.

We were all looking forward to seeing our little darling dance.

Four of my tickets had to be cancelled, when my daughter Emma heard that her father had reserved a ticket for the front row.

This made her even more angry, Kevin tried to console her; but nothing worked, she began to self-harm again; by cutting her arm with a razor blade, the medication had seemed to stop working and her flashbacks returned, slowly at first, then they became more intense.

Emma had asked to be discharged from her private psychiatrist as we needed to have someone local, so she had only been with her new Consultant for about a week.

She broke down in tears and disclosed that her father had also sexually abused her when she was little. Before Uncle David and then with her Uncle David.

"He knew Mum, he knew… he let Uncle David… and he helped him."

I tried to understand what Emma was trying to say in between the sobs, she was crying uncontrollably like she had never been able to do before.

Eventually Emma calmed down and explained everything to both Kevin and me.

She began to speak slowly and quietly,

"Mum, Dad…. I find it hard to call him that…"

"Why? What has happened? What has he done?

"He's abused me Mum; he raped me when I was little."

"What! You're Dad?" I could feel the blood draining away from my face, I felt I had just been kicked in the stomach, I was speechless, Emma was looking for some reaction, everything went blank, her words echoed over and over in my head; I managed to walk towards her I put my arms around her as I squeezed, I felt all my love and heartfelt sorrow being transferred into her trembling body, petrified of all the threats her father had made to her as a child.

"NOT TO TELL OR ELSE?"

"It was when my dad held my arm at the funeral it triggered off so many bad memories which I have buried for nearly twenty-five years."

The shock and horror of what I was hearing from Emma; made me feel physically sick I had my arms around her, I felt awful that I had to leave her for a few minutes to collect my own thoughts, I rinsed my face with cold water.

It was hard to contemplate what Emma was saying about her father, my ex-husband who I had been married to for thirty years, I trusted him totally with our children.

This incestuous abuse never entered my head, I did not know it existed in families like my own, I thought about my little girl being with that monster, her father, the person who was supposed to protect her from evil people like that and all the time he was the evil one.

I was heaving in the bathroom; my mind went back to when she was so small, so fragile, and so innocent; I could not protect her when she needed me.

I knew Emma wanted me, but I could not face her, luckily Kevin was with her. My body went numb as I went into their spare room, I collapsed on the bed; shaking, I buried my head in the pillow and sobbed trying hard not to let Emma or Kevin hear me.

Eventually I came downstairs, Kevin had made Emma a sweet cup of tea, as she had gone deathly white, and her lips were turning a pale colour of blue. He went to make me a cup of tea, while I apologised for being away for so long,

Emma immediately replied,

"Mum, you have nothing to apologise for,"

She was more concerned for me than herself. I sat down next to her, and she took hold of my hand and squeezed it; she looked me in the eye asking,

"Are you alright?" I replied,

"No, I can't get my head round it and every time I try to, I feel sick."

Emma gave me a look as if she were sorry that she had said anything.

"I feel so guilty Mum, for upsetting you and not being able to tell you sooner,"

The shock and upset had now turned into anger I said,

"Don't worry about me you have to tell the police."

That night I stayed in their spare bedroom; I could not sleep; my mind was racing my blood was boiling. It was early morning; I needed to calm down so I could plan how Kevin and I were going to organize things later that day.

The following morning: Emma started with serious psychotic intensity flashbacks, much worse than Kevin or I had ever seen; we immediately rang the Crisis Team, the team leader came as soon as he could and he suggested we get in touch with Emma's new community psychiatric nurse, in the hope she might be able to contact Dr. Bedfordshire, Emma's new psychiatric consultant: hopefully to have her anti-psychotic medication increased. Kevin and I knew this would help Emma. When she was presenting psychosis, the professor always increased her dosage of anti-psychotics; until her behaviour (intensity psychotic flashbacks) subsided.

Miss Rylands arrived I was so relieved, this was the first time we had ever had any help from a local CPN (Community Psychiatric Nurse), I explained a little bit of what to expect before I opened the lounge door. I asked her to sit down after introducing her to Emma and Kevin and offering her a cup of tea; she politely declined. She began to ask Emma all sorts of questions of which Emma could not answer.

I tried to interrupt and explain that when Emma presented these involuntary movements she was completely out of control of her own body and mind until she opens her eyes and comes back to reality.

"Professor Andrews had explained that Emma is having a dissociation with reality."

Emma was answering Miss Rylands questions to the best of her knowledge; when suddenly, Emma's head swung forwards then flung backwards, I grabbed a cushion quick and held it behind her head, and I explained to this lady it helps to lessen the impact.

The movements became much stronger and aggressive, then her head slowed down, it was if someone was pulling Emma off the settee; she slid down to the floor, then her back arched and her body was writhing up and down. At last, it stopped nearly as quickly as it had started.

Miss Rylands sat and watched in amazement as Emma was just opening her eyes. Kevin helped her get back up on the settee. She needed a cigarette, it always helped afterwards, she said,

"It brings me back to who I am and not that little girl."

Kevin slowly walked with Emma outside into the garden to have a smoke, she was always sore in between her legs after these episodes.

I spoke to Miss Rylands,

"This is what happens, she is actually reliving the sexual and physical abuse through these flashbacks, she doesn't need to go into hospital; we just need the appropriate medication to help take the edge off them so Emma can cope. We have seen and dealt with them for years, so we know what we are doing. Emma disclosed for the first time yesterday, that her father had raped her, and he had also helped his brother-in-law to do the same."

Emma came back in from the garden, she apologised for having to leave us.

Miss Rylands asked Emma how she felt and what had just happened? I had just explained to her hoping that Emma did not have to. She had not listened to a word I said. Emma tried to answer her question.

"I don't know anything, except that my neck hurts and my dad was pulling my hair." I interrupted,

"Emma goes back into the past when she has an episode like that."

Emma began to explain about her father abusing and raping her from the age of about four years old. It was extremely hard for Emma to speak about these memories which were very hurtful and.... traumatic. As it was only the day before that she had disclosed it to us. I felt so much empathy for Emma as she was talking to this woman, opening her heart out to a stranger; she had never been able to do that before as she always had a problem with trusting people.

Unfortunately, she should have gone with her gut instinct regarding the trust. I watched Miss Rylands body language; I was being too optimistic to expect her to understand what Emma was trying to say. I had hoped this lady would have been more empathic, but instead she started asking more questions. Little did we know then that Miss Rylands was also a Social Worker.

"Have you contacted the police?" Emma answered,

"I can't yet, I'm not ready," Before Emma could say anything else Miss Rylands asked,

"Have you got any siblings?" Emma answered again,

"Yes, I have a brother and a sister." The woman asked,

"Do they have any children?" Again, Emma replied,

"My sister has a little girl, Cindy."

CHAPTER 9

Katherine Meets Paul

It was quite a few years ago since Katherine had been discharged from hospital; she had spent six months on the Picu Ward (Psychiatric Intensive Care Unit). She had experienced a complete breakdown caused by the sexual abuse she had suffered at the hands of her Uncle David.

The strong medication helped, she eventually acknowledged what had happened to her and after months of denial, she began to face normality.

It was so upsetting to see her in the beginning as the Doctors had to sedate her. Visiting times were awfully hard watching Katherine walking about like a Zombie, her eyes were so dark and sunken into her prominent cheek bones. She was not eating very much, but the nurses provided a milk shake, which contained all the vital vitamins and minerals Katherine needed to function.

She could communicate in short sentences,

"What is happening to me Mum?"

I did not know how to answer, I just explained,

"I don't know, there is only you that can help yourself get better." I had to be truthful because she might never recover until she has acknowledged her abuse.

Unfortunately, her Uncle David; as we found out in her statement to the police, had drugged her with tablets he had taken from the hospital he was working in at the time. She was not compos-mentis at the time when the sexual abuse was taking place and so everything is hazy to Katherine; it is easier for her to go into denial as there is no complete memory.

The doctor's and the nurses were excellent, especially one that Katherine had taken to, it was not the softy, approach that Katherine needed, this nurse did not beat about the bush; she said it how she saw it and gently threatened Katherine by telling her.

"If you don't get better, they will send you to forensics." This had frightened Katherine, she had heard all kinds of rumours about forensics, and she did not want to experience it for herself...

Slowly those words helped Katherine come to terms with what had happened to her. The pictures that she made in occupational therapy were becoming colourful instead of black boxes which represented coffins. She asked me to fetch her favourite red top with me next time I come, that was something special to me, as she had been adamant about wearing black and dark grey clothes which were baggy and hung on her body. It had seemed she wanted to portray on the outside how she felt on the inside.

Ward round came, I was always invited, so was my husband, but he never attended. In fact, not once did he visit Katherine on the Picu ward.

The Consultant explained that Katherine would be moving back to the acute ward in a week's time if she carried on showing the same improvement. Katherine smiled at me, I could not show my true feelings; but I felt the tears welling up in my eyes and the lump in my throat, as the Consultant was telling me that they would also allow her to have some short time at home, maybe an hour or two at the beginning.

On my first visit after that ward round; I went to the usual place the Picu ward to see Katherine, I received a nice surprise when the nurse told me over the intercom to go to the acute ward.

They had needed Katherine's bed for an emergency and moved her earlier. She met me wearing a pair of pale blue jeans and a nice colourful top which I had brought earlier under Katherine's instructions.

She was smiling as she stood in the doorway to the acute ward. I gave her a hug, she hugged me back; so different from all the hugs I had given her when she was in the Picu ward.   I received so much more warmth with this one, which meant such a lot as Katherine had now managed to acknowledge her own feelings and emotions.

The day came when she had been given permission to come home for a few hours, everything went well on her first visit, she explained that she felt nervous and very insecure; but we took it slowly and when she felt ready to go back to the hospital, I took her in our car.

After a few weeks and quite a few short visits, the Consultant arranged for Katherine to spend a weekend at home.

I was full of excitement as I collected her small empty suitcase from the top of the wardrobe; knowing that it would be full of her clothes and personal belongings when I brought her home. Looking at her bed with her special duvet that we had bought on one of our shopping sprees. I had decided to make Katherine her favourite meal, Cauliflower, mashed potato, steak, and plenty of homemade cheese sauce.

We arrived home around lunch time; she went upstairs to unpack, while I made us a snack. I crept upstairs and stood in her bedroom doorway, she came over and I gave her a big hug, she responded smiling,

"Mum, I am a lot better, it won't be long before I can come home for good," I smiled back saying,

"I know love, I have been waiting so long for this day to come, I knew it would, I just didn't know when?"

We went downstairs together, her dad had just walked in from the garden, he was pleased to see Katherine; he walked towards her, opened his arms, and gave her a hug.

I was delighted that reunion went well; as I was apprehensive of them meeting, it had been a long time since her dad had seen Katherine.

He spent about an hour with us sat talking and laughing, reminiscing old times, then he stood up and walked towards the kitchen. I followed him; he was just taking the bottle of whiskey out of the cupboard, he picked up a glass and began to pour. I asked him,

"Not today Steve," ignoring my plea, he topped the whiskey up with water and whispered,

"Just the one."

I went back into the lounge, trying hard not to let Katherine know her father was drinking.

My mum popped round to see Katherine she stayed for a coffee and a chat; then left an hour later.

I asked Katherine what she would like to do. She replied,

"Let's watch a film on TV and chill out." That was a good idea, I could see she just wanted a nice quiet afternoon. While we sat watching the film, her dad kept going into the kitchen for the bottle of whiskey. I tried to stop him; but I was terrified Katherine might hear me, so I whispered,

"You are drinking too much." again, he ignored me.

Later, I made dinner we decided to eat on trays in front of the television. Katherine's face lit up when she saw what I had prepared.

"Thanks Mum, you haven't forgotten my favourite tea," I smiled knowing she appreciated it,

"Enjoy it," I said.

Katherine was halfway through her meal when her dad came staggering into the lounge, he tried to sit on a dining chair over the far side of the room; but he fell off and landed on the floor. Katherine looked at me, I said,

"Don't worry; eat your dinner."

Her Dad got on all fours and pulled himself up onto a chair, it toppled on top of him. I was so angry, I got up to help him; he pushed me away as he was struggling to get up.

Katherine started shaking,

"Mum! I need to go back now." I did not hesitate; I got her coat and the car keys and went back to the hospital. The staff nurse on the ward was nice, after I had explained the reason

Katherine had cut her weekend leave short. While I was saying good-bye to her, she said,

"Don't worry, we'll look after her."

I was livid, walking briskly to the car park and thinking out loud.

How dare he spoil Katherine's weekend?

When he was sober, I let him know how much he had upset me and Katherine. He apologized and said,

"It won't happen again."

How many times had I heard those words?

A couple of days later, I rang the hospital to see if Katherine could have some leave, the answer was,

"No, I am sorry Mrs. Colne; but Katherine can't come home while her dad is there, it is too upsetting for her."

That was it, I wanted my daughter home, my mind was settled; Steve must go.

I phoned his sister, asked if she would collect him and could he stay at her house for a while until he found somewhere of his own. I explained,

"I've had enough, I am sick of his drinking, I have tried to help him; but I cannot do it anymore."

I then went on to tell her about the weekend and why I cannot bring my daughter home if he is there. She understood and agreed to help me.

That was it, my marriage was over.

A month later Katherine was completely discharged from hospital, she just visited the

Outpatients at the mental health centre in town as and when she wanted.

One cold December night we were snuggled up on the settee, when the phone rang, it was about ten thirty; Katherine and I were watching a good film on the television.

It was Anne my sister-in-law she seemed drunk, screaming down the phone,

"He's raped me, when I was nine years old, my brother raped me."

I never spoke just listened as Anne was repeating the same words.

"Your husband raped me when I was only nine, my mum knew, she said he was only experimenting, it was pushed under the carpet, I'll have him one day; when my mum has gone."

Anne was crying and getting really distressed; then she started shouting the same words again. By this time, I had changed over to the far chair, away from the settee.

"Who's that on the phone?" Katherine asked, not really that bothered as she was enthralled with the film, oblivious to my feelings of utter shock and disgust.

I whispered so Anne would not hear me,

"Just a friend."

Anne's friend came on the line and apologized saying,

"Anne is really upset; I think she has said enough." Then she put the phone down.

I thought to myself, *so that is why he moved out of Anne's so quickly,* within weeks of asking him to leave he had found himself a flat about half a mile from my house.

I could not get those words out of my head, I had to speak to Anne again when she was sober; she denied it when I asked her,

"Was it true?"

She angrily replied,

"I was drunk, forget what I said."

But it was not easy to forget something like that.

It never came up again until Katherine's daughter Cindy was two years old.

Christmas was coming, I asked Katherine what she would like, and she answered,

"A dog."

What a brilliant idea it gave her something to think about. We rang the local RSPCA to look for a dog suitable for Katherine. There was quite a few to choose from, but nothing appealed to her. Then she contacted another RSPCA about fifty miles away, there was a German shepherd who had six puppies.

The Mother had been abandoned by her owner, and left to feed her puppies on her milk, she had not been fed herself for quite some time and the puppies had bled her dry. Katherine said,

"Mum let's go and see them."

She could not say no, they were all so cute and fluffy, especially one that Katherine had taken a shine to.

After all the necessary checks were made, we went to collect her puppy. I would love to have taken the mother as well, but she was so poorly. They said they will look after her.

Trixie, that was the name Katherine had given her puppy, she was now six months old and growing fast. It had given Katherine a new lease of life; she took her dog for a walk every morning and evening. Trixie was her responsibility; she loved every minute she spent with her. She regularly took her to a training school.

The Village Green was not too far from our house, she loved throwing a ball for her; she had trained her to bring it back.

Months passed, Katherine was becoming more like her old self, the daily fresh air was giving her a lovely complexion she looked so much healthier.

She mentioned she had met a man on the Green, he too had an Alsatian dog, they had been meeting regularly, while the two dogs were playing; they chatted together on the wooden bench.

I knew Katherine spoke about this man for a reason I asked,

"Do you like him?"

I could tell by the smile on her face that she did.

"He has asked me to go for a drink tonight."

Katherine took ages to get ready, she could not make up her mind what to wear and then she searched for a black pair of high heels to match her dark blue jeans and a pale blue sparkly top which brought out her vivid blue eyes.

Some of her long blonde hair was clipped up allowing the rest to look dishevelled. She decided not to wear too much make-up just a little mascara and lip gloss.

The night went well, and they began to see each other as a couple.

Katherine and Paul had been dating for nearly a year when he proposed, of course Katherine accepted, she was completely besotted with him.

Katherine also received her Criminal Injuries Compensation three months later. So, they decided to get married. They began to look for a house, Paul was a teacher, so they did not want to go far as the school was close to where we lived. They found a nice three-bedroom bungalow about a mile away in a quiet cul-de-sac.

"Perfect for when we have children, it will be safe away from the main road." Katherine said excitedly giving me a funny look. I asked with a quizzical gesture,

"Are you...?" before I could finish my sentence she replied.

"Yes," but don't worry I won't be showing on my wedding day, we only found out yesterday, I am six weeks pregnant." I gave her a big hug and told her how happy I was for them.

Katherine and Paul organized everything for their wedding day, I offered to help, but Katherine was so busy enjoying herself and keeping her mind occupied she said,

"Mum, thanks I will ask you if I need you, at the moment I am fine, and things are going to plan." And they did.

The day finally came, Katherine looked gorgeous in her long white dress ruched all around the skirt with tiny bows, the bodice was similar it tapered down to the waist with crossed silk ties at the back. She let me help her choose her wedding dress. I say that laughing, happy that she had become so independent.

Her bridesmaids, Emma, Jodie, and Paul's two sisters Susan and Jackie; they were all in dark purple which looked lovely next to Katherine's dress.

Paul looked very smart in his grey striped suit with Top hat and tails. He and his best man wore a purple cravat and matching handkerchiefs which were placed perfectly in the breast pocket of their suit jackets. They also had two ushers one of them was Liam; he and Paul got on well, they were both into football.

It was a lovely ceremony in the church and then onto a venue for the reception; where Katherine and Paul greeted their one hundred guests; Paul had a lot of family, there was about a quarter of the guest list from Katherine's side and then several friends that they have met since being together.

It was lovely how Katherine and Paul had organized everything. The tables were arranged so that each person had a view of the top table where the groom and his bride would be seated. The wedding breakfast finished, photos taken, and the happy couple were ready to leave for their honeymoon in the south of France for two weeks.

Katherine's pregnancy went well; with the award of the Criminal Injuries Compensation meant they did not need to worry about affording things for the baby.

A few months after they returned from their honeymoon, they decided to decorate the nursery, they knew from the scan the baby was a girl, it was easier to choose the colour scheme for her room.

It helped Katherine keeping busy, decorating then shopping for the necessities for the baby, such as a pram, clothes, although Katherine was hoping to breast feed, they still wanted a sterilizer and bottles.

The week of her due date, I was with Katherine every day. Paul worked as much as he could, as he was taking time off when the baby was born. She was having twinges; but nothing serious. I arrived at her house the day after her due date, she had woken up early, helped get Paul's lunch ready; he decided to take sandwiches every day so he could leave at any moment.

Katherine would not sit down; she was washing clothes, cleaning the kitchen floor with the steamer she had just purchased that week. Changing all the bedclothes and hovering. This was not like Katherine she was so laid back regarding the chores, she would do them but at her own pace I knew there was something different.

Lunch time came I told her to sit down while I made her a sandwich, she reluctantly agreed. A few hours later she began to feel pain in her lower abdomen; I rang Paul and suggested he comes home soon. Then I started to time these contractions they were happening every ten minutes, I decided to ring the hospital. The sister on the delivery suite suggested Katherine goes straight to the hospital.

Paul arrived just as I was collecting Katherine's case and some toiletries she may need.

We went in Paul's car, luckily Katherine went in when she did as Cindy was born just a few hours later, she was so small weighing 6lb 4oz; tiny fingers and toes, just a whisper of blonde hair.

Paul was with Katherine while the nurse asked me to dress the baby so she would not get cold, this brought back memories of doing the same for Emma.

I was nervous as I cradled her little head in my hand while I put on a small vest and a babygro I chose the lemon one to match the little white knitted hat with lemon ribbon threaded through the band, it fit perfectly.

A couple of days later after the doctor had discharged both mother and baby, Paul went to the hospital to collect his wife and their beautiful daughter to bring them home.

CHAPTER 10

Public Protection Unit

C indy would be nearly four years old when Miss Rylands questioned Emma about her siblings; regarding the alleged abuse of her father.

Miss Rylands, being a social worker felt it was her duty to inform Katherine about the allegations Emma had made against Cindy's Granddad. She had mentioned that Katherine should know, I agreed and asked her to wait as I would explain to Katherine and Paul.

When Miss Rylands left, I immediately rang Katherine and asked if I could go and see them at five o'clock, Katherine said,

"Mum, what's wrong? Is everything alright?"

I did not want to alarm her, she was doing so well and had been for years; but there is always that vulnerability, so I said,

"Yes, I just want to tell you both something."

Katherine replied,

"Can you make it seven o'clock when Cindy has gone to bed?" I agreed and told her I would see her later.

Before I had chance, Katherine had a visit from Miss Rylands at five o'clock and she had explained everything, I then received a phone call from Katherine at six o'clock; in tears, screaming down the phone,

"You are not welcome at this house, don't bother coming later," then the phone went dead. I was so shocked, I rang Katherine straight back, I needed to know why she was so angry with me,

"Why didn't you speak to us first, instead of sending a social worker round?"

I had to remind her that I was supposed to be seeing them a seven o'clock,

"You told me to come when Cindy was in bed."

Katherine was so upset,

"Mum, Paul's really angry and so am I, that social worker questioned Cindy about her Granddad and told us what Emma is saying about Dad. I have to let him know what she is saying about him."

I tried to explain on the phone, but it is so hard to put something like that into words, so I asked if I could go and see them face to face but again, she refused to see me.

I thought, *how dare Miss Rylands tell my daughter and her husband what Emma said and question Cindy?* I was so angry that she had told Katherine and Paul about the sexual abuse which Emma was accusing her father of when she was a child. Surely that is highly confidential.

They did not believe Emma; it was similar to when Cindy was nearly two years old. I had heard that her Granddad was going to babysit for her; Paul and Katherine were going out early evening and not coming back till late. The memory of what Anne had told me kept coming back to haunt me, I withheld that information for so long it had been eating away at me.

I contacted various helplines including NSPCC and the Social Services, hoping they would be able to help me. I rang each one asking the same question.

"How can I let my family know without upsetting them too much? My granddaughter Cindy is nearly two years old, and I am frightened for her safety knowing what her Aunty has said about her brother, Cindy's Granddad."

I proceeded to explain the detailed phone call and since then Anne has denied it. The lady on the other end of the line apologized and said,

"I'm sorry there is nothing you can do unless your sister-in-law admits to what she said."

I desperately needed some advice; her answer was the same as the others.

"It is hearsay, you are classed as a third party."

Anxiously I replied,

"How can I protect my granddaughter?"

Knowing that my ex-husband had arranged to babysit for Cindy put me in a difficult position. I had to tell Paul, hoping that he would understand and make up some reason for her dad not to babysit. I did not dare tell Katherine; I was frightened of what that information about her dad would do to her.

Paul did not understand he stated,

"I think Katherine should know, and you can tell her yourself."

I did go to their house Cindy was fast asleep in bed. It was so difficult having to explain what Anne had told me that Christmas time when Katherine had recently come out of hospital. I had never forgotten those words,

"He's raped me; my brother raped me."

I tried so hard to put it into a better frame of words, but you cannot flower it up, how can you make those words sound any different? I told them word for word. I also expressed how I felt and had done since Anne told me.

"I feel I have lived a lie all my married life. I had to tell you, I couldn't live with myself, if in the future

Cindy came and told you something had happened to her, and I hadn't told you."

Paul was not happy with what I was saying. I was so angry, I carried on,

"If someone had told me years ago, I would have had a choice, but that didn't happen."

They decided to see Anne and ask her if what I was saying was true; apparently, she admitted that she was raped, but it was not Katherine's dad. Paul and Katherine were angry with me for misunderstanding what Anne had said that night.

There was always an atmosphere after that, I had to promise never to say anything bad about her father or I was not welcome at their house.

Katherine told her dad what Emma was accusing him of; she went as far as she could to protect him.

The following morning, she visited the Mental Health Centre where Miss Rylands was based and spoke to her about Emma, explaining that Emma was telling lies about her father and that she was seriously mentally ill. Katherine had also been on the internet and researched Personality Disorder, which she was saying that Emma was diagnosed with. Katherine was making it all up Emma had never been diagnosed with Personality Disorder. She had printed off a load of information about it and handed it to Miss Rylands.

This was against all ethical and moral principles. Miss Rylands accepted this information and seriously broke confidentiality by speaking to Katherine about one of her clients. Unknown to us Miss Rylands also contacted an officer from the Public Protection Unit with this misguided information before Emma could speak to them.

With the information we had regarding Katherine and knowing that she was telling her father about the allegation; Emma had no choice but to contact the police straight away.

Emma made the phone call; and complained to the police about her father abusing her when she was a child.

A young policewoman came and took some details; she explained that the PPU (Public Protection Unit) would be in touch soon.

The following day a lady and a gentleman came to my front door, both were smartly dressed; no uniform, but they each held up an identification badge in their hands.

"I'm Detective Constable Sandra Cardinal and this is my colleague;" the gentleman showed me his badge as he introduced himself as, Detective Constable Graham Wilkins I asked them to sit down and offered them a drink.

Before they sat down, they told Emma that Miss Rylands had been in touch with them and that anything she had said would not influence their judgement on the case.

Unfortunately, Emma and I were completely oblivious to what Miss Rylands may have said. We just thought she had gone to the police because it was her duty as a social worker to let the police know as there were children involved.

"If you prefer you can postpone this interview and you can speak to someone else."

Emma looked at me, it had been hard for her to pluck up the courage to contact the police, now they were here she was better getting it over and done with. We both agreed that she would speak to them, with hindsight it was the wrong decision to make.

Their attitude was extremely negative in the way they questioned Emma; being the victim, I expected some compassion and understanding.

It was obvious that Miss Ryland's misguided information had been an influence on this criminal investigation which may have also prejudiced their judgement against Emma, as they did not seem to take her seriously.

Before the Detective Constables left, they decided with Emma to pick her up and take her to this special place where she would make an official statement. They had diplomatically tried to persuade Emma that her case may not go any further and did she really want to make a statement? But Emma was adamant, although she was not well and still suffering the after effects of disclosing the abuse; she still felt strong enough to want to make a statement.

The DC's were not very encouraging, this made her feel even more anxious.

DC Cardinal collected Emma the following Monday morning, she had been quite nervous over the weekend as she did not know what to expect.

Going to give a statement at this venue did not worry her too much, as she had already been to the same place many years before; she remembered it as if it were yesterday.

However, the two DC's that she had met a couple of days earlier did cause her some anxiety. She had felt intimidated by the questions they asked her. Her mental health was mentioned a few times which seemed to prejudice their opinion. I presumed the authorities should be impartial in such a case as this.

Emma had tried her best to remember, but that was it they were only memories, the police needed evidence, good hard practical evidence.

There was so much more Emma left out that has since come to the surface of her mind. She really was not well; we should have postponed it for another time.

Unfortunately, through the intervention of Miss Rylands, Emma had to inform the police of the abuse long before she was ready. How can you be expected to remember so much in such a short time? Especially when she had buried the memories, feelings, and emotions for so long.

When Emma mentioned Uncle David and that her father was involved at the same time, we had hoped they might have brought David in for questioning.

Unfortunately, the police explained that the uncle had already been charged and that they could not include him in their investigation.

We later heard that Steve had gone to the police station voluntarily before they could arrest him. He denied everything the Detective Constable was reading from Emma's statement and what she was accusing him of doing to her when she was just a child. The police believed he was guilty by the way he was accepting what she had said about him. He did not seem too shocked.

That is something I ask myself to this day. *If he had been innocent like he wants everyone to believe, why has he never showed any anger towards Emma for accusing him of something so despicable?*

A week passed Emma was waiting patiently to hear from DC Cardinal, she rang a few times but there was no positive response to her phone calls.

She began to re-live her abuse through flashbacks in her sleep. Kevin had to wake her up on numerous occasions during the night, she was whimpering, her arms were over the top of her head clasped tightly together; her body was stiff, but she was still trying to wriggle, the more she tried to move the more she whimpered. Kevin found it hard to bring her back to reality; he had to gently tap her face while he was whispering her name. When she finally did open her eyes, she explained what had happened to her in her sleep.

"My Dad was holding my arms above my head while Uncle David was hurting me."

This broke Kevin's heart to hear what his wife had gone through and is still experiencing. Emma desperately needed to see the Psychiatric Consultant Dr. Bedfordshire to ask him to increase her medication also provide her with something to help her sleep comfortably.

It was hard to get an appointment immediately; she had to wait a few weeks. The same flashbacks happened each night, she was terrified of going to bed; knowing that she would have to experience the trauma of the abuse again.

DC Cardinal rang explaining to Emma,

"I am sorry, but the CPS (Crown Prosecution Service) will not be taking your case any further, your sister is supporting your father and without her support for you they feel they would not receive a conviction."

The CPS had their own barrister, they questioned him as to whether they would get a conviction, the barrister had said, "The defence will use Katherine against her, without her sister's support Emma has no chance."

Emma was devastated and so were we, she has suffered for so long, burying all the hurt and pain; but her sub-conscious knew, it showed through the intensity flashbacks.

Instead of showing any emotion such as tears, or anger Emma just went incredibly quiet and turned the disappointment in on herself. This was the worst thing she could do, but Emma had never been able to show any emotion. Even when we, as a family had been watching a good comedy on the television and we were all laughing; there was no expression on her face, I asked her,

"Did you not find that funny," at the time I had no reason to think there was anything wrong. I remember she had fallen off her bike, she had literally gone over the handlebars and cut her leg quite deep; there were no tears. These are just a few significant incidents that I remember.

Emma was at my house when she received that phone call from DC Cardinal.

"I'm just going upstairs." I knew what she meant when she said that.

Kevin found it difficult to accept when his wife had to self-harm, so she spent some time with me when she needed to release the emotional pain that was going on inside her mind.

"Call me if you need me," I said to her, she nodded and went upstairs.

We had a carrier bag with everything Emma needed, razor blades, sterile water that I had managed to get from her GP, bandages, and sterile swabs; if the cuts were too deep, I helped using stere-strips to bind the skin together, then bandaged her arm. She cleaned the cuts herself with the files of sterile water. She always felt better after she had self-harmed; it was her way of coping as she could not express herself on the outside.

Being a mum to both my daughters and my son it was so hard to understand Katherine and Liam not wanting to support their sister.

I love them both so much and I find it difficult to speak to Katherine knowing that she has deliberately foiled any chance of her sister getting justice in the courts.

I do not think she realised the detrimental affect her attitude and telling lies about Emma's mental health would have on a criminal investigation.

Liam was also finding it extremely upsetting about the accusations that Emma was making against their dad.

"If he was guilty of this abuse, why have the police not charged him?"

I tried to explain that if Katherine had not interfered with the investigation, then that is precisely what may have happened.

The psychosis became a lot worse as it was beginning to intrude on Emma's daytime routine. Her nights were becoming a little better, so she was managing to get some sleep. It was essential as she needed all the sleep she could get to cope with what was to happen during the day.

Emma stayed with me so as not to let Darren see what a terrible ordeal his Mum was going through. It was awful to watch Emma's body endure so much torment at least every twenty minutes of the day.

She would get up, wash and dress herself without any trouble, come downstairs, have a slice of toast, take her medication with a glass of water. She was lucky to finish a cup of tea before the first flashback started.

We could be in an interesting discussion without any reference to her mental state, I tried to keep conversation happy and positive; she smiled so I knew she was listening and she also interacted with me. Then for no apparent reason her head flung backwards again then forwards with such a powerful force it was as if it was on a spring.

These movements were more violent; her feet lifted off the ground, the heavy Italian sofa was tipping backwards with the full force of her body. She was exhausted after about half a dozen of these flashbacks, so she laid down on the sofa, as soon as she closed her eyes; she was back in time with those monsters her dad and her uncle David.

First her arms flung behind her head, it was as if someone had just grabbed both her wrists and violently pulled them in position but there was no one there.

The next thing I saw was unbelievable; her legs moved into a position half bent and spread out between her knees, you could see she was trying to close them, then she began to whimper, I watched in horror as her back arched upwards and her stomach muscles moved in and out. She was being raped in front of my eyes again and again.

"Stop him! dad, stop him!"

those words were so clear; although they were only a whisper, I wasn't imagining them it sounded like a child's voice. This episode went on for about five minutes, I had to let her go through the whole ordeal, we had asked her psychologist at the time what to do? He did not know the full extent of each flashback, but he had explained that Emma needs to let these happen.

I noticed it depended in which position Emma was sitting or lying at the time depicted which flashback would happen. She explained when she sits up it is like when she sat on her aunty Anne's recliner chair, when she lies down, she is reminded of being on the floor in her uncle David and Aunty Anne's house with her dad.

I decided to borrow my Mum's camcorder and get these on tape, no one would believe this; if I had to try and describe in detail what was taking place. It was as if there was a poltergeist raping my daughter.

I was not the only one to see this happen, Kevin, my Mum, Peter, and I have all been present at such a time when Emma was having one of these flashbacks. They too could not believe what they were witnessing.

There have been times when it has become dangerous and really frightening. Lunch times were a worry, she needed to eat. This happened many times when we were eating, I was always frightened of her choking and had to be on alert. One time she was having a sandwich for her lunch when her head flung backwards; she had just taken a bite of her bread and it was still in her mouth. Immediately I got up from where I was sitting which was always close to her when she was eating; pulled her head forward and gently slapped her face continuously to bring her round and back to reality; when she eventually opened her eyes she was choking, the piece of bread was lodged in her throat.

The most peculiar thing about it; Emma did not know anything until she came back, she could vagely remember what had happened to her in the past couple of minutes before we brought her back to reality; she always complained that she was very sore in between her legs and the top of her thighs.

Emma was never told what we had witnessed, we just carried on as if nothing had happened.

Sometimes she asked questions and we would answer them truthfully but never to the extent to what we had seen. We felt it would have been too frightening and degrading for her to hear everything we had to witness.

These flashbacks were becoming a regular occurrence, we packed her up with cushions and pillows to protect her, as the day went on; her neck and throat began to swell with all the muscular movements; by 6.00p.m at night we were all exhausted.

I constantly phoned the Crisis Team from the local mental health, hoping for some help and guidance but they said,

"Go to A&E."

Kevin had gone home to look after their son, Darren was too young to understand. They only lived five minutes' walk from my house. My Mum had been looking after Darren while Kevin stayed with Emma and myself.

By eight o'clock I knew Emma had, had enough and I phoned for an ambulance. Again, it was difficult to explain to the paramedics what was happening, I just let them think it was involuntary movements and that if they wait, the episode will slowly stop and allow them to move her to the ambulance. How could I tell them what was really happening to Emma, I think they would have locked us both up in an asylum.

When we managed to get an appointment with Dr. Bedfordshire, I had taken with me the camcorder with plenty of film on it to show him the full extent of Emma's plight.

We had to accompany Emma's new Community Psychiatric Nurse, a gentleman called Simon, I had put in a complaint regarding Miss Rylands, and so they had found Emma someone else. I mentioned to Simon about the camcorder I had with me, he suggested I do not show it to Dr. Bedfordshire. I could not understand why; I ignored his advice and turned it on anyway. I asked, in fact I pleaded with Dr. Bedfordshire to watch and take notice of what I had managed to tape. He was not interested, he told me to put it away.

"We don't need to see anything Mrs. Colne,"

Emma did get her medication increased, the rest of her symptoms we had to cope with ourselves.

I was so angry watching Emma's repeated flashbacks and not getting any justice regarding her father. I decided to contact DC Cardinal myself after I had been on the internet and found some information about an Independent Police Complaints Commission, (IPCC).

I phoned them and spoke to a nice lady, she explained if I did not get any response, I should contact them again.

"DC Cardinal?" she answered the phone straight away,

"Speaking," I began with,

"This is Mrs. Colne; I am not happy with the way you and your colleague have investigated my daughter's case.

"I have contacted the IPCC..." before I could finish my sentence she interrupted…..

"You are not putting a complaint in against me, are you?"

"There is some evidence from the flashbacks of the abuse on tape, I have mentioned this to you before, but you said the CPS have closed the case."

DC Sandra Cardinal then said,

"I will speak To Mrs. Manning in the CPS and let you know, if I do this can you please put your complaint on hold."

I agreed and waited to hear from DC Cardinal.

She did collect the tapes and I believe Mrs. Manning from the CPS watched them, she had asked the DC to tell me,

"They are very worrying, but she is sorry she will not be re-opening the case."

Unfortunately, I expected too much, I decided not to complain to the IPCC. DC Cardinal did her best under the circumstances, I appreciated that.

Thinking back to David's court case and how that also had not transpired. I asked myself, if this had been a murder case would the CPS had given up so easily; looking at all the evidence in the statements made by both Katherine and Emma, it could quite easily have been a much more serious investigation, had this case gone to court.

Similar incidents were described by both girls, and to this day neither of them knows that it could have been an attempted murder case.

The girls never spoke about their abuse to each other, it was hard enough for both to accept their own trauma; they always protected each other's feelings.

Katherine could never have a bath or a shower without my presence in the bathroom; she was always frightened of her fears when she was in the bath.

At first, I did not realize there was any reason for me to stay with her, I just thought she liked my company as I used to talk to her while she was bathing. The conversation stopped while Katherine put her head under the water, as she surfaced, she needed me to talk to her about anything, so long as she could hear my voice. She panicked if I wanted to leave the bathroom for even a minute, I knew there was something else going on in her mind, but I also had to be careful not to mention anything and accept what Katherine needed from me until she was ready to speak.

Eventually, she allowed herself to disclose a very frightening experience,

"He tried to drown me Mum, Uncle David pushed me under the water and held me down and tried to drown me."

She was crying while she was trying to describe her memories as the feelings and the emotions expressed her near death experience. All I could do was listen and support her; as this terrifying ordeal was relived, yet again.

This was not the first time I had encountered this information; Emma had also experienced the same from Uncle David, only her memories of the drowning were physical, again I had to accompany Emma in the bathroom, she could not then and still cannot have a bath or a shower with the bathroom door closed.

As soon as I realized what had happened to both girls in the past and that their ordeals were similar, they both explained that it was Uncle David who had threatened them by drowning to the point of submission.

The next day I had contacted DC Williams, she was the lady that looked after us regarding David's case. I felt it was important to let her know that information.

"Hello, this is Mrs. Colne can I please make an appointment with you, it's regarding some new evidence that needs to be added to the girl's statements."

DC Williams did see me, I informed her of the details which had then come to my attention.

"I'm sorry Mrs. Colne we can't keep adding to the statements, it doesn't look good for the prosecution," I was appalled at that comment.

"What! He tried to kill both my daughter's and you can't do anything about it."

She tried to calm me down, I pushed for this information to be given to the CPS, but DC Williams explained again, the case was closed.

I had returned home disgusted at the system and how it lets victims down, I felt sure this was serious information that needed to be brought to justice as well as the abuse both my girls had suffered at the hands of this person.

I was angry, a niggling thought came from the back of my mind.

Had there been a conspiracy? A cover up perhaps?

The memories of my husband when he had stopped me from going to the police. Saying,

"We could all end up in body bags; run if you see a black cab."

I wonder, *could it have been true what he was saying. Was another source involved? Were we in danger? Had he really been in touch with Special Branch and passed information on to the authorities to protect David his brother-in- law, his accomplice in the abuse?*

He was charged; but not convicted.

David was arrested at his place of work, taken to the local police station and questioned for about six hours, according to Tracy the DC he kept needing to use the bathroom; he was extremely nervous and very tense when questions were put to him from the girls' statements; the horrifying abuse they allegedly accused him of. It was a long time ago, he must have thought he had got away with it; until his victims became empowered and ready to seek justice, mainly, to get some closure in their lives.

Questions were fired at him between Tracy and her colleague,

"Do you know a Katherine Colne and an Emma Colne?"

He hesitated for a second,

"Yeah, they were my first wife's brother's kids."

He then went on to deny everything.

Later we were advised that he had been charged with, 'Rape, Attempted Rape, and Sexual Assault.'

He was on conditional bail for twelve months; he was not allowed to go home as he had a daughter aged eighteen months. The Judge had stipulated he had not to be in the vicinity of any child under the age of sixteen without supervision.

The DC Tracy and her colleague Barbara had come to see us, we had been in touch with them over the past year; the court case had been postponed on numerous occasions, but this was different. I noticed by the way she approached me in the living room that things were not right.

"Please sit-down Jennifer," her dismal features looked towards Emma and Katherine.

"I'm so sorry the CPS have closed the case; it is not going to court."

All the blood drained from my body as I felt faint, I broke down hysterically, asking,

"Why! Why?" Tracy had tears in her eyes, even though she was there in an official capacity we had become friends over the time. She explained,

"When the CPS put the case to their barrister, he had concluded that there was insufficient evidence; that the girls had both received counselling which encountered a negative response." I interrupted,

"But the police charged him."

Tracy could see I was getting angry, she then went on to explain,

"His defence will use it against them, in the court of law the jury has to find the defendant guilty beyond reasonable doubt, otherwise the defendant walks free. The CPS cannot take this case to court unless they have enough evidence to get a conviction."

Emma never received any counselling till after she had been to the police; that was with Mrs. Fieldsend-Jones. Unfortunately, Emma lost her trust when she had to provide notes for the family courts. She felt she could not confide in her about certain aspects of her life.

Katherine did receive counselling sessions, as time passed; the counsellor suggested some hypnotism may help. She was also qualified to do this kind of therapy. Katherine was able to go under, but only for a few short sessions which did not lead to much.

DC Williams contacted Katherine's Counsellor, but she was unhelpful as she could not provide any notes for the prosecution.

Apparently, Tracy had an Ace card. She had asked a Paediatric Psychologist to see both the girls. I had taken Emma and Katherine had been escorted by two nurses as she was on the acute mental health ward at the time. After she had spoken to them, she was positive in her report, unfortunately she could not complete it as she was waiting for a report from Katherine's Consultant, who had abruptly handed in his notice and disappeared.

I cannot help thinking that these reasons were so trivial to stop two serious rape and sexual abuse cases going to court. The CPS would not take a chance; they wanted tight cases so they would receive convictions for both.

The date of Cindy's show was looming. I did not know whether to cancel mine and my mum's tickets, after all she is my granddaughter, we love her so much I do not see why we should not be there to watch her dance, she was so excited when she showed me her outfits and did her singing and dancing rehearsal.

I did not want to let her down or disappoint Katherine, if we do not go it will make her and Liam think I do not care. We decided to go.

Katherine had reserved our tickets for the balcony, she had known that it was hard for Emma to see her dad; we had booked them weeks before Emma's disclosure. It would have been nice to have had tickets for the front row with my family including Emma and her children.

We sat on the right- hand side of the camera man at the back of the small auditorium, we had a good view of the stage, including the front row.

He was sat there smug, clapping when my sweet innocent little granddaughter gave a curtsey to the audience.

I was proud as I stood with my mum clapping and hoping and praying to God to keep her safe from his clutches. *He has done it before; there is nothing to say he will not do it again.*

The thought of it made me feel sick, *how can I possibly protect her?*

The curtains closed, everyone stood up and made their way towards the exit.

I knew I would bump into him one day, I thought I could handle it. I caught a glimpse of him in the crowd, when I had him in full view I stared at his features, his greying hair and the face that represented evil to me.

He turned and smiled lovingly to my daughter Katherine and my son Liam who was holding hands with his fiancée Emma.

I was not originally from the close-knit village; however, my ex-husband was born and bred there. He was a pillar of the community, and voluntarily helped run a badminton club, he was kind and generous, helped to organize charity events; most of the villagers knew and respected him. He had many friends from his school days although they were all grown up and had families of their own; they kept in touch.

Unfortunately, they did not know the evil side of his personality.

The rage boiled up inside of me, I could feel my heart beating rapidly against my chest, I just wanted to race after him; shouting for everyone to hear what he had done. If I were carrying a gun, I would gladly have shot him; not to intentionally kill him, but to make him suffer for what he did to my little girl. Knowing my daughter had gone through hell in the last twenty-five years, at the time trying to love her father, who should have protected her and kept her safe, instead of being the monster in her nightmares, raping and sexually abusing her while my back was turned. Threatening her, not to tell anyone.

He looked up towards the balcony giving me the impression that he knew exactly where we would be sitting. We caught eye contact, he gave me such a smirk; his eyes narrowed, his cheekbones lifted, into a childish grin which said it all,

'I GOT AWAY WITH IT AND THERE IS NOTHING YOU CAN DO!'

The grin disappeared and his facial features turned to a scowl, which he channelled into my sub-conscious unbalancing my defence mechanism to the point of sheer panic. I felt physically sick and grabbed my mum by her arm and whispered,

"I have got to get out of here." She understood as she too had seen his sneer.

We immediately left through a side entrance. Sadly, we were unable to see our family and congratulate my three-year old beautiful granddaughter.

CHAPTER 11

Emma's Dream Came True

How many times I look back and see how some things can happen for a reason. I had a car accident, nothing serious, some whiplash and I was also left with some psychological problems as another car hit me head on.

I mentioned this to my uncle, he too had a bad car accident much worse than mine. He recommended his solicitor who successfully dealt with his case.

I contacted a Mr. Neville Turner who did an excellent job getting me the compensation that I deserved in a very quick and efficient manner.

While I was having a coffee with him and his staff, I enquired,

"Do you have any family solicitors in your company?" Neville answered,

"No, but I know where there is a good one,"

He gave me a phone number of a lady, Mrs. Sharron Rainsford. As soon as I got home, I rang Emma and told her of this person I had been recommended; I gave her the number to ring. She was pleased and she rang her straight away. Fortunately, there was an appointment available in three days' time. Emma asked me if I would take her.

The receptionist explained that Mrs. Rainsford will not be long, and would we like a drink while we wait. We both politely accepted a coffee.

Approximately five minutes later, Mrs. Rainsford asked us to follow her to her office,

"Bring your coffee's, with you."

After the introductions and the relevant forms were completed, Emma spoke of how her ex-partner had been with her and how he had abused her access with her children.

Sharron Rainsford was appalled at everything Emma was saying and how the court had given custody to Carl because of Emma's mental health problems. Sharron asked Emma,

"Were you a danger to your kids?" she questioned Emma abruptly,

"No," Emma answered meekly. Sharron said,

"Then why couldn't you have kept your children or at least have received shared custody?"

Emma then replied,

"I don't know."

We spent about an hour with the solicitor, she was good, she understood when Emma told her the truth about her mental health and that she had been in remission of these intensity flashbacks for nearly two years.

Jodie was now seven years old, and Zak was nearly five. Emma was having regular contact with her children but no overnights, Carl had been difficult in agreeing to the children staying, he never kept to the court order that stipulated Emma's access to see her children. Sharron looked at the clock on the wall and made a gesture as if the appointment were coming to an end,

"Leave it with me, I will see when we can get a court date and in the meantime, I will speak to a barrister that I have in mind."

She seemed positive and told Emma she will be in touch soon. The solicitor kept her word and contacted Emma,

"First, we need to get you overnight access, so can you be available in two weeks, 8th July at 10.00 am?"

Emma replied,

"Yes, thank you."

Sharron told Emma which courthouse and then finished her phone call with,

"See you then."

It was the same Court House as before, so we knew the directions.

Sharron met us half an hour before Emma was due in to see the Judge. Carl did not even have a solicitor. The Judge ordered that overnight access will be resumed and if Carl objected, he would be in serious trouble.

The children were so excited to stay with their mum, Kevin, and their little brother Darren, whom they had never been allowed to acknowledge at their father's house. According to Jodie, she had mentioned Darren to her dad, she had been told that he was not her brother and not to speak about him again. It was difficult to understand how Jodie must have felt, each time she came to her Mum's she and Zak would always see and play with their brother Darren; not to be allowed to talk about him when they went home, was unfair; to take that away from a child is unreasonable and detrimental towards their future.

After Emma made a special tea for her children and both her and Kevin had played with them, she said,

"Come on its bath time," they all ran upstairs excited as they each went into their rooms.

Emma had put new pyjamas on Zak's bed and a Disney Snow White nightdress on Jodie's bed. She had also bought Darren a Spiderman pair to match Zak's.

Emma put some warm water in the bath with some special bath foam that did not sting their eyes. She lifted Zak in first then Darren, they laughed and splashed each other, it was lovely to watch her two sons bathing together, *that is just how it should be,* Emma thought to herself.

When the boys were dressed and ready for bed, Emma filled the bath again for Jodie, she was growing up and did not want her brothers to see her undressed.

Emma left the boys playing while she spent quality time with Jodie having a girlie chat in the bathroom. Emma let the children ring Carl to say goodnight.

They all slept well; the children were in their dressing gowns watching children's programs on the television while Emma made breakfast. It all felt so normal. Kevin was still in bed. When they had eaten, Emma let them all jump on him to wake him up.

Around ten o'clock when the summer sun was beginning to warm up the early morning air, they all decided to go for a pleasant walk in the nearby park. The children ran towards the swings, Darren was trying hard to climb onto a small round-about, Zak shouted,

"Push me!" Kevin stopped speaking to Emma and briskly walked towards Zak and began to push him on the swing. Zak was delighted and shouted,

"Higher, Higher," Kevin laughed as he pushed more, also aware of the safety aspect.

Jodie was stood at the top of the slide shouting to her Mum,

"Watch me Mum, watch me." Emma turned, smiled, and waved to her. They spent about an hour on the park, on the way back Kevin bought them all an ice-cream. The children played in the back garden while Emma made a roast chicken dinner.

Before it was time to go back to their dad's house Emma managed to read a story to Jodie and Zak while Darren was having a nap. Then she and Kevin played snakes and ladders with them. She was also preparing them to go back.

"When we have finished this game you both need to get everything ready to go home to daddy. Nana will be here soon."

The children reluctantly agreed. They gave Darren a big hug and told him they would see him the following week. Kevin helped to put the children in the car, he fastened their seatbelts and waved them goodbye.

Carl had divorced Jackie; he was living with a girlfriend who already had three children from a past relationship.

When I parked outside the address Carl had given to Emma; we noticed it was a small three-bedroom end terraced property, with a back yard, there were cats everywhere, we got the children out of the car and walked them towards the front door, Jodie said,

"We have to go round to the back door; we are not allowed to go in the front way."

The bins were full; boxes of empty beer cans were strewn over the small piece of uneven concrete flags, with bits of weeds growing in between them. There were black bags tied at the top with holes at the bottom where the cats had been clawing their way in, they had managed to scavenge an empty tin of tuna and some used tea bags.

Emma felt sick at the thought of having to leave her children in such a dirty place, but she had to. Carl met us at the back door, his girlfriend still wearing her dressing gown and he looked rough.

She gave both her children a big hug and promised she would pick them up next weekend. Emma rang her solicitor the following Monday morning and explained the sleeping facilities at their father's girlfriend's house. Sharron questioned,

"Does your ex-partner not have a place of his own?" She replied,

"No, he has only known this girlfriend for two months."

The children had been staying overnight on a regular basis, in fact Carl had been leaving them with Emma much more than the Court Order had stipulated. They were settling into a better routine, Emma was taking them to school and interacting with their teachers, doing homework with Jodie, and helping Zak with his colors. There was such a happy atmosphere.

The children were pleased to see Kevin when he got home from work and Darren loved having his brother and sister at home. Carl still had control, although the children were now residing permanently with Emma and Kevin. Emma still had to contact Carl for him to agree to anything regarding the children, for example, making a hospital appointment for Zak as he wore glasses from an early age. Emma had noticed Zak's left eye was turning when he was only a baby, but when she mentioned it to Carl he did not agree, until a few years later. By that time Zak was permanently wearing glasses.

Sharron contacted Emma with good news; there was a slot in the courts timetable the following

Wednesday for the whole day, as the barrister was going for full custody. Emma was so excited; she had waited so long for this day. The number of times she had been through the heartache and upset of negative outcomes, changing solicitors, each time being given positive advice, but it never came true.

So, Emma was apprehensive, however; this time circumstances were on her side, Carl had no home of his own, he was not working at the present time and there was only Emma and Kevin who could offer Jodie and Zak stability.

Carl did not seem too bothered when the Judge gave Emma full custody of their children, she agreed to Carl having regular contact, things were so different now, she was in control; there would not be any more acceptance and bowing down to his demands how and when she could see her children. Her face said it all, her natural smile was not put on, it was real for the first time in her life she was able to relax and smile and be happy knowing that she was collecting her children from school and taking them home for ever.

The children had been happy and stable living with Emma, Kevin, and Darren for about eighteen months, when Emma surprised them all that they were going to Florida for a holiday. Emma had promised Jodie when she was only two years old.

"Someday I will take you to Florida to see the dolphins." Jodie had never forgotten and neither had Emma, now she can keep her promise. She had already spoken to Kevin first and he was pleased for Emma.

Since getting the children back they had been saving up for this holiday, there was now enough in their savings to book the tickets for them.

They had asked me and Peter if we would like to go with them, Kevin had preferred that just in case there was any problems, conscious of the knowledge that Emma may a have relapse at any time. She had to be practical knowing that Kevin would have support if it was needed.

Katherine and Paul had arranged to take Cindy to Egypt. We were so happy for them; they came to see me and Emma before they were due to fly the next day; Cindy was about three years old now and so excited; she had never been on an aeroplane before. We waved them off and told them to have a good time.

A week later Katherine, Paul and Cindy came to see us with gifts from their holiday; I asked them if they had a good time? They both said,

"Yes," but I felt something was not right with Katherine.

Although they had just got back from Egypt, Paul had to work, and Cindy was at Playschool. The following day I rang Katherine asking her to come for a coffee, she agreed and within an hour she arrived at my house.

I made us both a drink and we sat at the kitchen table,

"What's the matter?" I questioned her,

"Did you have a good time?"

Her face changed,

"Not really."

I could not understand, *why did she tell me she did? I needed to know.*

"I didn't tell you before that we were going with Aunty Anne, it was horrible Mum; she wouldn't stop pestering me about Uncle David."

"What!" I was shocked and annoyed; first that Katherine had gone on holiday with Anne and then she had the nerve to speak to Katherine about David; knowing that Katherine had suffered a severe breakdown from the trauma of the sexual abuse.

"Why on earth did you go on holiday with her?"

"She asked us to go and that she would pay, we had no money, so we accepted." All Katherine's compensation had been used and there was no spare capital.

I had already told them twelve months earlier about the things Anne had said about her brother my ex-husband.

That awful night came flooding back to me, when Anne screamed down the phone at me,

"He raped me; my brother raped me."

Since then, my relationship with Katherine began to deteriorate. Emma found out about Anne going on holiday with Katherine. The thought of Cindy being in Anne's company caused stress for Emma, she did not realize why she became so upset about the whole situation. Her intensity flashbacks returned, they only lasted a week, but it was enough for Emma to suffer trauma to her nerves in her lower back; a week before we were due to fly to Florida.

Painkillers, muscle relaxants, we tried everything, but Emma could not walk. Slowly she got back a little movement in her legs, which meant she could walk a few paces, but she had to sit down most of the time. We managed to purchase a wheelchair, I rang the airport to let them know about the changes, that one of the passengers would be needing wheelchair assistance boarding and disembarking.

The staff at the airport were extremely helpful from the minute we left the taxi, they escorted us all through passport check-in and all the way through to the departure lounge.

When the plane was ready for boarding the passengers, Peter pushed Emma escorted by two aircraft officials on to the plane before anybody else.

I stayed with Kevin and the children until it was time for us to board.

I felt a little empathy for Emma, she was missing out on seeing and hearing the excitement of all the children, they had a small rucksack each; Emma had packed some activities and sweets for the flight.

When we boarded the plane, Emma was already sat comfortable waiting for her children, they all sat close to her and Kevin, Peter and I were in front.

The children were so eager to take off their seat belts and turn on the screen in front of them; they could not decide what to watch, in the end they decided to play on the drop-down tables with the activities from their bags and eat their sweets.

The flight was magnificent. Eventually, we landed at Orlando Airport.

Everything went well till me, Peter, and Zak got a cab and Kevin collected the hire car from the depot, which was not far from the taxi rank.

I asked the cab driver if he would wait until Kevin was behind us so he could follow the cab; things do not always go to plan, I should have prepared myself for the unexpected. I left all the luggage including my handbag with all our passports with Kevin and Emma. I just put one hundred dollars into my jeans pocket. I gave the cab driver the address of the holiday apartment, expecting him to know where to go; he set off without waiting for Kevin. I tried to explain, but he spoke with an accent I think he was Mexican; it was difficult for us to understand each other.

We were told by the travel agent that our apartment was approximately a thirty-minute drive from the airport in Orlando, we had been driving for over two hours, I am sure we passed the same landmark on more than one occasion.

It was getting dark and the lights from other cars were blinding me while I tried desperately to see any towns that resembled the apartment's address. We were on the same highway, first heading east; then west, then east again. I was beginning to panic; I knew we had no money or passports with us. We were lost. We had no idea where we were and neither did the cab driver. I asked him to stop at the nearest supermarket; I ran in, conscious of clocking up the fare. The people in the shop could not help, but someone pointed to a police traffic control just around the corner.

The officer put the address into his computer and showed me how to get there. I thanked him so much, he guessed I was becoming quite stressed and asked me if I wanted a drink, I thanked him and mentioned I had family waiting.

We were just entering the gates of our park when I heard Jodie's voice,

"They are here! They are here!"

It was so nice to hear Jodie; knowing that they had managed to find the apartment. By the time we arrived, the cab had clocked up nearly three hundred dollars. *Great for our first day in America.*

We had planned on visiting most of the popular sights, Disney World, Hollywood Studios, Animal Kingdom, Water Parks and much more.

Although Emma could not walk very well, we took her wheelchair with us, but most of the places we visited provided battery-operated scooters for the disabled. Darren sat on his Mum's knee while she was able to steer it herself.

The car which we hired was equipped to seat seven people, so it fit us all in comfortably. The apartment was fantastic: the only problem was it was on the first floor, I tried to change it before we left.

It was an effort for Emma to climb the stairs but with the help from Kevin and Peter they managed to get her up and down.

The bedrooms were huge the boys shared one, Jodie had her own room, Peter and I had a master room en-suite. Emma and Kevin also had a room en-suite.

The kitchen area had a large dining table big enough to seat everyone. The electrical appliances consisted of a washing machine, dryer, microwave, toaster, dish washer, and a huge cooker with six rings. They also provided all the crockery, cutlery, bedding, and towels and lots more to make our holiday brilliant.

There was a beautiful heated outdoor pool, the children loved it. Emma was able to get into the pool with some help from me, but when she was in the water, she was fine and able to play a little with the children.

One day we visited 'Discovery Cove' what an amazing place. We all went snorkelling, through my goggles I could see the wonderful sight of the Rays gracefully swimming in their own environment and the tropical fish diving in and out of the coral reefs. I was frightened at first but with Peter giving me confidence I made myself dive down towards the bottom; what an experience.

Peter also helped Emma; he took her hand and swam next to her while she floated on the surface wearing her snorkel with her head face down in the water, she was able to see most of the tropical fish including the rays, they were all different sizes some were quite big, they were so graceful as they skimmed the surface, then gradually submerged to join the rest of them, I tried to touch them but they were too fast.

The price included a meal, the food was so good. We sat on one of the tables outside. The weather was lovely, hot but not scorching.

After lunch we went to some of the pools; one was fantastic it was outdoors, it had exotic birds flying about and at the edge of the pool there was plenty of greenery, fabulous plants with a fine net overhead to stop the birds from getting out.

Next, we went to a huge pool with waves; I picked Darren up each time one was coming towards us. Jodie and Zak were with their Mum and Kevin jumping the waves and laughing when they fell over.

The time had come for us to go to the pool which we had to book for when we first entered Discovery Cove.

'The Dolphin Pool' Yes, we were going to swim with the dolphins. Another experience we will never forget. There were a few more people, so we were put into groups. Luckily, we were all together. The first dolphin swam over to us, the trainer gave us each a fish to give as a treat and allowed us to pet him.

He did a little display to say thank you. Peter, Jodie, and I had to swim out into the middle of the lagoon, a young female dolphin joined us and one by one we swam back while holding onto her fin. Emma, Kevin, and Zak stayed in the shallow end of the pool with the dolphins, as Darren was too young to be with us, he was being looked after and entertained by one of the staff, sitting on a rock watching us whilst eating ice-cream. Then Darren joined us in the pool as the dolphins grouped together and did a fantastic display for us. To finish the whole wonderful experience, we all had a group photograph taken with the dolphin. They had also taken photos of each of us swimming with them.

What a marvellous day, we were all exhausted so on the way back to the apartment we stopped off at the 'Golden Coral' an eating place where they provided a variety of good food, the children loved helping themselves especially Darren; before he had finished his main course, he always made room for his desert. He came back to the table loaded with ice-cream covered with chocolate sauce and lots of sweets.

The following day we went to SeaWorld, another amazing place to visit. First, we watched a show which was brilliant, the star attraction was a sea-lion, the background scenery was an old galleon, the children loved it; they laughed so much when the sea-lion soaked a gentleman in the audience.

Later we walked over to where the Killer whales displayed, we had missed the show, but we were able to see through the large glass windows below the pool, what a fantastic sight: watching those beautiful creatures swim with their trainers.

One day we had gone to Disney World, it was getting dark, people were queuing up for the Mickey Mouse Halloween Party, we decided to stay longer and join in the fun. The whole atmosphere was unbelievable; there was a full procession of all the Disney characters on floats and music was played and some of the characters were dancing in the procession, one came over and shook Zak's hand.

Jodie had started collecting autographs, she had one off Mickey Mouse and Minnie Mouse, most of the Disney Princesses, Woody from Toy Story and before the end of the night she managed to get one off Tigger.

Then the firework display started, what a magnificent sight, lighting up the Disney Castle in all different colours.

Kevin was pushing Emma, Darren was sat on his Mum's knee and trying his best to stay awake he was tired, it had been another long day. The following morning, we decided to rest and stay at the apartment and spend the day in the pool.

We had a fantastic two weeks, Although Emma had to use a wheelchair, she did not let it spoil anything, she was determined to give her children what she had always promised, a holiday in Florida.

Thinking back to the cabbie in Florida; whenever I go travelling with Peter we always seem to end up in a predicament.

Three weeks after we started courting, I received a phone call from him,

"Would you like to go to the Lake District for a day out?" I replied,

"Yes, I would love to."

We were going with his cousin and his ten-year-old daughter; little did I know she was an expert at climbing mountains.

I had never visited the Lake District; I knew it was up towards the north of England. I had seen it on the television and read about it in the Country Life magazines. I believe it is one of the most beautiful places in the United Kingdom, mountains, lakes, and picturesque villages. I imagined a bit of sightseeing, Beatrice Potter Cottage, Lake Windermere, and Coniston Water where the Bluebird had reached over 300mph tragically killing its pilot Donald Campbell the fastest driver on land and water at the time.

Peter had suggested I wear good walking shoes: I only had a pair of trainers. Luckily, the weather was warm; I decided to put on jeans and a sleeveless top. I had a fleece with me in case it became cooler.

We parked the car in an isolated car park, miles from any lakes or picturesque villages.

I watched as Mark, Peter's cousin gathered a length of rope, I thought nothing of it, we began to walk, over stiles through streams, carefully managing to step on boulders which were luckily placed close together; I did not fancy getting my trainer's wet, not wanting to squelch all the way back, which must have been quite a few miles.

"There it is!" Mark shouted to his daughter Lorna,

"What is?" I asked Mark,

"Helvellyn, Striding Edge," he replied excitedly.

I looked towards where he was pointing, it was a mountain notorious for accidents across its very

narrow path with a thousand foot drop on either side.
I looked at Peter,

"Did you know we were going to climb a mountain?" He shook his head,

"I'm sorry I should have realized this is what Mark and Lorna like to do."

I felt the blood draining from me, as the thought of walking towards my death.

I said to Peter,

"But I am terrified of heights, I can't even walk across a motorway bridge without going dizzy."

Peter did not want Mark or Lorna to know of my fears he just whispered,

"Don't worry, I'll look after you."

This mountain must be quite popular for climbers as there was quite a few groups of people. We had been walking uphill for approximately half an hour when we came to the narrow path, Mark was tying a rope around Lorna's waist making sure she was safe.

I kept letting people go in front of me knowing that I would hold them up. Peter waited until I was ready, my heart was beating fast, he went first; he was wearing the backpack full of drinks which unsteadied him a couple times, I took a deep breath, I was absolutely petrified as I began to tread slowly along the narrow path, I could see down to the bottom which made me feel lightheaded, Peter said,

"Don't look down," Too late, I was already imagining my fate. I had my back to the edge of the path and my hands steadied me as I pushed against the rock face a bit at a time. My heart was still pumping like a drum against my chest, I think it was the adrenaline that kept me going, Peter held out his hand, but I persuaded him to carry on.

"I'm alright," I said, as I felt the beads of sweat on my forehead, I could not wipe my brow. I did not dare let go of the rock face. I was also terrified of Peter falling to his death. Eventually we came to the end, climbed up a steep rock face which was a doddle to the

Striding Edge which I had just accomplished.

I felt so exhilarated and proud of my achievement. It was all worth it when we walked onto a large flat surface where the view was tremendous; a wondrous blue sky without a cloud in sight; the sun shining over the peaks. I never imagined how I would feel experiencing such a beautiful scene, this was nature at its best. That was it; I had conquered my fear of heights and when we were on our way back, I asked excitedly,

"When are we going to climb another mountain?"

Over the next six months we had managed to do, Mount Snowdon in Wales, Scar Fell in the Lake

District which is the second highest Mountain in the British Isles and the piece de resistance Ben Nevis in Scotland, which was a brilliant experience.

We had travelled right up the north of England over the border into Scotland and passed Loch Lomond, through the highlands to our destination, Fort William, a nice quiet little town close to Ben Nevis. We stayed at a lovely Bed & Breakfast, after a good night's sleep and a full English breakfast we set off on our expedition. It was quite busy when we arrived and well organized, we were given brochures that showed the direction to the peak. It was a lovely clear day, so we were hoping to get a good view from the summit; an official told us that people are lucky to have a clear view on their first climb.

We climbed higher and higher watching the cars become minute until they disappeared. I remember as we climbed higher looking down at the peaks of other mountains close by. Up we went; it was beginning to get a bit cooler with the oxygen levels.

And after about five hours of strenuous climbing, I could see and hear people in the distance, someone was playing a guitar, others were dancing it was so exciting and overwhelming for everyone who had conquered 'Ben Nevis.' To top it all; it was a clear view as far as the eye could see.

'What an experience!'

Unfortunately going back down became a bit steep at times, with boulders everywhere and I could not stop myself from walking faster, my feet were treading each boulder; until I missed my footing, although I was wearing good strong walking boots, I went flying forwards hitting the boulders with my hip and all down one side; I managed to put my hands out to save my face.

Peter came to my aid as soon as he saw what happened and others came over, I heard one shouting,

"There's blood," that seemed to bring me round; I had to let them know I was alright. I had banged my lip and my mouth was bleeding, my hands were stuck in between the boulders.

I began to move slowly, Peter and another gentleman helped me to my feet, I was very sore, my body ached with every step I took to get down off that mountain; fortunately, we did not need the mountain rescue. Peter held my hand all the way, what took us five hours to get to the summit took us six hours to get down, I did not think we would ever make it. What was worse; I was dying to go to the loo and by the time we had reached the bottom the toilets were all closed, and everyone had gone home.

There was another episode I had of a near death experience. Peter and I had planned to go to Canada and see my relations. My cousin was excited as we had not seen them for twenty years, so she rented this beautiful cottage at the side of a lake with its own jetty and a pedal boat. We entered via a private road for about a mile, surrounded by woodland, completely isolated from the towns and the main road. Northern Ontario was beautiful in the fall as we were there towards the end of September beginning of October.

All my family came, and we had one big reunion, it was fantastic to see everyone and listen to their interesting way of life, Peter got on well with them all.

One morning after breakfast all the family decided to go to the nearest mall and do some serious shopping, food, but mostly clothes. They were going to be out for some time. Peter and I declined the offer of going with them, I asked if we could take the boat out. One of my cousins shouted,

"Only stay in our cove, you don't want to get lost."

We set off pedalling, watching the cottage and keeping it in view, most of the time. It got a bit boring round and round so we decided to venture a little further into the huge lake, the water was getting a bit choppy; we started to head back; but we could not see our cove they all looked the same.

The water was beginning to come over the edge of our little boat, the sun had gone behind some dark clouds and the nice cool breeze had turned into a wind which was making the waves crash against the sides.

We pedalled faster not bothering which way to go we just needed to get into some shallow water, we were getting closer to land, approximately fifty meters away, the water was now up to our knees as we pedalled faster and faster, I was preparing to jump; Peter was putting his wallet into his top pocket as he did not want his dollars to get wet. He had brought all his money with him.

We did not jump ship we just pedalled on adrenaline as the water was coming in faster my shorts were getting wet, I could feel the ice-cold water hitting my thighs as we kept going.

Peter was much taller than me he shouted,

"I think I can stand up here, so he jumped, his feet touched the bottom, not before giving me his wallet. Fortunately, his head stayed up above the water line; I was relieved as he pulled the boat and me to safety.

When we reached land, we tipped the boat upside down and drained all the water, when we had rested and got our breath back, we jumped aboard and began to pedal staying awfully close to the water's edge till eventually we reached our own little cove.

Great, nobody was home we were so cold we stripped down to our undies and jumped in the warm Hot Tub that was on the veranda.

About an hour later everyone returned, asking us if we had a good time and had we enjoyed being on the lake, we both replied,

"Yes thanks, great experience."

That is the thing I liked about Peter he was so kind and considerate, always putting other people before himself. I remember the time I met him.

Katherine was recovering; she had met Paul. Emma was happy with Kevin and Liam was getting on with his life.

I felt so helpless after the effects of the Crown Prosecution Service letting my girls and me down; by closing the case against their Uncle David.

My Mum asked me one Sunday morning if I could take her to church. I was pleased to, as she had been my rock through everything; I spoke to her when things were getting me down and her words of comfort helped me cope.

We decided to go to early morning communion, which we both enjoyed and each Sunday we would do the same; go to Church then back to my Mum's for tea and toast.

We became friendly with the same crowd of people; we also spoke to the Vicar after the service. I asked if he would say a prayer for my children, he invited me to the vicarage if I needed to talk to someone.

I appreciated that, so I made an appointment the following afternoon. I had not spoken to anyone about my feelings and anger towards the whole situation of their Uncle David and the suffering my daughters endured. The Vicar was so understanding; he told me my anger was justified, but I needed to channel it into something positive.

That is when I decided to go to college and begin a counselling course.

There was a good one available with two other vocational subjects, IT which meant I could learn how to use a computer and how to send and receive emails, surf the internet for information. The other subject was an assertiveness course, which I recommend for anyone who has got little confidence. It really made me feel good about myself.

I thoroughly enjoyed the courses and passed with flying colours. One morning while I was taking part in an assertive class, I spoke of my feelings to my fellow students, and it was so helpful to get some positive feedback.

I soon signed up for the Level 2 counselling course which was due to start after the Xmas holiday.

I sailed through that and signed up for my Level 3. Unfortunately, it had to be cut short as I could not financially afford to carry on, so I put it on hold and got myself a job; thinking I could save up and pick up later from where I left off.

I managed to get on bank as a nursing assistant on the mental health wards at the hospital in the city. With the experience I had; I felt I could help someone in a similar situation to my own. It was there I met Peter.

He was a staff nurse in charge of me and other nursing assistants. He was different to other staff nurses; in the way he would ask you to do something; he had manners and he showed his appreciation by calling us the foot soldiers of the ward.

After a few months we had become friends and chatted to one another when we got chance at a break time.

One of the staff nurse's daughters was getting married, we had become good friends with her, and she invited us to the evening do. I met Peter at the bar, and we began to talk, he asked me if I would like to get a table, we talked and talked about each other's future, what we both intended to do with our lives. The funny thing was we both wanted to travel. I had never been out of England except for when I was fifteen years old and was fortunate to go to Switzerland on a school trip, where the teachers were in charge, so we had to do everything and go everywhere they had planned.

"Don't get me wrong," I said,

"I loved it and wanted so much to experience travelling again."

My husband never wanted to leave the Country. We always went to the same place for our holiday so that he could watch the planes landing and taking off from the nearby RAF station. Luckily, it had a nice beach, so the kids and I enjoyed swimming, sunbathing, and making sandcastles.

Peter mentioned he had been travelling since he was eighteen; I was impressed when he told me tales of his experiences in America and how he had travelled from state to state via a Greyhound bus. He had a good friend in Australia, and he was planning on going to see him in the winter as it would be their summer.

"I also have relations in Sydney and Perth," I mentioned that I was expecting to go to Australia when I had finished my Level 3 counselling course. He laughingly said he would wait, and we could go together.

That was it, when I was saying goodnight to him, Emma and her husband had come to pick me up Peter put his arms around me and kissed me on the lips.

Eight years later; I am still waiting for my Australia trip!

I had been seeing Peter for about six months when Emma had a relapse, she only had Darren at home she had not got full custody of the children then, but she was having regular contact.

Each time Emma had a relapse Kevin phoned me and I would immediately leave what I was doing, it was difficult for him to look after Darren and watch Emma's every move. Her involuntary movements happened at any time, if Jodie and Zak had come to visit, we always protected them from seeing anything.

Emma and Kevin only lived a few minutes' walk from my house, so I could be there as soon as he needed me. When Emma was presenting psychosis, we all thought it was better for her to stay overnight with me. That was when the flashbacks were at their worse and she was dissociated from reality.

I had explained to Peter about Emma's intensity flashbacks and how they cause these involuntary movements.

To see it for himself was another thing he said,

"If I hadn't seen it, I would never have believed it," he explained that it was like witnessing someone possessed.

He watched as Emma's body began to twist into all kinds of different positions and he too realized what was happening to her as he witnessed her stomach muscles moving and her legs were being spread apart, she was unconscious and not able to close them although she was trying hard to stop whatever was happening to her in her dissociation episode of the abuse. Peter was so understanding and helpful, after a short while the flashbacks stopped; but again, it left Emma with a sore back which causes her sciatica to return.

Peter was good at motivating, it did not matter whether she needed to use a wheelchair, and he pushed her when we went out, as he said,

"The sunshine is good for you, and it builds up your serotonin." I learned quite a lot from him, as Emma could manipulate me and Kevin, we did things for her whereas Peter explained,

"She needs to do things for herself, you have to be cruel to be kind," I appreciated that. When Peter and I were alone, we spoke about what would be good for Emma; she was in pain from her back and becoming depressed.

We decided to take her to London for a day out on the train.

With our support, she had to organize the tickets, also to let officials know that there would be a passenger using a wheelchair. Emma did most of the preparing on the computer and when she had to speak to someone by phone, she did it with confidence. Kevin was pleased, it was giving Emma something to think about and look forward to; also allowing him to have some time for himself.

The day came we were all excited it had given Emma a whole new goal to achieve and she had coordinated it well.

Kevin gave us a lift to the station in the city and attendants came and waited with a ramp until we could board the train, they were extremely helpful to Emma, when she was able to get out of her wheelchair, they showed us to our seats which she had reserved for all of us.

When we reached Euston station another attendant was on hand to help us with Emma and her wheelchair. The service Emma received from British Rail was magnificent.

We had set off quite early so we could spend the whole day in London. We arrived around ten o'clock.

Peter pushed Emma towards the sights, Buckingham Palace via St. James Park, and the Mall.

Then the British Museum, we managed to have a bit of lunch before visiting Madam Tussauds, Emma and I were amazed at how life-like the models were.

Celebrities, famous sportsmen/women, world leaders, the Royals, Pop stars of the present and the past and so much more. Conscious of the time, we flagged down a taxi which took us to the Tower of London where we saw the Crown Jewels. Then on to Selfridges in Oxford Street; Harrods in Knightsbridge the largest Department Store in Europe with its three hundred and thirty departments. We visited both stores, not all the departments may I add! The atmosphere in London is so different; extremely metropolitan; to see it is a magnificent experience.

We were travelling back home, Emma was so happy and talked excitedly about everything we had seen and done, it was so satisfying to see Emma relaxed and making conversation about something interesting. I suggested we should do it again,

"Let's go somewhere else, Emma you can decide," before I could finish my sentence she interrupted,

"Hey, can we go up to Scotland?"

I looked at Peter, he nodded.

"When because I've got to work?" I replied,

"End of the month, when you're not working, hey let's go every month."

Peter and I decided to put our social life on hold and put the money towards our little expeditions.

Emma was now buzzing with lots of enthusiasm. Later that week she rang us asking,

"Can we go to Edinburgh?" We both agreed it was a good idea.

Again, Emma organized everything, it was working; the psychology behind it all, was giving her something to look forward to, at the same time keeping her occupied and redirecting her thought pattern.

British Rail were excellent again they were prepared for us at each station.

Peter pushed Emma from the railway station, up Princess Street towards the famous Edinburgh Castle; although Peter was around six feet three inches tall and built like a Viking with biceps that could lift a car; he stared upwards to the castle. Sighed, then he pushed harder, he stopped a quarter of the way up to get his breath and then forced himself that little bit further.

We arrived at the gates to pay admittance, I enquired if they had any kind of lift as I expressed the need for some assistance. The gentleman behind the counter beckoned to another gentleman dressed in uniform, I watched as he signaled back.

Within minutes this vehicle came towards us, stopped beside Emma, the driver opened the side door for us, then pulled down a ramp and proceeded to push Emma and her wheelchair safely into place.

The driver explained to us while he was transporting us to the top of the castle,

"This is the way the queen comes when she visits the castle. We felt very privileged. It was most enjoyable and interesting exploring the castle rooms and the outside courtyards.

Luckily, we were able to see the cannon and all the protocol of it being fired at a certain time. After leaving the Castle we focused on a little shop which advertised kilts in the window, with a sign inviting you inside.

It was surprising as we made our way through the shop, along a small parapet and down to a large workshop.

There were racks of kilts in all different colours of tartan. We were invited to watch the pieces of cloth being turned into kilts using one of the large machines. It was also amazing to learn that the surname of a person or their ancestor who was born in Scotland whether it began with a Mc, or a Mac determined which cloth would match their clan.

That was interesting especially for Peter having the surname Mackintosh; we tried to discover which clan he and his ancestors belonged to. We managed to find out, fortunately Peter's cloth was out of stock; and where in Little Beddington would he wear it?

These trips were proving to be therapeutic for Emma as the amount of preparation kept her mind occupied. She did well to organize everything, we planned on travelling by rail again. The staff were so helpful each time we needed their assistance. This outing, we had decided to visit York.

The York Minster is a magnificent Gothic building dating back as far as the year 627AD. It is one of the greatest cathedrals in Europe and attracts many sightseers from countries all over the world. The experience is one not to be missed.

We spent a short time in the Treasure's House where we were escorted down into the cellars.

Legend has it that when the workmen were down there, they saw a frightening apparition of Roman legionnaires marching past, apparently the ghosts could only be seen from the knee upwards. It was an eerie feeling but alas; we did not experience any ghosts.

The Shambles is a maze of narrow lanes with overhanging timber-framed buildings dating back to the fourteenth and fifteenth centuries. The first and second floors seemed to lean towards each other on the opposite sides of the street, apparently, they were built like that to protect the meat from the direct sunshine.

It was fascinating to see the quaint little shops and houses with their tiny narrow-paned glass windows. Imagining the butchers with the freshly killed rabbits and pheasants hanging on hooks in the street outside the shop. Standing back and absorbing the atmosphere.

It was thirsty work walking the streets of York and taking in all the sights. We decided to sample a glass of Shandy in the most haunted pub in the city; where it is known that in the early hours, the late Lady Pecket wanders the endless corridors and staircases.

The following month Peter and I made it even more exciting, after looking at our finances we found we were able to fly to our next destination.

It was lovely to see the surprise on Emma's face when we told her to book a flight. I had already found an Airline which had some good offers to Europe.

We all decided to visit Rome and it would be Emma's responsibility to find a hotel for one night and book the flights.

Four weeks later we arrived at the nearest airport. Peter and I followed Emma towards the elevator; because we each had a small overnight bag; we could go straight to the departure lounge; Emma had already checked us in online. It was so easy being prepared. She did so well to find all the information on the internet. The more responsibility she had the more she excelled.

The best of that trip was that Emma was able to walk.

We stepped off the plane to thirty-four degrees, the heat hit us. There was a line of taxi's waiting, so it was good that we did not have to wait.

Emma had been studying some Italian language, she tried to tell the driver the hotel's address; fortunately, he understood English. Both Peter and I were impressed with the Star Hotel, a lovely large L shaped room, with three single beds.

We could not afford another room; Emma was comfortable with us all being together. The room had en-suite, two wardrobes and a dressing table.

It was 10.15am Italian time when we arrived at the hotel. We could only check in at 2.00pm so the assistant manager allowed us to leave our small amount of luggage in a room where there were other suitcases.

Firstly, we made our way to the Vatican City which was only about fifteen minutes' walk from our hotel.

What a magnificent sight, it was packed with tourists, some were praying in front of the steps underneath the balcony from where the Pope blessed the crowds of people in St. Peter's Square. Many were busy taking photographs. There was a queue waiting to enter the Vatican we did not have much time as we also wanted to see the Coliseum.

The heat was tremendous; people were queuing up to refresh from the cool water the fountains provided around the Square.

The last couple of months Kevin had been patient, Emma mentioned that she would love to go to Ireland and take Kevin and her children with her. Her confidence was growing, her self-respect had improved so much so that she did not need mine and Peter's support, but she wanted us to be close by.

We agreed, Kevin was a bit apprehensive; but we convinced him that Emma would be alright.

Dublin in Southern Ireland was going to be their destination; Peter and I decided to stay in Cork which is further south. There was plenty of time to organize passports for the children and Kevin as the trip was arranged for the summer holidays.

Emma had booked a nice apartment for them just outside the City of Dublin. Fortunately for them the same one had been double-booked; the proprietor was so apologetic he offered them a much more expensive penthouse suite with a roof garden for the same price.

Peter and I set off for Cork the same day as Emma and Kevin arrived in Dublin.

We stayed in a lovely Bed and Breakfast for the week, did all the sight-seeing including 'Kissing The Blarney Stone' which was an exhilarating experience, you must lie down on your back, lean as far back as you can while a gentleman holds you by the waist; at the time you feel a sense of vulnerability as you are suspended from a great height headfirst, looking down at the ground almost forty metres below.

At one time they held visitors by their ankles and lowered them down to the Stone; nowadays they are more cautious, they have provided an iron railing from the parapet walk.

For over two hundred years, world Statesmen, Literary giants, and Famous Celebrities of Stage and Screen have joined the millions who have climbed the steps of the high tower. Legend has it that if you kiss the stone, which is a block of bluestone built into the battlements of Blarney Castle six hundred years ago; you gain the gift of eloquence.

Whilst we were enjoying ourselves, Emma and Kevin also did some sight-seeing with the children. They loved Dublin Zoo, from Ha'penny Bridge over The Liffey they visited Grafton Street: famous for the Buskers who generally play music and sing in the street. Emma and Kevin enjoyed watching Irish dancing in a pub while sampling some of Ireland's famous Guinness.

Unfortunately, unforeseen circumstances caused Emma to try and contact us in Cork.

That day we decided to discover Peter's ancestors on his father's side; instead of returning to our room, we sampled the Guinness in a couple of the Irish pubs, the live music was deafening, people were dancing, the atmosphere was terrific.

After a late night out, we slowly made our way back to the Bed & Breakfast; the manageress had kindly waited for us to return,

"Your daughter has tried to contact you on at least four occasions."

Immediately I rang Emma I was not bothered about the time, I needed to know what had happened and why she rang the B&B; straight away all negative thoughts were flowing through my mind.

Emma and Kevin were watching a late-night film on the television, Emma answered the phone,

"Hi mum," before she could say anything else, I interrupted,

"Is everything alright?" the tone of my voice told her how anxious I was,

"I'm sorry Mum, I did panic a bit, there was some trouble with the children's passports, but everything is fine we have sorted it out ourselves."

No one can imagine the relief I felt when I heard Emma's voice, it was so normal, whatever normal is; there was no sadness, hesitation, or negativity. It was pleasant, happy, and content with life.

CHAPTER 12

Monty

E verything was going well, everyone was happy; but Emma needed something else, a hobby. She reflected on her childhood, the happy times when she went horse riding with Katherine and Brandy the pony, they both shared for a short while until he had to go back to the Horse Sanctuary as he developed a bad condition with his stifle, unfortunately Emma had not been well enough to look after him. Katherine was also busy studying for her exams.

Emma began surfing the internet day after day she searched for the right pony.

Until she noticed an advertisement; there was no photograph of the pony just a small description and how he needed a new home. Emma automatically phoned me,

"Do you fancy driving up to York this afternoon; I think I have found a pony." She sounded so excited,

Jodie too, as she was also taking after her Mum with a love for horses.

It was now two thirty, I was thinking about the length of time it will take to drive up to York and back; but I could not let Emma down, so I replied,

"Yes, if Kevin is happy to stay with the children?"

With it being a weekend, he could take both boys to play football. She said,

"Of course, he is." I knew he would be, that was typical of Kevin anything to please Emma, if she was happy, then so was he.

Jodie, Emma, and I piled into the car, I had already checked the water and oil, and I just needed to fill the tank with petrol to travel the long distance up north.

The journey was alright a bit busy when we hit the tea-time traffic. We arrived later than expected as it was difficult to find the address; it was a farm, miles from anywhere. The sky was beginning to darken, so the owner suggested we watch her lunge him in the paddock.

He moved well to her voice commands; Emma then led him back into his stable. Both Emma and Jodie fell in love with this beautiful chestnut gelding, only three years old and just recently broken and backed which meant they could ride him, but he also needed a lot of schooling.

A week later a truck pulling a horse trailer drove into the driveway and down towards the yard where Emma, Jodie and I were waiting. Emma had been lucky to find a nice friendly farmyard that took liveries, it only accommodated ten horses which was perfect, as Emma and Jodie did not want a big yard with lots of horsey people. They were not into competing, just hacking, and enjoying looking after Monty.

Emma put the new head collar on their new pony and led him down the ramp onto the cobbled yard. Jodie tied him up to a piece of bale twine attached to the railings that were provided for that purpose.

After paying the owner for bringing Monty and seeing them off the yard, they began to brush him and give him lots of TLC.

When Monty's coat was gleaming and the golden highlights shone in his mane and tail, Emma lead him into his nice, clean comfortable stable with plenty of straw for his bed and hay hanging in a net for him to help himself; a bucket of water inside a tyre so Monty could not be mischievous and knock it over; like some of the other horses on the yard had done. Emma learned this through speaking to the other horse owners, she felt comfortable being in their company as they were friendly and glad to help; also offering advice when she needed some information, especially when she tried to ride him in the school.

Jodie also got on well with some of the owners' children, as they were a similar age to Jodie, and they had plenty in common.

The satisfaction Emma felt from getting Monty and the responsibility of looking after him was extremely therapeutic; again, this gave her something to keep her mind occupied during the day whilst the children were at school.

Over the past ten years, there were times that she was unable to venture outside alone, not interacting with anyone other than her family and a few close friends, staring at the same four walls and not having the opportunity to hold an interesting conversation unless it was about something she had seen on the television.

Emma and Jodie were spending more quality time with each other, there was no distraction from her siblings; this meant she could have her Mum all to herself.

Over the next couple of months Emma's confidence grew, it was summertime the horses were in the fields and the weather was glorious. I noticed Emma was wearing a long-sleeved jumper, whereas everyone was walking about the yard in strappy tops as the heat was unbearable. I commented,

"Are you not hot?" she answered,

"Yes, I am, and I can't wait to go home so I can change."

I questioned her why she was wearing the jumper she replied,

"Mum, look at my arms," she was referring to the deep scars left from her self-harming.

"I can't wear strappy tops; people will see my scars." I felt sorry for her as I had never thought at the time; when it helped her to cope with her emotional pain that it would have such a bearing on her confidence. I automatically said,

"But people don't see them, when you speak to them, you give them eye contact, they have no need to look down at your arms."

My statement made no difference to how it made her feel.

"Mum I know they are there, and I don't know what to say if someone mentions them." I thought about what she tells her own children.

"Why don't you explain the same thing that you have told your own family? That the cat scratched you, it worked for them." She listened, but I could see she did not agree with me, she said,

"I think I will mention it to Janet."

Janet was the owner of the stables, she and her family were so obliging, friendly, and easily approachable.

The following day Emma arrived at the stables wearing a strappy top and a thin cardigan which covered her arms. She began her daily chores, around the corner Emma heard Janet's small Jack Russell yapping, knowing that she would not be far behind she plucked up enough courage to attract Janet's attention so she could mention her arms. She got such a surprise when Janet showed empathy towards her and stated that Stacy her cousin had the same need to self-harm.

"Take your cardigan off, Stacy doesn't bother, she walks around in her strappy tops, if anyone asks about them, which they won't, you will notice the people on this yard are understanding; they have manners not to mention anything like that. However, if the kids ask about your scars tell them what you said, the cat did it."

Emma was so relieved to hear the way Janet spoke to her about the fear of people seeing her scars.

The next day the sun was blazing, some of the girls were even sun-bathing sat outside their stables, and

Emma felt comfortable joining them in her strappy top without the camouflage of her cardigan.

Every day she was gaining serotonin from the sunlight which enhanced her mood, and her complexion was like a peach with a hint of strawberry covering her cheek bones, she looked radiant from the daily fresh air she was now accustomed to. Emma was so happy with her new life, still being a housewife and a mother but also enjoying time for herself.

Kevin and the children occasionally visited the stables, Kevin was so happy to watch Emma relaxed, confident and content; he also met up with some of his old friends from his youth, so they took it in turns to look after the children.

Monty was so good when he was on a hack either on his own or with other horses, but in the school he would bolt.

The first time it happened was a frightening experience, but Emma managed to hang on. The second time she was not so lucky, she had given Monty a good schooling on the lunge hoping that would have taken enough fizz out of him to be ridden in the school. She mounted him outside the arena, I walked at the side of Monty till Emma felt comfortable to walk alone, I stayed over at the gate with Suzanne a friend off the yard, she also had her horse stabled close to Monty.

A helicopter came from nowhere it was flying quite low and the noise from the blades frightened Monty into a canter, Emma was controlling him well until the helicopter flew over again and Monty went galloping towards the fence then came to an abrupt halt swiftly turning to the right; where Emma unfortunately lost her balance and came flying off, hit the ground and rolled out of the paddock, over the ten-inch steel barrier which separated the sand from the grass in the next field.

Suzanne and I ran over as fast as we could; Emma was not moving, my first thought was ***Oh my God she has broken her neck,*** I screamed at Suzanne,

"Quick! Ring for an ambulance," she immediately ran towards the farmhouse hoping someone would be around; she was shouting that loud Janet and her husband came running out of the house, Suzanne tried to explain between breaths what had happened, Janet immediately rang for an ambulance while her husband followed Suzanne back to where we were.

Meanwhile I was knelt beside Emma she had opened her eyes and muttered something,

"I can't move my legs," she was beginning to panic; I gently spoke words of encouragement that she was going to be alright, but all she could whisper was,

"Mum, I can't feel my legs."

It seemed ages before the Ambulance arrived, three paramedics ran towards us, followed by Janet.

They had brought a back board with them hoping to transfer Emma on to it and take her to the nearest hospital; realizing that Emma could easily be paralysed by travelling over uneven roads before reaching the main road which led to the hospital, the paramedics concluded that it would be safer and more beneficial to contact the air ambulance.

Immediately Janet and Suzanne made sure the horses were safe by taking them back to their stables.

The paramedics administered pain relief through placing a mask over Emma's nose and mouth and allowing her to breathe in gas and air, which helped to relieve some of the severe pain she could feel in her lower back and the middle of her spine.

When the Air Ambulance arrived and was hovering above, the paramedics asked each one of us to stand in a certain place in the field to enable the helicopter to land safely.

Soon Emma was being transported to the helicopter after being strapped to the back board and her head and neck safely supported.

It took us well over an hour to reach the hospital with all the traffic, being a Friday afternoon most of the huge business premises closed early so the roads were hectic. Suzanne had accompanied me, she knew I was a nervous wreck so she drove my car, I appreciated that as I could not help thinking the worse, *was Emma paralysed?* Before we left the stables, I asked Janet if I could use her phone to contact Kevin.

We eventually arrived and made our way to the Accident and Emergency dept. I gave my details to a lady over the desk, and she politely asked us to sit down while she got a nurse to assist us. Within a few minutes a nurse came,

"Your daughter has been asking for you," she then asked us to follow her to a cubicle where Emma was lying on a trolley, she had already seen a doctor and all the relevant tests had been done including X-rays for her neck and back.

Luckily, she suffered no broken bones, just severely bruised; her back had gone into spasm from the trauma of the accident which in turn caused her to be unable to move her legs.

Emma was admitted and had to stay overnight for observation.

About ten minutes later Kevin arrived, he had such a worried look on his face, until he saw Emma; she was now slowly beginning to sit up and looking much better than she did.

It took a few weeks before Emma returned to the stables, Jodie and I were looking after Monty while Emma was slowly recovering, she was black and blue all down her right side. Her confidence had taken a battering, she never felt the same again at the stables, she tried her best to motivate herself, but slowly she began to lose interest in Monty.

Jodie also felt uncomfortable without her Mum being there, I think it was the quality time she spent alone with her Mum which she missed.

However, Zak did show an interest in Monty, although he was only ten years old, he seemed to have a natural way with horses and loved accompanying me to see Monty, he helped me muck out, fill his nets and his water bucket. He even enjoyed searching the field with a fork and a wheelbarrow for droppings from Monty and the other horses, we all took turns, it was one of Janet's rules for looking after the farm.

It was nice spending time with my grandson, we spoke about lots of things; but Zak kept on repeating how much he missed his dad and wanted to go and live with him.

Meanwhile, Emma had become involved with the dance group of which Jodie belonged to. Jodie's drama teacher had approached her and asked if she would like to help behind the scenes, she had already met her from collecting Jodie after practice. This gave Emma something else to focus on and Jodie was really pleased when her Mum accepted the offer.

She joined them on a coach trip when the dance group were invited away from home.

When Emma and Kevin were searching for the appropriate high school for Jodie, they took into consideration her interest in music and dance.

Fortunately, close to where they lived was a school which specialized in the Arts. The Auditorium provided special sound equipment and all the relevant material to allow the staff and their pupils to present productions of both Musicals and Plays.

Zak was getting frustrated, he was also becoming quite aggressive towards his Mum, being cheeky to Kevin and fighting with Darren. This kind of behaviour carried on for about three months; then Emma discovered she was expecting another baby. Kevin and Emma were delighted with the news and could not wait to tell the children, they were also pleased that they were having a new baby sister or brother. Zak seemed quiet for a while; Emma thought he was settling down; she had arranged for him to see his dad on a regular basis.

One early evening when Carl had brought Zak home, Zak began shouting,

"I don't want to live with my Mum and Kevin, I want to go back with you."

He screamed to his dad as he was trying to get him out of the car. Emma was there, with tears in her eyes; coaxing him to come into the house. Carl had a few words with Emma, they decided he could go back with them, stay the night, and come home the following day.

Carl presumed that something more serious was causing Zak to behave in that way.

He rang the police.

Approximately two hours later; Emma and Kevin were completely shocked when the police arrived at their house with Carl, his girlfriend Helen and Zak. They stayed in his girlfriend's car, while the police entered Emma's home.

The police explained in short that Zak's father was concerned about his son, and would they investigate? They began asking very personal questions, of which both Emma and Kevin answered with a positive attitude.

Then Emma explained that recently Zak had been asking to live with his father, Emma new and understood Zak was not happy; but there was no room at his girlfriend's house as she had three young children of her own and now, she was expecting Carl's baby. The police were satisfied that the serious concerns of the father were unfounded. They left soon after. Emma described the situation to Zak and both Kevin and Emma had tried many tactics to make Zak happy, he had joined the local cubs in the village which he enjoyed every Monday evening. Emma knew how much Zak enjoyed his football, they had bought him his own goal post for the garden, he and his friends played regularly if the weather was good. Emma had found him a Football Team who took him on as a young player to teach him the rules of the game. They had also put his name down at a High School which specialised in Sports. His bedroom was decorated with his favourite team, he had a huge picture on his wall with all the Teams signatures, his quilt cover and pillowcase were covered in the Team, he was loved so much; yet still he could not understand his own feelings. Although he had spent most of his young life with his dad, his primary caregiver and not had a great deal of contact with his biological Mum. This deeply upset Emma, when she was given full custody of both her children. She was so happy thinking she could make up for all the years she had not been allowed to be a proper mother to her babies; she did not foresee that it was too late for Zak, he was already emotionally confused. Jodie was different, she always wanted to live with her mum, she also understood her own feelings as she was older than Zak, when their dad got full custody.

Zak accepted things for a while staying with his Mum and Kevin and seeing his dad every weekend.

When Carl was working and he could not have Zak, he was really upset and unfortunately, he took his anger out on his little brother Darren. He punched and kicked him on a regular basis, then he teased Jodie, she just went to her room. His behaviour was getting worse, Emma and Kevin were constantly telling him off for hurting Darren. They understood that siblings fall out and fight at times, but Darren was always covered in bruises.

One Saturday morning Emma asked Zak to fetch his dirty clothes down for washing, he ignored her comment and Emma asked him again, thinking he may not have heard her properly the first time; she then received a mouthful of abuse from him, he came towards her and deliberately punched her in the stomach, immediately she experienced pain, straight away she thought of her baby; she was now five months pregnant.

Kevin phoned me to look after the children while he took Emma to the hospital after she had spoken to the maternity ward for some advice.

The Sister suggested they need to do a scan to make sure the baby was alright and there was no damage. The results were fine and she could go home.

Then, the sister began to quiz Emma on how it had happened, when she first contacted the ward Emma had just explained in short that she had an accident; how could she possibly tell them the truth?

But the sister was empathic when she saw how upset Emma became when she mentioned this.

Suddenly the tears came, and she explained everything in detail and how Zak's behaviour was uncontrollable. The doctor was called for, and he decided to keep Emma in hospital for her and the baby's safety. There was nothing Emma or Kevin could say or do.

The doctor explained it was their duty of care for the unborn child. The Social Services were then informed, Emma was not allowed home until Zak was removed from their house; he was now ten years old and strong for his age. Emma's unborn baby was their priority.

Emma reluctantly contacted Zak's paternal Grandparents, I was too close, he did not want to stay with me, I understood after all he did not emotionally recognise me as his grandmother, even though I saw him every day since Emma had got him back, it was those missing years from being a young baby that caused so much heartache for him.

However, Carl's parents had played a huge part in Zak's life, it would be the best place for him to stay. Emma just wanted him to be happy.

Zak's paternal grandparents were happy to oblige after she had mentioned the situation to them, they were never too keen on Emma; it had always been difficult when the court cases were happening and both sides were fighting for the custody of the children and naturally

Carl's parents would be there to support him and vice versa, but because it was for Zak, they happily went to collect him that same day.

In the eyes of the medical profession the doctor would not even allow Emma to come home to say goodbye to her son.

So, I looked after the children and waited for Zak's Granddad to come for him, I had to explain to my grandson that he would be staying with his grandma and granddad. He asked,

"Why?" *How could I tell him the truth?*

It was difficult for Emma she had fought for so long for her children and now, when she finally got the chance to show how much she loves them and provide the stability they so desperately need, it was too late, the only consistent thing in Zak's life has been Carl's parents.

He loves his grandma and Granddad, if he cannot live with his dad, he wanted to live with them. Emma could see how unhappy Zak was, she understood how he felt; after all Jackie, Carl's ex-wife had told him he had come out of her tummy and that she was his real mummy. This must have confused his little mind not knowing what to believe at such a young age; *who was his Mummy?*

Emma had been asking for a while if Carl's parents could accommodate Zak; just for a short time while things calm down, but with their busy schedule it was awkward for them to agree.

She tried desperately to keep in touch, she bought him a mobile phone so she could speak to him, or he could ring her. It worked for a few weeks; then he switched his phone off. She rang Carl's parents asking to speak to him, fortunately Zak came to the phone, but there was little conversation; Emma asked him all sorts of questions.

"How are you? How's school? Have you been to watch football with your Granddad?" It was all a one-sided conversation; the answer was always the same,

"Yeah," it felt as if he did not want to speak to her. Emma was heartbroken, every week for month's she rang Zak, but nothing changed, his mood was the same, there was no response, no feeling, no love, nothing.

The week she was due to give birth she rang Zak to tell him and that he could come and see his baby sister; they knew it was a girl. Kevin, Darren, and Jodie had asked Emma if she liked the name Virginia. She said,

"Yes, we can call her Ginny for short." They all laughed.

Virginia was born, out of all the four children Emma had given birth to, Ginny was the easiest, the caesarean section was booked; this time Emma did not go into labour which was so much better for her back. Kevin had been with her the whole time; they were both so happy everything went well, their baby girl was a healthy 7lb 3oz bundle of joy. While Kevin left Emma and his baby daughter to sleep, he went home to tell his other children the good news and I went back to the hospital to stay with Emma.

When Ginny woke up Emma automatically looked after her, fed her when she was hungry and changed her when she needed to, it was so nice watching her being a Mum, so normal, no pain, only from the caesarean. It was such a wonderful experience watching mother and baby bond, Emma had Ginny in her arms, held her close to her breast and kissed her on her forehead; lovingly she rocked her till she fell asleep.

I felt so much empathy for Emma, there was no sign of a visit from her sister or her brother; I knew she missed them being there with her to celebrate their new little niece.

Kevin came every visiting time either with Jodie and Darren or his niece Jade; she was a lovely girl. Emma was upset the way her brother and sister had treated her.

Visiting time was nice it gave me a bit of a break; I went outside to get some fresh air as the wards in the hospital were overpowering with the heat. I had offered to stay with Emma so Kevin could look after the children. The nursing staff were kind, they brought me a fold-up bed, some sheets, and blankets; they made me feel welcome and extremely comfortable.

A couple of days later Emma and Ginny were discharged from the hospital.

Kevin had cleaned the house and prepared a nice meal; Jodie and Darren cleaned their own rooms which was a lovely surprise. It was a miracle to persuade a thirteen-year-old to clean her room. I had entered weeks before while I was helping Emma with household chores. It was like Aladdin's cave, a mixture of a hair salon, a beauty parlour and not to forget a clothes rehearsal, posters of her latest heart throb, jewellery strewn over her dressing table along with hair straighteners.

A hair dryer and all the hair products that she needed to keep her beautiful long dark curls at bay. Then there was her make-up she loved experimenting with all colours of eye make-up and various foundations. Her Mum would not let her wear it outside, but Jodie did not mind she just enjoyed trying it out.

She loved dancing and singing, her Mum and Kevin had bought her an electric guitar for her birthday and an electric keyboard from one of her Xmas presents; they were neatly stacked next to each other in one corner of her room. CD's covered part of her carpet, I presumed at the time she could not make up her mind which one of her pop artists to listen to.

Jodie took so much pleasure in reading; her books were kept immaculate on the shelves above her bed.

'Her bed' everything was in its place; pink velvet cushions rested perfectly against the pink velvet headboard, the latest pop band printed on her duvet and her soft toys she had collected over the years sat proudly at the foot of her bed.

We were always proud of Jodie when she received a good part in any of the shows that were organised for the year ahead; she deserved it as she worked hard towards the auditions.

I used to love hearing Jodie sing, many a time when we were alone in my car; she would say,

"I'm bored Nana," I knew just what she meant. It was 'our thing' and I would tell her to sing, she suggested some songs that she knew I liked. And she would sing, without any music; she could always find the right tune, the right beat, then she would blast those lyrics out. Sometimes it brought tears to my eyes when she sang something soft like, 'What If' by Kate Winslett. Then she sang a tune that she liked with a lot of beat, she was also brilliant at rapping. How she managed to remember the words so quickly and say them so fast was unbelievable?

The school productions began, it was the first opening night and Jodie was nervous but excited. We were all there to watch her; she performed brilliantly. Her Mum was so proud of her, we all were. Even Darren had sat quiet while Jodie sang her heart out.

She was gifted with such a beautiful voice, her Mum had questioned her as to what she would like to do as a career and if she would like to go to Rada which is a school for the Arts where teenagers learn to act, sing and dance along with educational subjects, most are destined for the Stage, Film, Television, and the Theatre. Emma had told Jodie she was more than willing to spend money on sending her to Rada if that was what she really wanted.

I had told the rest of the family, Katherine, Paul, and Liam about the show and asked did they want any tickets? But Katherine had changed dramatically towards her sister.

This attitude was not like Katherine. Her kind and considerate personality had disappeared.
Since Emma had disclosed the truth about her father, Katherine had disbelieved everything she said, even some of the involuntary movements that Katherine had witnessed.

"See Mum I can do it; Emma is putting it on for attention."

Then to my horror she had sat back on the sofa and proceeded to bang her head backwards and forwards.

This made me so upset, Katherine did not know the pain and torture Emma had experienced while she was going through these horrible movements. I could not believe what she was saying about her own sister, she had changed so much. Then the anger spilled out.

"When Paul and I were getting engaged she was ill, she couldn't be bothered to make an effort for us."

I wanted so much to interrupt, but she carried on,

"Then my wedding, I had asked her to be my bridesmaid, but the same week of my big day she decided to be ill; you were all caring about Emma and whether she would be able to perform her role on the day. You said you were frightened that she might collapse in church. Mum I was so upset, it was my day, and everyone was more interested in Emma. Paul thinks she is jealous and wants the attention herself, so that is why she is always ill whenever anything exciting is happening in my life."

I never realised Katherine felt this way, she interrupted my thoughts,

"When I was expecting Cindy, I wanted Emma with me as my sister and do things together, she never went shopping with me to buy baby things," I managed to say something,

"I did," she was getting upset.

"Mum, I know you were there for me, but I also wanted my sister."

Fortunately, I protected Katherine from seeing the horrible flashbacks, I was frightened that they may set off Katherine's mental health problems; she was doing so well I could not let her see her sister going through that torture.

I tried to explain to both Katherine and Paul, I had not realised they did not understand.

How was I able to describe the terrible ordeal that Emma was experiencing? Unfortunately, Emma was always ill, not just around those important times in Katherine's life. Emma had not wanted to let her sister down, she tried so hard to make the effort which she accomplished as best as she could; but at the same time, she needed my support. I thought I had given Katherine a great deal of attention at the same time, she had Paul in her life, and she was happy, I was not aware that Katherine had felt this way.

Years ago, when Carl was living with us Katherine's relationship with him was good, they both had the same sense of humour, apparently through information from Zak she is now in touch with him and good friends with his girlfriend; she also sees Zak on a regular basis, he spends time with Katherine, Paul, and Cindy. Emma also learned that they had all gone on holiday together and that Zak had slept in the same caravan as his Granddad.

No one had asked Emma if Zak could go on holiday, let alone stay in the same caravan as her father.

She was so angry, she had full custody of Zak, they should have respected that and spoke to her, but Carl had a parental right, he gave his permission; Katherine just took Zak away without Emma's knowledge.

When Emma's dad was questioned by the police, Carl supported him, this caused an inconsistency in Emma's statement of which Carl was indirectly involved. At the time the police believed Carl, not realising that Carl did not know everything about the situation. Since that time, Katherine and Paul have become good friends with him and his family.

Both Emma and Katherine used to be close and so did her brother Liam; now he does not want anything to do with Emma or her family. He does not send them birthday cards or gifts not even a Xmas card. There are times when Emma is at a low, she thinks, *was it all worth it?*

She states,

"If I hadn't disclosed what my father did to me, I would still have my brother and my sister especially my niece Cindy who I miss dreadfully." I thought about what Emma had said and replied,

"You had no choice, it was either you recover from the trauma and move on with your life or I wouldn't like to think of the other choice, as you have said in the past you could not have lived with the emotional pain you were suffering. Have you not realised your intensity flashbacks have stopped since you disclosed your father's sins?"

Emma rang Zak to let him know about Ginny, he did not seem too bothered, she asked him to come and see her and perhaps stay for tea. She told him how much she missed him and how much she wanted to see him. He reluctantly agreed to see his Mum at the weekend, but he controlled the situation by demanding that Kevin, Jodie, and Darren will not be there.

"Yes alright, I will ask them to leave us alone for the afternoon; I just want to see you."

Emma was becoming quite anxious regarding this visit from Zak she was so looking forward to it but at the same time apprehensive.

It was the first time Zak had come home since she was five months pregnant with Ginny, she had asked him to come to see her after school, but he had declined and gone straight to his dad's girlfriend's house.

Emma had asked me if I would stay with her while Zak was there. I agreed as I had also missed him.

There was a knock on the front door, immediately Emma went to answer it.

"Come in,"

Emma said excitedly, Zak was standing next to his grandma, she looked down and asked,

"Will you be alright? I will pick you up in two hours."

I noticed the look on Emma's face that she was not happy with that comment from his grandma, she replied in a friendly but diplomatic way,

"Of course, he'll be alright, he's with his Mum and his Nana,"

Emma gently took hold of Zak's hand and led him into the lounge.

"Come and see your baby sister Ginny."

Zak's Grandma shouted,

"Bye," as she walked through the front door, which I held open for her. I was very polite as I said,

"I think he's excited to see his baby sister." She nodded and returned to her car. It was lovely to watch Zak with Ginny, Emma had put her into Zak's arms, he was gently holding her close, smiling down at her tiny features, and touching her fingers one by one.

Emma took some good photographs of them together.

I asked Zak if he would like to see Monty some time, he shrugged his shoulders. Emma suggested she picks him up from school and takes him to the stables; he did not say anything, to break the silence I said to Zak,

"You can always ring your Mum if ever you want to go, can't you?" Zak nodded. Emma asked him if he would like a drink, he answered politely,

"Yes please," you could cut the atmosphere with a knife. This was also the time when Emma learned about Cindy seeing Zak and how they all regularly go to the park on a Sunday afternoon.

There was another silence, then Emma exclaimed,

"Give Ginny to my mum and come in the kitchen I've got something to show you." I took Ginny from Zak while he went towards the kitchen.

Emma had baked a cake and iced it with a boy in a red football T-shirt and black shorts kicking a football on an oblong piece of flat green icing, she had also made two goal posts.

This represented Zak and the football team he supported.

"Do you like it?" Emma waited eagerly for a response.

"Yeah, did you do that?" she nodded, as he smiled, it was like turning the clock back a few years when Zak seemed happy.

"Do you want a piece?" she asked him,

"Yes please, can I have one with the boy on?" Emma smiled and nodded,

"Yes." The ice broke and they began to talk and laugh about the old times, steering away from the reason why Zak left in the first place.

Time went fast, his grandma turned up and Zak quickly put on his coat, gave his Mum and me a hug, kissed Ginny on her forehead and ran towards his grandma's car.

Emma enjoyed the short time she had spent with her son; unfortunately, she has not seen him since.

It did not take long for Emma to get Ginny into a routine; she was such a good baby. Both Jodie and Darren were there to help. Jodie was more than capable of picking her up, making sure she always supported her head. Ginny was a bit boring for Darren, except for bath times when he was allowed to splash water onto her tiny body, he also helped his Mum by getting her things needed.

He was fascinated when she began to chuckle and watch him when she was able to focus properly.

There was only the one visit from Zak; Emma still carried on texting him weekly; she never got a response either from his mobile phone or his Grandparents landline phone.

The only consolation she had; was that she had done the right thing letting him go, knowing that he was much happier.

CHAPTER 13

Torment

I n the beginning I expected this feud between my children to last a short while and then make up like siblings should.

I remembered the barbecues I had in my garden in the summer, Jodie, Zak, Darren, and Cindy played together in the large swimming pool while Katherine, Emma and I organised the food on the large wooden picnic table I had in the centre of the decking. Kevin and Paul looked after the barbecue and chatted together, putting the world to rights; whilst we girls talked about family stuff.

Liam and his fiancée Emma were speaking to my Mum about their wedding which they had recently booked, eighteen months before the actual date.

My Mum and I found it hard to accept the way the family had been split apart from the sexual abuse Emma's father had inflicted upon her as a child.

I have a cousin my Mum's brother's son Michael who is married to Alice they have two children a boy and a girl, Dean and Millie.

When Emma and Katherine disclosed the sexual abuse by their Uncle David, my ex-husband Steve decided to be the one to tell everyone what had happened, I remember him saying,

"I will let Michael and Alice know; it will save you having to tell them." At the time I could not understand why they had to know so soon. He also told the rest of the family on both sides.

We were close at one time to Michael and Alice; they used to visit us regularly as they only lived approximately five miles away. Slowly they stopped coming round, they used the reason that it was the dog, but I could always have put the dog in another room. When the girls were admitted to hospital, they did visit Katherine, but never asked about Emma.

Over the years my Mum got upset with the way Michael was towards Emma and her children. We always visited them at Birthdays and Christmas's with presents; Emma always sent something for their children. One day my Mum asked if we could bring Emma with us, the answer was,

"No, we would rather you didn't." There was no explanation; my Mum was annoyed as Emma had done nothing wrong to deserve this negative attitude towards her. She spoke at length saying how she felt about the whole situation and that she was disgusted that he had never supported Emma through the turmoil of her Post Traumatic Stress caused by the abuse.

He replied,

"We don't believe anything happened to Emma only Katherine that's what her dad told us, and that she tells lies and makes things up. I remember when I came back from living in Australia, I was staying with you, she was telling lies then, and she stole your jewellery and hid it in the garden." My mum was so angry she retaliated with,

"Emma was only ten years old at the time, she was trying to tell us something; because years later I found a pair of knickers buried in the garden."

He tried to finish the conversation, but my mum would not let him, she carried on,

"Unfortunately, I threw them away, at the time I just thought she was a naughty girl, I wish now I had mentioned them, maybe they might have found some DNA."

Michael just listened and when my Mum had calmed down and said what she needed to say she changed the subject as she did not want to fall out with her nephew, she had already lost her brother Edward, Michael's Dad to a fatal sailing accident.

My Uncle Edward, his wife and their two small children had emigrated to Australia in the mid 1960's, they were referred to as £10 pommes.

In a conversation years later with my Mum, Aunty Norma told her about the long horrific journey by boat, but it was worth all the heartache.

Uncle Edward made a good life for them and himself, it was not easy at first, but over the years he had established well with a good job and a nice home. They had settled nicely in Albany, south of Perth, close to the Indian Ocean.

The dreams of building his own boat and sailing back to England; were slowly becoming a reality. Michael and Annie had grown up as Australian citizens; they were accustomed to the Australian way of life, living in a house with a swimming pool; able to cool off when the heat became unbearable.

Uncle Edward and Aunty Norma were strict with their education and made sure they both went on to university, achieving excellent results, which enabled Annie to become a Veterinary Surgeon and Michael to excel as a sports instructor.

The day finally came when my uncle finished off the fine details of building his beautiful boat; he named her 'Familia 2nd.'

He arranged a small gathering of some special friends and his family to celebrate the launch with a bottle of Champagne which he gave the honour to his wife Norma to perform. After all, she had tolerated all the times he came home, had his evening meal, and then tirelessly worked on his relentless ambition to sail the seas.

My Mum and I were so happy when we received a letter from Uncle Edward letting us know that their adventure had begun, he and Norma had set sail for England.

Michael and Annie were staying in Australia as they were both happy with their careers, their friends, and their home.

Apparently, Uncle Edward and Aunty Norma had left Australia eight months earlier, they had already sailed six thousand miles to South Africa by way of Christmas Island, Cocos Keeling Island, Mauritius, and Reunion Island.

Over the last couple of months Michael decided to join his father while his Mum flew back home as Annie was having a few problems and needed her mother's support.

They were in a small port north of Durban while they waited for Michael and then, Father and Son planned to sail from Cape Town to St. Helena a small Island in the Atlantic Ocean and then on to South America, Rio de Janeiro, Salvador, a look at the Amazon and then the West Indies for Christmas.

Whilst he was writing this letter, he said he could not believe how lucky he was at being able to travel the world, do these things and think these thoughts.

He wrote addressing this to my Mum, his sister.

"The Gods have been kind, I can but hope they will continue to smile upon us and look after us through the dangers ahead."

"Why do we all have to grow old and look it? Why cannot we remain active and vibrant and forever eighteen – until our number is up and then go. Quickly, painlessly, with no fuss, with no regrets, with no tears.

Like having a jolly good go at batting, scoring a century and enjoy every minute of it until, 'Hey Presto!' you are out, and you retire amid a burst of applause. Well, I do not know about the applause, but I think I would like to have a go at the Century- so long as it is fun. So now you know why I am sailing my little boat around the world. It would only be partly true to say that it is my dream come true, that having designed it, planned it and built it at the side of the house, there is nothing more to do except sail away.

The truth of the matter is that I want to be a Peter Pan, I want to pretend forever that this world of tropical islands and far distant landfalls is the real world and that I will – like

'The flying Dutchman' sail the seven seas ad infinitum."

Uncle Edward expected to reach England twelve months later; he was going to keep us informed of his whereabouts.

My Mum and I were planning a huge reception, all the family, including three generations of cousins, half cousins etc., The Media would be waiting to take photo's when 'Familia 2nd' was to finish her long journey home and sail into Plymouth harbour.

Alas, it was not meant to be sadly my Uncle Edward lost his life when he and his son Michael got into difficulties close to Port Elizabeth.

After ten hours in the sea Michael was rescued by a fisherman and taken ashore; two weeks later my uncle's body was found washed up on a beach close by.

Years later after dealing with the tragedy of that dreadful night, Michael decided to pack his bags and come to England. He met a nice young lady Alice through regularly attending the gym. Two years later they married and had two wonderful children.

Peter was shopping in the city, when he accidently bumped into Alice; he had met her a few times on special occasions. She asked how everyone was and how proud her and Michael was of Katherine and how well she has done and moved on with her life.

"Why can't Emma do the same?"

Peter was taken aback with this comment, he said it was nothing to do with him.

He was loyal to Emma; he just politely made his apologies and walked away. Peter did not show any feelings of anger towards Alice, after all she had not heard and seen what he had; he thought, *if only she knew what torment Emma had gone through as a child and now as an adult.*

Katherine did not want anyone to know not even her father when she was feeling mentally unwell. There was only my mum and I that supported her through the bad times.

Slowly Katherine drifted further apart from me, my mum and Emma and her family. She had changed since she met Paul.

It was heart-breaking to see how good friends and family can snub a person who is the victim in this horrific life changing situation.

Yet, the person responsible, the perpetrator who caused so much hurt and conflict can just sit back and do nothing. I ask myself. *Do they have any feelings? This is his daughter who is suffering not just because of the evil things he did to her when she was a vulnerable little girl who just wanted to please her daddy; but how she is being tormented now as if she has done something so terribly wrong.*

Questioning all of this,

Is this the profile of a person who does these things to a child? Where he manipulates people into thinking the worse of the victim and all the time it was him, he was the evil one. Do they really believe in God? I know for a fact my ex- husband did not, did this allow him to sin without a conscience? He earned the respect where people would never think that he was capable of such atrocities, as he always offered his time to help. Over many years he became well liked in the community. If there was a rumour about him, he kept a low profile, till after the rumour had died down.

According to Emma's memories, when the sexual abuse first began with her father, she remembers him tickling her and then it hurt so badly between her legs.

It was mainly at bath-time as the true episodes of abuse have visions of the bathroom and its surroundings; she also recalls a significant memory of the burgundy bath.

She recollects the air shows when she was alone with her father in the white van, he orally raped her; she still experiences the taste of his semen, irrationally believes her teeth will fall out if she does not clean them regularly, a bit like OCD (obsessive compulsive disorder) she repeats the cycle from morning till night-time at least eight times a day. She panics if she is in a situation where she has not got the opportunity to keep up with her daily routine.

One experience I will never forget, I had gone to the hospital to visit Emma when she was presenting bad psychosis. I was sat on the bed whilst she sat on the floor.

A nurse was present as Emma was on a one-to-one observation. For no apparent reason

Emma picked up a small towel folded it, then rolled it into what resembled a long thin pipe. She then put it into her mouth and proceeded to move the rolled towel in and out, as this was happening Emma seemed to be dissociated with us and her surroundings. I was aghast at what I was witnessing in front of my eyes. I do not think the nurse saw anything, as Emma had her back to her. It was like watching a little girl, playing. I did not mention it, within a few minutes she was back to her adult state; unaware of what she had just been doing.

Colours are a trigger, each time Emma saw a car resembling a red Capri she would have a flashback of her father saying to her Uncle David,

"Bring her back when you've finished with her."

Then her Uncle David would regularly take her to a lay-by set back from the main road. Emma remembered the feel of the seat belt keeping her fastened down, her knee banging against the side of the door. The memories are not of a full story; her sub-conscience throws out bits of information at a time, she explained,

"It's like a jigsaw puzzle."

She was reminiscent of the time her father and his sister Anne walked her back to her grandmas from Anne and David's house. Emma began to cry with the pain she felt after her father had held her down while her Uncle David raped her on the lounge carpet.

She remembers her Aunty Anne's scolding words,

"Stop crying, don't be so soft."

When she reached her grandma's house, she wet herself and her Aunty Anne told her,

"You dirty girl."

These are just a few of the many traumatic memories of Emma's true experiences.

One weekend while Steve and I were at an air show. Anne and David had offered to look after the children.

Emma still has nightmares of that weekend; in her sleep she recognizes the red and white kitchen and certain ornaments on the windowsill.

She remembers crying and wanting to go home. Uncle David showed her the fridge full of goodies.

"You can't go home we have made a bunny rabbit jelly."

She recalls in her dream, seeing a jelly in the shape of a rabbit.

The memories of that weekend still haunt her. Upstairs, she remembers not feeling well on the bed... then the bath where he tried to drown her by pushing her head under the water, the heavy palm of his huge hand on her forehead.

My Mum had accidently broken her hip, to make her more comfortable I bought a reclining chair; when Emma first noticed the chair, she felt physically sick and began heaving, then she started to shake uncontrollably, for a few minutes I had a dreadful thought; that her intensity flashbacks were returning.

It was a panic attack; I quickly found a paper bag and told her to breathe into it, when she managed to calm down, she explained,

"Uncle David and my father used my Aunty Anne's reclining chair, when they were abusing me." Apparently, her father was behind the chair, while her Uncle David forced open her legs and raped her; she was approximately eight years old at the time, she remembers telling her daddy,

"Tell him to stop, Daddy, he's hurting me."

She remembers her father's words,

"Just open your legs, it will be over soon."

She tried to scream but her father put his other hand over her mouth. The flashbacks have been seen on video, she can be heard whimpering, you can see her stomach muscles moving under her jumper, the film has captured her desperately trying to close her legs, but alas her tiny little body is forced to give in to such a huge monster as her Uncle David.

Then she comes out of the dissociated state, she gasps for air, she has tears in her eyes, complaining that her mouth is sore where her father had been pressing down with his hand trying to muffle her cries; she is also seen gently rubbing between her thighs. Again, complaining that they are sore.

Then she explains between her tears and shortness of breath what has just taken place, "He was tickling me Mum,"

"Who was?"

"Dad, he was tickling me and making me laugh and then he pulled my arms up and held me tight, I couldn't move, he was hurting me, Uncle David was hurting me I told my dad to tell him to stop, but he didn't."

Emma needs a cigarette, this action seems to bring her quickly back to reality *(young children do not smoke*) slowly she makes her way outside, still feeling the physical pain of what she has just experienced. Her father had held his young daughter down by pressing his hand onto her left arm with her right arm stuck firmly underneath (each time Emma came out of one of these horrendous flashbacks, I had to help her bring her arms back down into a more comfortable position).

This is a significant memory as her left arm has always been the main one, she self-harmed; by cutting with a razor blade deep into her skin to get the feeling of her father's hand away.

She would gladly have had it amputated.

It was at the funeral after her father took hold of her left arm, when all the horrendous memories came slowly flooding back.

Now she has got a beautiful tattoo of an Angel she calls Petra, concealing her scars and the gruesome memories of her past.

CHAPTER 14

Petra

E mma always had fond memories of Petra my sister, she remembers a teddy bear she bought for her on one of her visits; she named it Petra. She also bought one for Katherine.

Every time Emma experienced sexual abuse either from her father or her Uncle David, she always searched for her teddy bear Petra, she would hug it, love it, as it gave her so much comfort; something she could not get from anyone, as no one knew, no one could ever know.

She was threatened not to tell anyone, she was told that no one would believe her, she will be sent away and never see her Mummy again. That was what her daddy had said. Uncle David told her that he would kill her, he had already shown her how in the bath; so, she talked and clung to Petra her teddy bear.

One afternoon in April 1981 I received some heart-breaking news. Petra my sister died in a car accident on one of her journey's up north. This time she was not driving, she was a passenger training an assistant. She was showing him the many outlets of the Company and introducing him to the Managers, as Petra needed to delegate some of her workload to give her more time to visit potential buyers overseas.

She was so excited when she rang my Mum to let her know that her Managing Director had asked her to be their leading representative. She was close to her 25th Birthday and had the rest of her life to look forward to.

The police let us know about the accident. Steve had collected my Mum and brought her to our house, they were waiting for me to return from picking Katherine up from school. I had taken Emma with me.

I will never forget that feeling of shock. When they told me I just fell to the ground, unable to believe what Steve and my Mum were saying. I remember the screaming and the howling that comes with the devastating news of suddenly losing someone so close.

My Mum will never forgive my ex-husband for that sad- time, she and I desperately wanted to see Petra; tell her we love her and to say our good- byes. But Steve thought he was helping, by protecting us from seeing her, he told me that she had broken her neck and died instantly which would have turned her face black. We believed him, and reluctantly allowed him to do everything, including identifying her body. He said he owed it to Petra as he was not nice to her when she was alive, so he felt he was making up for the way he had treated her when she came to see us. He was the one to tell the rest of the family, organise the funeral. It was hard as my Mum wanted so much to speak to everyone who turned up to her funeral, there were so many friends, colleagues, bosses, her Managing Director who had been wonderful, making sure that all the funeral expenses were taken care of. Unfortunately, Steve bundled us into a waiting car as soon as the funeral was over. Except for some of Steve's family and a few of our own we went back to our house for sandwiches and a cup of tea which Steve had already prepared. It would have been nice for me and my Mum to invite some of the people who were an important part of Petra's life.

Years later, my Mum was disgusted to learn that Petra had not died instantly, apparently the ambulance had picked her up and she died on the way to the hospital.

This proves that Steve had been lying as he went to identify her body almost immediately. Her face would not have been black as he had stated. ***Why did*** *he not let us know so we could have gone to see her for the last time?*

My Mum and I needed to feel she was still with us, we held each other tight, we were praying together, my psychic abilities felt she was all around.

My husband did not understand, he was quite angry; got up from where he was sitting and stormed out of the house.

We could not collect Petra's ashes to scatter them where we would have liked. Steve had told the Vicar in the Crematorium; to scatter them to the wind. He never asked us, never mentioned them. I understand we were still in shock, we appreciated everything he did for us at the time. However, it would have been nice to take them to a place, where both my Mum and I knew. A place Petra liked not far from where we lived.

She used to come and stay at Mum's when she was on her annual leave. She loved walking. Early in a morning my Mum and Petra would go up into the hills and walk for miles, and then return for a hearty breakfast.

One morning she rang and asked if she could take me and the children out for the day Emma had just turned three at the time and Katherine was five, Liam was not born then.

"I want to show you something,"

It was a lovely time of the year, late spring everything was turning a beautiful green, baby lambs were frolicking in the fields not far from their mothers.

Trees in pink and white blossom, daffodils with their yellow petals swaying in the cool breeze; but where Petra took us was the most beautiful spot you could ever imagine.

On either side of this waterfall was a mass of bluebells, you had to go through a gate and along a path leading to a stream coming down from the waterfall.

The sunlight caught the water as it trickled slowly over the glistening rocks and stones that were naturally placed in the stream. Petra took Emma and carried her in her arms, while I walked slowly up with Katherine close to the water's edge, holding her hand tight.

"Do you like it, isn't it the most beautiful place?" Petra's face was so pleased that she had been able to show me this. I smiled, and I had to agree.

So that is where Mum and I would have scattered Petra's ashes, to help us deal with the disappointment, we believed that they would have found their own way there.

Every year on her anniversary we go to the stream and throw daffodils for each one of our children and our grandchildren. This is not a morbid gesture, we have lovely memories of Petra when we do this, we always took the children with us; they loved watching their daffodil make its way down the stream.

A month after the funeral my Mum and I were going through some of Petra's belongings. My Mum found a diary, she scanned through the pages. On one of them there was something very strange, it was Petra's handwriting, most uncharacteristic of her. She never seemed religious to us except that in the last twelve months she had been visiting a spiritualist church.

On one of her visits, she had come downstairs at my Mum's house so excited saying,

"Mum, I have just seen my own aura."

Mum had not taken too much notice at the time until she found this piece of writing on one of the pages between January and the date of her accident; we tried to decipher when she would have written this. Reading it, it seemed like she was prepared.

I place this day, my life, my loved ones,
My work, in The Lord's hands
There is no harm in The Lord's hands

Only good, whatever happens,

Whatever results, If I am in The Lord's hands

It is The Lord's will and it is good

It was written with a special pen, of which Steve and I had given her for a Xmas present only a few months earlier.

We decided it would be lovely if we had that inscription put in 'The Book of Remembrance'

We each had a copy of the inscription made into a beautiful card that we both treasure. I decided to put mine into a heavy dictionary to keep it flat. Without a word of a lie, the page I opened at the time had the word 'Sister' on the top left-hand side. A huge shiver went through my body. I also kept one of her books, she had lent it to me before she died.

"Read it," she had said.

'The Third Eye' by Lobsang Rampa

Published in 1956 the year Petra was born.

One day while Katherine was at school and Emma was quietly playing with her toys, I had the television on just for the sound, I was not taking any notice of what I was watching, until I noticed a vision of Petra's face appear on the screen.

I was so overwhelmed at what I had just witnessed. It only happened for a split second, the racing was on and there was a man in a dark suit, nearly taking up the whole of the screen. I needed to make sense of this, and looked for the book Petra had given me before she died,

"Some still have the gift, visions of a loved one can be seen looking into.

A large flat bowl of water, a dark screen etc……"

I had shown my Mum what I found in the book and explained what had happened on the television screen. So, one day she was at my house, the children were out with their father. We both sat in front of the blank television screen and after a short while a vision of Petra appeared; she was sitting cross-legged I remember her shoulders, neck, and face. Then as quickly as it came; it disappeared. My Mum had tears in her eyes, I knew she had seen her.

For a long time after, I used to have quiet conversations with Petra while I was ironing, no one was about, just me and my thoughts.

I would love to have been an Aunty to her children, but it was never going to happen.

I miss that. Whether she had a boyfriend, or someone special we would never know. Approximately twelve months later I did not feel her presence anymore, but I know she deserved to be happy wherever she was. She was a lovely person with a fantastic personality.

Petra was always truthful. She gave to many charities for wild and domesticated animals.

I know it sounds like a cliché, but she constantly mentioned how much she was against war, she always wanted worldwide peace. One night I could not sleep I had gone downstairs to make myself a drink. Steve was fast asleep in bed. I decided to look at my book again and on one of the pages it read something like this.

We all have a psychic ability, some more than others. Many thousands of years ago the whole of mankind had the gift of being able to use the third eye, God took it away, as many used it for the wrong purpose.

This took me back to the first and last time I visited my son in laws spiritualist church.

Paul's parents helped organise the meetings, they were always inviting me, but I had to decline except for this occasion.

There was Katherine, Liam, and me. This day was a Good Friday. Frank and Barbara, Paul's parents were there preparing things when we turned up; they were pleased to see us and showed us where to sit. Most of the chairs were situated in a big circle, there was also a few rows. I think those were more for people who were not taking part in the group. Barbara told us to sit in the circle on the far side of the room.

The meeting had begun, the Medium was a lady she was standing at the front of the circle; she had been speaking and going round slowly to each person, when I felt my heart begin to beat fast, my right arm which I had comfortably resting on my lap fell.

I lifted it up with my left arm as it felt so heavy. It fell again. My heart was beating much faster, I could hear the medium in the distance still talking, but by now my heart was banging against my chest wall. I was beginning to wonder what on earth was happening to me.

I fell onto the floor, I have a memory of trying to get up, and seeing Liam and Katherine's faces they were disgusted, Liam whispered in an angry tone,

"Get up Mum."

I was half conscious about what was happening, but I could not do anything about it. I could not stop it.

My left arm was stretching out towards a man in one of the rows; I was trying to shout his name in another language, he knew who I was and came over towards me.

He stood over me as I was saying something to him; I later found out I was speaking polish; my arm was reaching out for him. He speaks the same language back to me, but it is not me; I am his dead wife who died of a stroke.

It did not last long, when I came back to reality, he sat with me for a few minutes holding my hand, he told me in a broken English accent that he and his wife were polish and his name was Joe and then he said,

"Thank you so much." I felt honoured knowing that I had made a sad gentleman happy.

Paul's parents were there with me, the medium was helping me to understand what was happening. I was frightened; but also exhilarated by the whole experience. Someone kindly made me a cup of tea. People who I had never met before came over to me and thanked me.

Liam and Katherine were really embarrassed, we left soon after.

The next day I met Peter, we had both been invited to a friend's wedding. We knew each other from work, but we decided to start seeing each other as a couple. I remember telling him all about my experience the day before, as I was still excited from it all.

Peter could not understand how I felt, in fact, he was quite shocked, I promised him that I would never to go back and never enter that spiritualist church again.

A few months later I was working. I had just entered the office of the ward I was an assistant on; when there was a phone call, immediately I answered and tried to say,

"I will get a staff nurse to speak to you, as it wasn't my place to take any phone calls.

The voice on the other end of the line spoke with a broken English accent and said, "It's Joe, thank you." Then he was gone, a shiver went straight through me, I recollected the gentleman named Joe I had met for just a short time.

CHAPTER 15

Richard

I appreciated Emma giving Monty to me when she found out she was expecting Ginny.

Although I had ridden horses when I was young, I had not actually owned one. Yes, we had Brandy when the girls were in their early teens, but he was on loan from a Horse Sanctuary.

My parents paid for a couple of riding lessons, but most of the time I rode my bike to the horse shows while my boyfriend rode his horse, I think I was attracted to him for his horse, I was thirteen years old at the time. He was fourteen. I was more like a slave to him than a girlfriend, but it did not bother me as I loved mucking out and everything it entailed looking after his horse, he would let me ride him in the paddock.

I lacked confidence when it came to riding Monty, I had heard of some stables about ten miles away.

They had a good name, apparently there was a young lady who had five horses of her own, she was good with green horses that had problems; that is a term which means they have a got a lot to learn and need plenty of schooling. I spoke to Emma, she agreed that it would be good for Monty to move and have some special training.

We had tried various other horse trainers, one that visited the yard, unfortunately she kept missing the appointment time. Another, we had to send Monty away for a week, that was unsuccessful.

I rang a telephone number I had got from a friend; she too had moved her horse there and she had so many positive things to say about the yard, the horses, and their owners, especially this young lady called Justine.

We moved the following week, it was sad to leave as we had made good friends with everyone, especially Janet and her family; but we had to think of Monty and what was good for him.

It did not take long for Monty to settle, as soon as he was put in the field with the other horses, he galloped off, his head held high, and his tail raised showing that he was happy in his new surroundings. The other horses soon accepted him into their herd, there was one horse in particular; he was the leader, proud and protective so Monty learned to respect him and curb his behaviour if he got too frisky with the others.

Justine was a lovely person, friendly and extremely helpful, although she was much younger than me, we seemed to get on well.

Over the next twelve months Justine worked Monty well until he obeyed her commands both verbally and through body language.

She also taught me how to recognise his behaviour when he genuinely did not understand what I needed him to do, or when he was taking the mick!

Slowly I gained the confidence to ride him out on hacks with Justine and her horse Lucy.

She owned a few horses on the yard, one was heavily pregnant and due to foal anytime.

Unfortunately, her Mum had a bad accident, she fell down the stairs and broke her ankle. So, it was impossible for her to help Justine with the pregnant mare. I offered to stay a few nights in case she had her foal in the early hours of the morning. There was nothing much to do except stare at the video of the mare in her stable, watching for anything out of the ordinary.

So, we talked about ourselves and general stuff. Night after night we waited and I began to tell Justine things regarding Emma, what she had been through and how she keeps having relapses.

It was then that I learned of Richard; Justine's dad, she mentioned he was a psychotherapist, she suggested I speak to him.

The following day I collected her from home; she had already spoken to her dad about me, and he came outside to meet me.

We spoke for twenty minutes regarding Emma, he was so in tune with me when I explained her behaviour (the involuntary movements) he understood everything I was saying about her changeable mood, her phobias, paranoia, self- harming etc.,

He gave me his mobile phone number, asking if Emma would like to see him.

The next night I thanked Justine for mentioning Emma to her dad, around midnight she could not keep her eyes open, she began to fall asleep. Finding it hard to sleep, I just stared at the television screen that the owner of the stables had kindly set up for Justine.

An hour later the mare was becoming quite fidgety, then she lay down, I could see something happening I shouted,

"Justine, I think she's having her foal."

Justine dived off the makeshift bed got the torch and ran; I followed her outside to the mare's stable.

The mare was standing up by this time, but the foal was only halfway out, I cannot remember exactly what happened next, as the mare was beginning to get anxious, so I talked to her and calmed her down. Justine was so excited watching the tiny foal make its way into the world, then it seemed like it was stuck,

Justine began to panic,

"What do I do?" (This situation took me back to when my Mum had told me a tale of when and how she had helped bring a foal into the world at her sister's farm in Canada) All I could think of was,

"Pull both legs together, pull gently, pull!"

She did as I suggested and with the adrenaline, she gave a couple of gentle pulls; the foal came sliding out still half in the protected bag of amniotic fluid. We watched the little foal slowly get to its feet while her mother licked her clean, she stumbled a few times before she was able to stand on her long spindle legs. I managed to film most of the experience while still consoling the mare. Justine immediately rang her parents and within fifteen minutes they arrived, they were all so excited, her sister had come too, so I left them to make us all a well-earned cup of tea.

The next morning I could not wait to tell Emma about Justine's dad being a psychotherapist and how he had understood everything, also the excitement of seeing the foal being born. Emma rang the mobile number I gave her and Richard; Justine's dad answered they had a short conversation before making an appointment for Emma to go and see him. He said,

"If you don't feel comfortable, you're not under any obligation."

Emma had nothing to lose so she accepted his invitation.

The first time Emma spent thirty minutes with Richard, she was certainly impressed and agreed to see him again and again, until finally she was making regular appointment times with him.

Emma had experienced many different Psychotherapists, psychologists, and Psychiatrists. She had been administered all kinds of anti-psychotic medication and anti-depressants. There was nothing that gave her a permanent solution.

She was now stable enough to learn how to get in touch with her own feelings and emotions. Richard helped Emma to find the courage to do this.

Over the last twelve months of seeing him she had managed to deal with the abuse. The triggers that cause an abreaction; that is the term Richard uses for when Emma lapses into an unconscious state and goes back to the past when she was a little girl.

He explains to Emma how her brain is reacting before she has a full abreaction.

She listens and tries to understand the way he describes what is happening to her and why.

Compared to the other kinds of psychotherapy that Emma has encountered; Richard's way of therapy works for her.

When Emma was experiencing her involuntary movements her head was reeling backwards and forwards and her back was arching into a position that only a double-jointed gymnast would find easy, completely unaware of her surroundings. It was difficult to bring her back, literally to wake her up.

Richard explained it as a dissociation from reality, this meant the brain was performing a protective mechanism; at the same time re-enacting the abuse through a flashback. When Emma was experiencing a flashback, which was too distressing and traumatic the brain would realize this and automatically remove it from her conscious mind.

Like what she would have done when she was a child and had to experience the abuse at such a young age. Then she buried it deep in her subconscious mind. This does not mean she will never recover her memories; they can come through in dreams or triggers of any description, colours, places etc., she regained many of her memories through her senses, touch, hearing, visual, taste and smell. For example, Emma's father wore a protruding wedding ring he never took it off. When he was in the act of sexual abuse, he pushed his fist into Emma's lower part of her back; causing pain from the shape of the ring being pushed against her skin. The slightest touch to her back is a trigger which brings back so many horrific memories.

Then there is taste, this is quite sickening and revolting when I tell you that when Emma was to take a certain type of anti-depressant the taste brought back memories of when her father and her Uncle David forced her to swallow semen; she began to heave as soon as she put the tablet into her mouth.

Kevin and I noticed for a long time that Emma's features on her face moved quite frequently, mostly during a stressful situation; I can only describe it as though she was sucking something in her mouth like a sweet, but her mouth was empty. Fortunately, Emma was not conscious of this happening so Kevin and I decided not to mention it, hoping it will cease in time.

It is not very often we notice it now.

Since being in therapy with Richard, Emma's memories began to surface in bits at a time, like pieces of a jigsaw puzzle. He explained,

"As a child she had subconsciously built huge strong walls and she needs to break down each one; although behind each wall represents for Emma evil, horror and uncertainty."

When Emma buried the memories of the abuse, she was also suppressing the feelings and the emotions; which stopped her from emotionally developing; this meant her inner child stayed the same age of when the abuse took place. For example, Emma was between the age of four and five years old when her father raped and sexually abused her and then when she was about twelve months older, he allowed his brother-in-law to do the same with her father participating. This abuse stopped when she had just turned ten years old; fortunately for Emma her father had a bad accident.

Many child abuse survivors are hyper vigilant, security is something Emma is paranoid about, she makes sure the doors back and front are securely locked late afternoon; the windows are not allowed to be open during the day. She also feels insecure when she is left alone; although Ginny is with her and sometimes Darren if he is not at school.

Kevin or I cannot leave her for a long period in her own home as she begins to panic. The fear of the threats from her dad and her uncle still haunt her;

(she has now told, the secret is out of what they did to her as a child).

To someone who has not been traumatized as a child it is extremely hard to understand when you are dealing with an adult. Because that person is an adult, people expect them to behave with a logical mind. You look at the person and you see the adult, but the inner child is pressing all the buttons emotionally and physically.

Going shopping, meeting new people, and visiting places which are unfamiliar causes many problems for Emma. Trust is a huge issue for her in men and women.

The inner child of herself has a great deal of influence on the adult being of Emma. A child thinks impulsively and when the child wants something it cannot wait for it. This is not an excuse for Emma's behaviour, but it was consistent with Emma's thinking; if she saw something that she liked, it seems like she must have it; she did not think about the consequences, i.e.: whether she could afford it.

It is true in the right sense of the word, 'Retail Therapy' it works.

Although she was awarded a substantial amount of compensation, regarding her Uncle David, her money is looked after by the deputy appointed by the Court of Protection.

So she must be careful with her finances as it is not always available to her without permission from him. He also understands Emma and how impulsive she can be, so he is not afraid of saying,

"No" he is incredibly good at his job and looks after her assets.

Richard explains to Emma that this inner child must be nurtured and accepted by Emma for the inner child and the adult to be as one. To enable Emma to think for herself as an adult without the influence of her younger self she must acknowledge her inner child.

Unfortunately for Emma this is extremely hard to do as this represents for her everything that is bad.

Emma explains that she believes that the child is evil, passed on through her father. Richard tries to convince her that this kind of thinking is irrational. For him to have explained this she told him,

"I saw a little girl, she looked so lonely. She was kneeling by the cemetery gates as I was walking Darren to school. I mentioned it to Kevin and his niece Jade who was with me.

I was pointing towards her. They both said,

"There is no one there."

"I did see a child who was looking so sad, I wanted to go over and make sure she was alright, but Kevin wouldn't let me."

Richard had confirmed to Emma that he believed her and that it was herself that she was seeing, she had projected the image away as she could not accept her inner child.

Her psychotherapist enlightened me as to what was happening to Emma. I always went with her when she had an appointment, so if it were necessary, he would ask me in so he could explain her recent behaviour.

~~~~~

Darren was eight years old and extremely clever for his age.

As Kevin was about to take Darren to school; Emma shouted,

"Don't forget to see Mr. Stephen's the Head teacher."

I was already at their house, Kevin had rung me earlier asking if I could stay with Emma and Ginny while he took Darren to school, Jodie was doing her own thing as she was becoming a very independent teenager; she shouted,

"See ya' as she shut the front door behind her, she had not far to walk as her school was just round the corner.

A couple of days earlier Darren had won a competition involving a poem he had written.

'Travel Back to the Past' he wrote about Florence Nightingale and his Mum was so proud she wanted him to be recognized in assembly the next day.

I asked Emma why she called Darren's Head Teacher Mr. Stephen's, she replied,

"Because he is." I explained that the Head Teacher at Darren's school is Mrs. Evans.

Emma frowned and argued,

"No, it's Mr. Stephen's."

She was adamant she explained she had never heard of Mrs. Evans. I told her,

"Mr. Stephen's was your old Headmaster,"

She explained that he is at Dobson Lane, Primary School.

Emma then blew my mind by saying,

"That's Darren's school." I argued,

"Darren goes to Little Beddington Primary School."

"No." She said in angry tone, I will show you a picture of his friend, 'Karen' in his school class photo, she explained that Darren was not present at the time.

"He must have been ill when it was taken."

Then she told me that Karen was sat next to her friend.

Apparently, Emma the adult had seen this picture from Karen's Facebook taken when she and her school friend were only eight years old at the time. Emma had no recollection that the child in the picture was herself.

Kevin and I were getting quite concerned as Emma's state of mind began to deteriorate.

We questioned her on the present day such as,

"Do you know who this is?" I pointed to a photograph of Zak. She replied,

"No, should I?" I hesitated before I answered,

"Yes, he is your eldest son."

Emma was finding it hard to understand what I was saying, I explained that Zak was living with his paternal grandparents through his own choice.

After having a much-appreciated cigarette we walked back into the lounge from the conservatory and there was a photograph of Jodie, Darren, Kevin, and herself.

She frowned as she looked at the picture and enquired,

"Who is that?"

"That's you," I replied.

Ginny was now around twelve months old, she was playing with my keys, on the key fob was a small photograph of Emma's family, Peter, and I;

she picked up the keys and noticed a dolphin in the picture and all the palm trees around a beautiful, landscaped lake.

She asked,

"Who is that in the picture?"

I explained everybody to her, but she did not recognize herself, she then enquired,

"When was this taken?" I replied,

"When we all went to Florida."

"What." She laughed,

"How on earth can we afford to go to Florida?"

I told her that we all went a few years ago; but unfortunately, she could not remember.

I explained that she owned her own house, she replied,

"No, we have a mortgage with Churchtown."

Then I said she had bought and paid for it.

Again, she argued and laughed. It was becoming quite fascinating to realize what she could remember from the present day and what she was bringing up from the past.

She decided it was time to get washed and dressed, I followed behind leaving Kevin with Ginny, as she was climbing the stairs she said,

"This feels weird when she reached the top step and began to walk forward onto the landing, she walked towards Darren's bedroom; she opened the door and stated,

"This is different," she put her head around the door of the bathroom, frowned as if she was seeing it for the first time.

"Isn't it big?" she exclaimed, she then opened Jodie's bedroom door, it was a mess as usual.

Emma pulled the door closed as if she should not be looking in.

We came to Ginny's room, by this time she was in total shock. Although Emma and Kevin had been living in that house for the past four years, everything seemed new to Emma; she was seeing it for the first time.

The last door she walked through was her own and Kevin's. She just sat on the huge king size bed; looked around her, completely mesmerised by the size of the whole house. After all she and Kevin had bought this when Zak was living with them. His bedroom was downstairs, it was left the same in case he ever changed his mind and came home.

Where she was seated on the bed, she caught a glimpse of the en-suite; she laughed,

"Oh, my goodness we have got a bathroom in our bedroom," she walked towards the door. Turned round and gasped,

"We have a double shower."

Back in her bedroom her imitation fur jacket came to her attention, she took it from the coat hanger and whispered,

"This is nice, is it mine?" I replied,

"Yes."

She tried it on, and we laughed as I said,

"Do you like?"

Emma decided to get dressed she began to look for something to wear. I felt embarrassed for her when she had to ask,

"Where is my underwear?" While she was exploring her home, she seemed excited, like how a child would react.

Later we were downstairs having a coffee, for some reason I found myself asking her name, she replied,

"Emmy." I frowned and she stated,

"Emmy Babe, that's what everyone calls me."

This was too much for me to accept and I said to Kevin,

"I need a cigarette," I had to get some air, my hands were shaking as I lit it.

According to Emma's memory, the name 'Emmy babe' was used by her father and his family while the child abuse was happening. Emma would never mention that name and it was forbidden to speak of it in Emma's company.

For some unknown reason Emma pulled her legs up to her chest and began to rock, soothing her legs at the same time. She then put both hands over her ears; shut her eyes tightly as if she was blocking out noise; we spoke to her but there was no response she was completely dissociated from reality. This behaviour continued for approximately two minutes and then she opened her eyes, she seemed like she was back in the present. I asked her which school her younger son attended, she smiled,

"Little Beddington Primary," *Yes! That was the answer I wanted to hear.*

However, things were not normal Emma was different, she could not remember how to use her cooker, or her microwave, she felt unable to cook a meal, which a few days earlier was automatic to her. We decided it would be better for everyone if Emma stayed with me that night, so as not to arouse any suspicion from her children.

I took Emma outside she did not recognize my car and she looked back at her house, frowned, and said in a childlike manner,

"Isn't it big?" she questioned,

"Where is your white van," I did not want to confuse her anymore and it was becoming quite exhausting having to try and explain things, so I just replied,

"I sold it," she accepted that.

We arrived at my house, again she did not recognize anything, she said,

"It's nice," and walked through to the garden,

"Where is the big tree and the back gate?"

She asked as if that is what she expected to see. Those things: the tree and the gate were taken down about twenty years earlier when an estate was built on the land behind my house.

"There was a big greenhouse there." I agreed,

"Yes, that's right."

I noticed she used the past tense. I thought, **Good, I am somehow slowly making her realize that the present time is around twenty years later.**

We went back into the house I gave her the remote control, I said,

"Here play about with this, because you are going to need to know how to use it in front of your children."

She was pressing buttons and confusing the large flat screen television that was mounted on the chimney breast.

I rang Richard to let him know what was happening to Emma, I wondered how long it was going to take before Emma came completely back to the present day. He explained,

"Don't worry this can be expected with the work Emma has been doing over the last couple of weeks, she is dangerously close to merging with Emma the child."

I came off the phone feeling so much better, trusting in the information that Richard had conveyed to me. It had been a long and an exhausting day I found a funny film for us to watch, as Emma needed to relax from all the confusion.

During the night I kept a close vigil on Emma, she seemed to sleep well; no aggressive movements or whimpering like she normally had in her sleep.

I woke early and took two cups of tea into the bedroom; my daughter seemed more relaxed than usual. She stated that she wanted to go home to see Kevin and her children. I rang Kevin and dropped her off soon after we finished our tea.

It was a weekend and Emma's children had plans for the day, Jodie had stayed over at her friend's house and Darren had kickboxing for two hours.

Emma received a text from Jodie just after lunch; asking her to pick her up from the McDonald's car park close to her friend's house. Emma rang me and asked if I would not mind driving. I was pleased to accept as I had no plans that day. Whilst we were on our way to collect Jodie Emma exclaimed,

"I feel weird,"

When we were near to our destination, I asked her to text Jodie to let her know we would soon be there.

Emma began to panic she could not remember how to use her phone, I said,

"Don't worry I will sort it out when we get there." I heard her whispering,

"Why are my hands so big?" she cried out,

"My feet won't touch the floor."

I began to worry about Emma's state of mind when we arrived at the car park, I needed to console her and try and calm her down before her daughter got in the car. I tried desperately to contact Richard, I had not brought my glasses and Emma could not remember her password, I can see the humorous side of things now when I look back, but it was a very harrowing time for me. Luckily Kevin rang to see how Emma was, I was so relieved, and I explained everything. He would ring her psychotherapist immediately to ask him to ring me. I waited, the phone rang within minutes; Richard was so good, he told me to bring her to see him as soon as I could.

Jodie was late turning up, she jumped in the back. I explained I was dropping her mum off first as she had an appointment.

She was fine with that; oblivious to the situation, she was so absorbed with chattering about the things her and her friends had been doing the night before. Richard had seen us come round the corner, so he came out to meet us; although it was a weekend, he still made time to see her.

I arrived back half an hour later after dropping Jodie off at home. Emma had already shown her therapist two or three bouts of past and present behavior.

Richard explained there is nothing to worry about,

"The wall Emma had built all those years before had started to crumble and the child was visible in Emma's conscious mind. Emma the adult was now able to accept the other part of herself."

I can never thank Richard enough for what he has done for Emma, her family and me, to work with her the way he did, gave her the confidence to help herself.

To break down those walls each one which were holding back all the thoughts of horror, uncertainty, and total blackness.

Emma had subconsciously put them up when she was a little girl to survive the gruesome memories she had to endure of the physical and emotional pain of the abuse.

Especially from her father who was supposed to be her hero and protect her from the very thing that he inflicted on her as a small innocent child.

The memories of her abuse were now bad memories never to be forgotten but will never again cause so much anxiety and emotional pain which in turn caused the involuntary movements she has experienced for so long.

We both walked out of the therapist's room laughing and happy. Emma was now 100% an adult, ready to face the world for the first time.

The inner child who was the emotional and creative side to Emma's being has now been set free, instead of being hidden for all those years. She has her own personality and can be the person she was meant to be.

She has now found a new strength and wants to help others the way she herself has been helped to build a new life.

CHAPTER 16

Jodie

As a family we had decided to go to a holiday resort on the east coast. Jodie was now in her fifteenth year; her mum thought it was a good idea to ask if she would like to take a friend with us so she could do activities her own age, such as disco dancing in the evening.

Jodie and her friend Stephanie were enjoying themselves, doing their own thing, while Kevin, Emma, my Mum, and I took Darren and Ginny to the fairground which was situated inside the resort. The girls were safe as there was security around.

Emma was content that Jodie had her mobile phone with her so if she or Stephanie needed us, she could always contact her.

Things were going well, they went dancing, swimming in the large pool which was also part of the resort. When they arranged to do certain activities, such as climbing a huge wall and jumping thirty feet from a platform we were all there to cheer them on. Both girls were so excited that they achieved their goals.

When the girls decided that they were not going dancing they came with us to the show which provided fantastic entertainment. Jodie wore a new dress that her Mum had bought her before the holiday, she looked lovely it suited her slim figure.

It was always difficult to tell Jodie she looked nice, she found it hard to accept any compliments.

Unfortunately, Stephanie, unable to understand how Jodie felt she said,

"That dress is gorgeous, you look beautiful in it."

Jodie was very abrupt with Stephanie and immediately changed into something else. They went to the show with us, but Jodie had changed towards Stephanie. Her attitude became intolerable. Emma and I tried to convince Stephanie that Jodie was not being personal and that she can be difficult at times. Jodie seemed to think we were taking sides and she stopped speaking to us. Emma and I felt sorry for Stephanie as she was away from home without her mum to talk to. It was understandable that when Jodie decided to stay in the apartment and not involve herself in any more of the activities, we took Stephanie with us while Jodie changed her attitude towards her.

We tried hard to encourage Jodie to participate in the rest of the holiday, but she was reluctant, although she accompanied us, she would not allow herself to enjoy it.

Days later we arrived home, Jodie's manner never changed. She questioned her Mum about her Granddad; she could not understand why she was not allowed to see him after she had heard that Zak her brother had been on holiday with him.

Emma sensed there was something wrong. She had not realized that Jodie knew. It was not something that Emma wanted to talk about, it had brought lots of unhappy feelings back, when she first learned that Katherine and Paul had taken Zak on holiday with them and that he had slept in the same caravan as his granddad. Apparently, there was not enough room for Zak as she had also taken Paul's niece Jemma who was sharing a bedroom with Cindy.

Emma and I had already explained to Jodie why her Mum felt uncomfortable with her seeing her granddad.

It had been explained in a diplomatic manner, hoping that Jodie would accept it. The subject was very delicate and was not something Emma or I wanted to speak about in detail.

The wedding of my son Liam and his fiancée was looming. I asked if Jodie would like to go shopping with me, I was quite surprised and delighted that she accepted my invitation. She loved going into London with me, so we made a day of it. While we were in one of the large department stores in the city, I decided to look for a dress. She questioned me,

"Is it for Liam's wedding?"

I should have realized she would guess why I was in the lady's section. I hesitated for a moment; then I replied,

"Yes." I felt so sorry for her when she exclaimed,

"Do you think Liam will let me come to his wedding?"

The empathy I had for her was so strong I said,

"I don't know sweetheart; would you like me to ask him?"

With a big smile on her face she said,

"Yes please, I would love to go."

Knowing that Liam was in the same frame of mind of his sister Katherine regarding Emma, he had given me an ultimatum at Christmas,

"Do you want a relationship with me and Emma? Only you and Nan I do not want to see my sister or her children."

It was the worst possible situation for a mother. At the end of the day, I was his mum, I did not want to jeopardize our relationship, so against my principals I complied with his rules.

Later that day I went to see him and put the question to him and his fiancée Emma, I begged him to think about it as Jodie was innocent in this feud between him and his sister and that my Mum and I would look after her. Eventually he agreed. I was so pleased he had realised that Jodie was his niece and that she genuinely wanted to be at his wedding; after all Zak, her brother would be going.

Emma was pleased when I told her that Jodie was invited. Without letting Jodie know, Emma was quietly upset that she was not going to see her little brother getting married.

She would not even have been able to have a sneak look as they had decided to abolish the thought of a church wedding and have the ceremony and the reception at the same venue. The excitement Jodie felt at being accepted again into the other side of the family lead her to texting her dad's girlfriend, asking if she could see her dad; she was over the moon when she received a positive reply. When she was younger and her mum received the custody of her two children, Jodie was so angry with her father that she would not see him; although Emma had tried her best, she could not force her to speak to him.

Emma was happy for Jodie, thinking maybe this will help Jodie's behaviour as she was clearly unhappy at that present time.

When she did see her father, he questioned her,

"Why did you not want to see me?"

Jodie was immediately put on the spot and said the first thing that came into her head,

"My mum wouldn't let me see you, she wouldn't give me the phone when you rang to speak to me."

This caused a lot of problems for Emma, the lies got worse as Jodie was having to make up more lies, she did not want to be seen as the bad person in this situation as she was getting an enormous amount of attention and it felt good at first.

Then Katherine became involved, Jodie had to make up more lies. She had told her mum she would be home after tea, she had been invited to stay with Katherine and Paul; Cindy was so happy to see her cousin.

Eight o'clock, Emma decided to ring Jodie on her mobile, she said she had gone on to her friends and will not be home till nine. Emma was not happy about this and told her to come home immediately.

Over the last week Jodie had been visiting her father and Katherine, her attitude had changed for the worse; that night, Jodie arrived home from school she was in a foul mood and had caused an argument with her mum.

She had stormed upstairs to her room screaming,

"My granddad is innocent till proven guilty, I don't believe anything you say about him, Katherine is going to take me to see him."

Emma was livid and shouted back at her,

"You are not seeing him, and you are not seeing Katherine if she is putting these thoughts into your head!"

Emma was so upset, she asked Kevin if they could go for a short drive, just to get out of the house.

They had only been gone half an hour; the door was unlocked but Jodie was nowhere to be seen. She had gone to Katherine's.

That same night at ten minutes past nine Emma and Kevin had a visit from two police officers. Emma was so upset when the police explained that it was her sister Katherine who had put in the complaint against her regarding Jodie. Apparently, she had been telling lies to Katherine that Emma locked her in the house, Katherine felt she needed to act on this and consequently rang the police.

Kevin automatically rang me explaining the situation, I immediately got my coat and my keys and sped round to Emma's house, something like this can set Emma back that was the last thing we wanted to happen with all the stress going on with Jodie.

Emma was in tears when I arrived, I rang her friend Gerry from across the road asking if Emma could come over, explaining the situation in short.

Since moving to their address Gerry had been a close friend to Emma, she knew everything, including what Emma had allegedly said about her father.

Gerry's youngest son was in the same class as Cindy and when parents and grandparents were invited to attend, sometimes Emma's dad would be there with Katherine.

Gerry explained,

"I had to sit opposite him, I literally felt sick knowing what Emma was allegedly saying about him."

Gerry was a very loyal friend to Emma and knew about Jodie's recent behaviour.

As soon as I put the phone down and began to explain to the police how things had gone too far with Jodie and that it all started with the fact that she was not allowed to see her granddad. The police automatically enquired,

"Why not?"

That was it, Katherine had started something now and I had to finish it. I began with Emma, I tried to cut a long story, short. I told them that the Social Services could not do anything, after Emma's father was questioned by the police regarding the allegations of child sexual abuse towards his daughter. He was allowed to go home without being charged.

I continued to explain why Emma was so reluctant to let Jodie see her granddad.

"She was protecting her and has been since she was given full custody."

I also mentioned my concerns for Cindy now six years old and extremely vulnerable.

"She spends time with her granddad after school while her Mum goes to collect her husband from work.

I believe Cindy is close to her granddad she speaks about him when she comes to visit me." I also told the police,

"I babysat for Cindy about two weeks ago and during that time Cindy talked about her granddad and that she doesn't like it when he tickles her."

The policeman seemed to be listening to what I was trying to say. I continued;

"When I first heard that I felt sick to my stomach, this was mainly because when Emma spoke about the abuse it began with her father tickling her."

The police officer enquired,

"Why didn't you mention your concerns when Cindy's parents returned home?" I explained,

"I tried to tell them, but the words would not come out, after all I have spoken to Katherine and Paul many times about my concerns for Cindy, but they just tell me to be quiet and not to mention it again. So, against my better judgement I abide by their rules."

I could not wait to get out of their home as I was trembling; my mum was with me, she also heard what Cindy had said about her granddad and understood when I said to her,

"Mum what can I do? They won't listen to me."

I told the police officer,

"Katherine and her husband don't believe anything happened to Emma regarding the alleged abuse of her father and I have been told never to discuss it again, especially regarding the risk to Cindy, or I will not see my granddaughter again, apparently she has a lovely relationship with her granddad they are very close."

I continued with the facts and when I had concluded they mentioned the safeguarding of Cindy, Zak, and Jodie as they are all under the age of sixteen.

"We have to pass this information on to our Sergeant and it will probably involve the Social Services."

The following day Emma and I went to collect Jodie to take her shopping for some new school shoes. On the way I noticed Paul's car slowly coming towards us, I flashed my headlights at him and beckoned him to stop, he did as I got out of my car and went over to speak to him, thinking that Jodie might also be in the car; he pushed down his window lock, consequently locking all the doors. It was difficult to understand what he was thinking.

There was no intention on my part to open them. Trying to converse with him through a closed window was impossible until he began to make a phone call on his mobile. After returning to the car, we continued to Katherine's house.

We had just parked the car in front of Katherine's house when Paul came racing round the corner, the brakes screeched as they came to an abrupt halt just close to where we were standing; he quickly got out slamming the door behind him.

Emma and I were smiling as we walked closer to the front door, Cindy had seen us, and she was waving to us from the lounge window. Paul's words took us back as he was just opening the front door.

"I don't know what you're smiling at," astounded at his attitude, I began to say,

"We have come to collect Jodie..."

"You are not taking her anywhere until she has seen Social Services; I am ringing the police."

Then he shut the door.

We decided to wait and speak to the police ourselves explaining the whole situation. Two police officers arrived, Emma spoke to one, while I spoke to the other, we brought them both up to date. The senior of the two proceeded to ring his Sergeant and then Social Services. When he had finished his conversations, he turned to Emma and said,

"You can take her home if you want to." Jodie came out shouting,

"I'm not coming home Katherine and Paul said I can stay with them." So as not to upset the situation any further; Emma reluctantly decided to leave her with them until the next day, hoping that Jodie would return.

Jodie never returned home. Social Services did visit her at Katherine's house; she was really annoyed as they were more concerned about Cindy, Zak, and herself regarding their granddad, than the teenage problems she was experiencing.

Jodie never forgave us for turning the whole saga around towards her granddad and taking the attention away from her.

Katherine and Paul should have sent Jodie back to her Mum soon after things had calmed down. That never happened. Gerry was brilliant the way she had supported Emma. Having children of her own, a young son Neil and a daughter Elizabeth two years younger than Jodie she could empathize with Emma.

However, she had her own issues of an experience. Gerry called in for a coffee just after she had completed a ten-mile run. This was becoming a constant routine; Emma was worried as she was conscious of Gerry being so slim.

She tried to encourage her to eat a good diet if she was persistent in this strenuous activity. To please Emma, Gerry agreed. She would never intentionally say or do anything to upset her friend.

One time when they were alone and there were no children around to disturb them, Emma asked Gerry,

"Are you alright? I am worried you are losing too much weight." To that she replied,

"No, I am finding it hard to cope, I didn't want to tell you anything, but you are my friend and I trust you."

Emma knew there was something wrong, but she never expected Gerry to say what she said in the next sentence.

"Something happened to me when I was younger, and it is coming back to haunt me."

This was too close to home for Emma; as much as she loved her friend she could not listen to anymore, she had to look after her own mental health. That was when Emma suggested she spoke to me, knowing I have a small knowledge of counselling she thought I may be able to offer a listening ear.

A few days later, Gerry knocked on my front door. We knew each other through Emma but we have had little contact. Whenever I arrived at Emma's house and Gerry was there, she would politely make her excuses and leave, she was not being ignorant she was just being well-mannered.

Gerry accepted a cup of coffee; it was already made as Emma had let me know that Gerry was on her way to see me. Just to break the ice I made a small amount of trivial chit chat, but I sensed Gerry urgently needed to talk about something, she sat in the corner of the sofa, and slowly she began to open up; I recollected my counselling skills and used them naturally.

For a short while Gerry went quiet, I was conscious of her body language, her hands were clutching each other and then she spoke.

"I can see his eyes! I can see his eyes and he is looking at me."

Not saying anything, I waited for Gerry to make sense of what she was experiencing. Then gradually she explained,

"I am sat in the back seat, he is taking me home, he keeps looking at me through his rearview mirror and then he stopped the car."

She had tears in her eyes as she describes,

"He opened my door; my friend was sat on the front passenger seat completely out of it as she had too much to drink."

Gerry puts her hands over her face and sobs; I did not try to console her as those tears were pent up emotions which have been suppressed for years.

"Weeks later, just after my seventeenth birthday I found out I was pregnant."

Before I could say anything, it felt as if she was trying to imagine what I intended to say and so she interrupted my thoughts,

"There was no other man in my life at the time so it could only have been from the rape of that terrible night that still haunts me in my dreams." She remembers the Nun taking her to the hospital from the Catholic College she attended.

The Nun was so empathic with her she has memories of how nice she was during and after the crisis.

"The pain was excruciating, the sister on the Accident and Emergency ward explained to me that I was having an ectopic pregnancy which is where the fetus was growing in the fallopian tube."

After a few minutes past I went to put my arm around her as she was still sobbing, I said,

"These are the tears for the little baby you lost."

Later, she felt so much better, that was the first time she had ever released her feelings and the emotions of that dreadful time in her life.

Gerry explained that she could not tell her parents, they would have been devastated,

"I was somewhere I shouldn't have been, and only sixteen at the time; my parents would have gone mad knowing that I had gone to a Nightclub with my friends." I interrupted.

"So, all these years you have kept your secret and all the feelings and emotions have been buried with it." She agreed with me, nodded, and said,

"Yes, but it has been hard, I could not eat, and I ended up in a hospital for people with eating disorders. My mum and dad had tried their best to understand, but they never knew the underlying reason; how do you tell someone their daughter was raped? I was frightened that if it came out it would kill them both. So, I decided not to tell anyone."

For years Gerry was able to cover up her feelings and emotions of that frightful night; until her twelve-year-old daughter mentioned this girl's name from the Girl Guides she attended. She had a double barrel surname which was quite different to other surnames. A shiver went straight through Gerry she had not heard that name for the past twenty-three years and it had devastating consequences.

Apparently, the previous year Gerry had to spend some time in hospital and Alan her husband had accidently seen her medical notes which had been left open on the table at the side of her bed, 'Termination' was printed on the top page he had questioned Gerry about it. She was not prepared to speak about her past; she explained in short what had happened that terrible night. Her husband was so angry and upset for his wife knowing that she had to experience such evil; he asked her,

"Who was it?" but Gerry would not divulge his name to him or anyone else. She had managed all these years to put it behind her and had no intention of letting it ruin her life.

Back to the present time, I mentioned that she was losing weight I asked her,

"Have you eaten?" Gerry was truthful with me and said,

"I can hardly eat anything; I have no motivation to do any exercise."

This upset her as jogging was part of her routine to cope with her feelings; she would easily run ten miles every day.

We spoke about how she needs to go to the police, tell her husband and see her doctor. She agreed with me, I supported her while she made the appointment to see a female GP, she felt she could not speak to a male about something so sensitive.

Then she rang the local Police Station and asked to speak to someone regarding making a complaint against her perpetrator.

That same night Gerry disclosed to her husband who it was and how it had affected her since hearing his name. She asked Alan if he would take Lizzie to Guides that night to save her accidentally bumping into him. She also asked him not to say or do anything about the situation as she had already contacted the Police.

The following day we went to see a doctor at her local Medical Centre who was concerned for Gerry's state of mind and referred her on to another Professional regarding her eating disorder.

A couple of days later I accompanied Gerry to the Police Station, she explained why she was there, the Detective Sergeant took some details and a description of her complaint.

When Gerry had answered all the relevant questions and completed the necessary paperwork, he told her that someone from the Public Protection Unit would be calling to see her.

It was not long before Gerry had a visit from the PPU, a lady took her to the same place both my daughters went to all those years ago to make a statement. She was away for a few hours. It was such an ordeal having to remember the detailed memories from that awful night which was imprinted in her mind. The questions were very explicit of what happened and where the rape took place.

Gerry was mentally exhausted when she returned home, hoping that was the worst of what she would have to experience. Unfortunately, there was more humiliation and upset to come.

Alan her husband could not keep Gerry's wishes not to do anything about the person who had violated his wife's body all those years ago.

He had followed him back to his address when he had gone to collect his stepdaughter Elizabeth from Guides. Apparently, the following day Alan had contacted this person and before the police could question Gerry's assailant about the alleged rape, Alan had verbally torn into him reminding him of what he had done to his wife.

Eric Buxton-Heath could barely remember what Alan was talking about. Then he laughed in his face and according to Alan he said,

"Mate, you know what it's like when you're that age, yeah I had a fumble in the back of my car with some bird."

This arrogant response had angered Alan so much he wanted to hurt this man the way he had hurt when he found out what had happened to his wife; he wanted him to tell his own wife what he had done, or he would let her know the kind of person she was married to.

The stranger hardly knew who Alan was referring to; he had never expected repercussions from that night when he had forced himself upon an innocent pretty girl.

That same night Eric Buxton-Heath went to the Police and put in a complaint regarding this person who was accusing him of something he had to make believe he knew nothing about; to safeguard himself when this person's wife goes to the police to accuse him of this crime.

Alan plucked up the courage to face his wife and tell her that he had found Eric Buxton-Heath; Gerry was livid she had asked him not to do anything, she had told him that she was going to the police.

After Gerry had made her statement and the police had received all the medical evidence, she was told that she had a strong case.

The police charged Gerry's assailant and they were waiting for the court case which could take twelve months. Eric Buxton-Heath could go home without any bail conditions. This upset Gerry and her mental health plummeted as she was so frightened of bumping into him when she went to collect her daughter from the Girl Guides.

Time was moving slowly, Christmas was looming; fortunately, Gerry had bought all the Christmas presents for the kids a couple of months earlier while the things they were asking for were in stock and she was able to buy them online which meant she did not need to leave the house.

Gerry made the effort to give her children a nice Christmas, she made a lovely Xmas dinner with a turkey and all the trimmings.

Two months later Gerry was preparing to go to court, a lady from victim support was helping her, she had taken her to see the inside of the courtroom so on the day it would not be such an overwhelming experience. She would be giving evidence behind a screen for the jury to hear.

It was Friday afternoon, and the trial was due to begin on the following Monday morning. I would have been a witness for the prosecution, until I received a phone call at 2.30pm.

"Jennifer Colne?" I replied,

"Yes, can I help you?" The voice on the other end of the line was about to pass on some unpleasant news.

"The court case Stockton Vs Buxton-Heath listed for Monday 3rd March will not be going ahead, there has been some more evidence from the defence, and the case has now been closed."

It was unbelievable to hear what this person had said. It has been a year since Eric Buxton-Heath was charged, and Gerry has suffered so much; to accept that the case is not going to court would be devastating for her.

Immediately I rang Gerry to find out whether she had heard anything, apparently she had been to the police station, the actions from her husband regarding the perpetrator has had a negative influence on Gerry's case and also that someone had made a statement saying that this person can remember Gerry ringing her up the following day after the incident twenty three years ago; Gerry never rang anyone, especially at the time and she never told anybody what had happened, she wanted to protect her parents from finding out as she was so frightened for their wellbeing. She told the police she had no knowledge of her husband intending to see the accused.

How could this witness remember a phone call from such a long time ago it just is not possible unless it had a personal significance to the lady in question.

Gerry and I cannot believe that these lies can determine whether a criminal case can go to court.

At that present time Gerry had the fight in her, I was pleased about that; without that anger and determination she would not have been able to cope with the devastation she felt when her world came crashing down for the second time in her life.

It is so sad that there are so many victims when a historic crime like this happens to a person like Gerry; it has been a complete life changing situation.

Gerry and Alan found it hard, it affected their married life and eventually they got divorced and the family split up.

There is no deterrent for these people, I am determined to let them know how their victims suffer years of torment.

The statistics must be extremely high as I have two daughters Emma and Katherine who have been sexually abused. A friend Gerry in her teenage years raped before her life had even begun.

My Mum's friend's daughter Stacy, who was abused at the age of eleven by her uncle her father's brother. When she disclosed what had happened to her as a child her father did not believe her. Fortunately, her mother did, she tried to support her daughter, but Stacy left home when she was just seventeen. She could not stand being in the same vicinity as her perpetrator. Distress and humiliation caused the family to break up.

Christopher my younger cousin was also raped by his teacher from a Private Boys School at the age of eight years. His class were going on a day trip, unfortunately Christopher turned up late and his teacher had said,

"I am going to teach you a lesson and you will never be late again."

He decided to punish him by way of raping him.

The headmaster was told, and my cousin was punished for telling lies. Years later Christopher went to the police regarding the incident and was told not to waste their time as he had no evidence.

He is now forty-four years old, still living with his parents, he suffers panic attacks and mental health problems. He has had numerous amounts of counselling but to no avail. Christopher has tried many times to work, unfortunately the stress and the pressure beats him every time. As far as relationships go, he has never had the chance to meet anyone who will understand his predicament.

CHAPTER 17

Liam's wedding

L iam's wedding was only a few weeks away.

I had to find the right dress for my son's wedding. I wanted him to be proud of me and most of all I needed to show I was not going to be intimidated by anyone.

I dragged my poor Mum around the streets of London, I was not satisfied with anything when I took Jodie with me. We had spent time in a considerable amount of high street stores.

My dress had to be sophisticated, classy and above all me.

Eventually we found the perfect one, I remember seeing a film with Demi Moore, she wore a dress with a black cross over slightly above her breast I had always thought it had looked extremely sophisticated. I caught a glimpse of one similar, it was white with a black stripe down either side matching the crossover.

I collected two sizes and walked towards the dressing room, my mum as patient as ever followed me carrying three more.

I tried on the smaller of the two, *yes it fits.* I scooped my long dark hair up and put it in a clip. *Perfect, now for the shoes.*

"Just try these dresses on in case you prefer a different one."

To please my mum I did, after all she had trapesed round London with me. Two of them were put on the peg without attempting to try them but my mum had chosen a Japanese style with large red flowers on a black background, it was nice,

"Very nice, now I am confused as to which one shall I choose?"

I decided on the black and white one, I would have been a little too conspicuous in the other. My mum laughed she had my best interests at heart and did not mean to confuse me.

I bought all the accessories to match my outfit, I rang a friend who was a hairdresser; she was happy to style my hair on the day of the wedding. I needed to organize everything in plenty of time so I would have nothing to worry about, except the anxiety of seeing my ex-husband Steve and the rest of my family.

My Mum was also pleased; we chose a nice outfit for her that she felt comfortable wearing; a flowered blouse with an orange background which matched her beige trouser suit.

We visited Liam and Emma two days before their big day and took them a little gift and paid towards part of their honeymoon.

They were very understanding about the whole situation; Emma was pleased to say,

"We have seated you both with my parents and grandparents, directly in front of the top table."

I appreciated the thought that they had considered our feelings.

The day came and I was pleased with my appearance. Emma my daughter had taken me to have my nails done which also made me feel confident; she said it would, it always works for her.

We decided to drive to the venue; I had no intention of drinking any alcohol.

As I was parking the car, I noticed a lot of familiar faces. I took a deep breath and stepped out of the car, after making sure my mum had everything, she needed we walked over to Liam who was smiling and making his way towards us. He told me I looked nice and thanked us for coming.

"I wouldn't have missed it for the world, you are my son and I wanted to be here to see you get married."

He said a few nice words to my Mum before one of his Best Men came over with buttonholes for us. The traditional number is one; Liam had three he did not want to let any of his friends down, so he asked them all.

My son was shaking like a leaf, I told him he looked so smart in his pale grey suit with a white shirt and a pale blue cravat to match the same colour as the bridesmaids. I gave him a big hug told him I loved him and how proud I was of him.

Then another of his Best Men came over, apologized to us looked at Liam and said,

"I'm sorry Mate, you're needed; you have a got a wedding to attend."

We laughed as he walked away smiling.

In the distance I saw Katherine dressed in a long pale blue gown, she looked beautiful with her long blonde ringlets falling over her shoulders, Cindy looking so pretty in a knee length white dress, she was wearing a blue headband with white flowers which pulled back her blonde curls.

My Mum and I entered the room where the ceremony was taking place. One of the ushers dressed like Liam's Best Men showed us where we were sitting. On the left side of the room were Emma's parents and family and on the right was Liam's. We were three rows back from the front where Liam was standing waiting for his bride to be.

I glanced further along the front row passed his |Best Men and seated next to them was Liam's father my ex-husband Steve.

For a few minutes I felt physically sick, but I was soon given something else to think about. Jodie and Zak came to sit on the second row in front of us. Jodie was directly behind her granddad, I watched as she put her arms round his shoulders, he turned and smiled at her and Zak. I tried to make eye contact with my grandchildren, but they did not look round, until I patted them on the shoulder and then they had to acknowledge my me and my mum we smiled at each other, I told them they looked nice and then the music started they turned and looked to the front just as Paul came to sit next to them.

Emma looked beautiful in her long white dress which had bows at the back and her train was spread out which gracefully followed behind her. Cindy was leading the procession carrying a basket of rose petals and sprinkling them as she walked towards her Uncle Liam.

It was all well organized, the bridesmaids followed, then took their place on the first row on the left. I looked over to try and catch eye contact with Katherine, but she was too busy looking towards the happy couple who had now been joined together as Man and Wife, a shiver went through me as Liam's wife was now known as 'Emma Colne' my daughter's name before she married Kevin.

The weather was beautiful, we were fortunate that the sun was shining while the photographs were being taken.

Luckily Liam had asked for my side of the family first, the photographer took some lovely ones of my Mum and me with the bride and groom.

Then I had to walk away as Jodie wanted a photo of her granddad and Zak. She was making a big show of it. I watched from the distance; Paul and Katherine with her arm around her dad having their photograph taken; they looked so happy.

The reception went well, it was nice to sit with Emma's parents and grandparents, we had so much in common as Emma's family were also interested in horses; there were no uncomfortable silences; we talked most of the time except when the speeches were made. My ex-husband was on the top table next to one of the bridesmaids, luckily, he was hidden from view, I found it extremely hard for me to be in such close vicinity to him, but I did it for Liam.

After the Toasts were made people slowly moved away from the tables and into another room where the bar was becoming quite busy.

My Mum and I spoke to various family members who unfortunately had supported my ex-husband believing my daughter Emma was telling lies about her father.

My cousin and his wife and their children shared a table with my mum and I, Cindy came over to join us, it was lovely to see her and speak to her.

The focus was more on the children, we never spoke of anything except small conversation of the ceremony and how Michael was so happy for Liam.

Me and my mum stayed to watch Liam and his bride have their first dance and then we made our apologies that mum was tired, and we needed to go home, just as we were saying our goodbyes on the dance floor Katherine, Jodie, Zak, and Cindy came over, we hugged each other and smiled, then we made our way to the exit.

When the wedding celebrations were over, Emma asked me how it all went, and did we have a nice time? Hesitantly I answered, feeling so sorry for her, her own brother not wanting his younger sister and her family to be at his wedding. I know she was upset it was difficult to understand how she must be feeling, when the whole sordid situation was none of her fault. It was all down to one person, her father who had caused so much pain in her life. From such an early age she had buried the feelings and emotions of the rape and sexual abuse. How it has affected her, the amount of suffering mentally and physically.

The mental scars will always remain, but through the help and guidance from Richard her psychotherapist she is now able to speak about her feelings towards her father. He is her father in biological terms only she will never forgive him for what he did to her as a child and the pain he has caused her through her lifetime.

The lies he has told to family and friends was the foundation for them to believe Emma was mentally ill and making it all up.

The way Carl Emma's ex-partner the father of her children had not supported her and now Jodie being fifteen years old she also believes the lies about her Mum.

Carl and Katherine are good friends; they all see each other regularly and visit Emma's father. Carl had always stayed in close contact with Emma's father.

No wonder Emma's mental health deteriorated over the years; the involuntary movements we now know as intensity flashbacks has caused her to suffer permanent nerve damage to her lower back.

The orthopaedic consultant said she has the back of a seventy-year-old. I get so angry when I must witness the pain she has to endure when her consultant tries his best by giving her fascist injections into the bone in her lower part of her back, he cannot use any anesthetic as she must be able to feel the pain until she cannot stand it any longer and that is when he knows he is in the right place. Also, she will no doubt have neck problems like a person who has experienced whiplash.

She had tried so hard to forgive her father and move on with her life, but her subconscious mind would not allow that to happen.

The times I have witnessed her fall backwards into the bath or suddenly go completely under the water, to a normal eye it would look like an accident.

What I saw was indescribable, unbelievable unless you were to see it for yourself.

I feel I must describe the things I have seen so if there is anybody who reads this and it has happened to them, then they are not alone.

Never, will I forget such a horrifying experience. Emma was sat upright in the bath water using her sponge, enjoying bathing herself and in small conversation with me, when suddenly her head went violently backwards under the water, I jumped up! Wondering and thinking, *what on earth is happening?* I tried desperately to lift her head from the bottom of the bath, but the force was too strong; her head was stuck to the enamel. It was impossible to get my fingers underneath as the power of the flashback was tremendous!

Emma was literally being drowned in front of me.

I pulled the plug and screamed for Kevin,

"Help! Help Kevin she's under the water."

He had taken the stairs two at a time and before I could stop shouting for him, he was in the bathroom trying his best to lift her head and get her out of the water. The water had started to subside it was now below her nose and mouth. Using all his strength he managed it. When Emma did open her eyes; she was choking, coughing, and shaking. We never spoke about what had happened to Emma, we were that relieved that she was alright, Kevin stayed with me for a while then went back downstairs and I guided her cautiously into her bedroom. I made small conversation about anything except what I had just witnessed and how I had to pretend to be normal; I was petrified inside but I could not let Emma see as she did not know what had happened and I was not going to tell her, it was bad enough for me to accept this visual phenomenon I did not know how to explain it and certainly not to Emma.

It was just like there was somebody else in the bathroom and he/she was pressing her down under the water and holding her there; when I had tried to lift her head, her forehead seemed to be the place of where the pressure was.

After that experience Emma never had a bath on her own again, we encountered the same problem on more than one occasion. It became a constant nightmare each time she had to have a bath. We took plenty of precautions she never had too much water in.

She was always frightened of being on her own and expected Kevin or me to stay with her, but she never realized why? Until she experienced the full flashback of what happened to her as a child.

It was her Uncle David; he had carried her into the bath of water when she was only about six years old and threatened her not to tell anyone or he would drown her; to frighten her into silence he had literally shown her how.

Slowly this information came to the surface through her flashbacks.

Emma had suffered a life and death experience, being a child; she had the ability to bury her feelings and emotions deep within.

Emma has been unable to live a normal life her subconscious mind knew the truth and eventually it had to come to the forefront of her conscious mind.

Unfortunately, the subconscious cannot logically decipher in what order things happened to Emma as a child and so it throws things out like a puzzle.

This is why the involuntary movements happen, she is literally reliving the abuse; physically through the intensity flashbacks she has suffered. It is only since she acknowledged what they meant and disclosed the abuse have they been able to subside.

The bathroom is not the only place where these flashbacks occurred. There have been many times we have had to send for an ambulance when Emma had been walking upstairs and fallen backwards landing in an awkward position at the bottom; she has always seemed to have been unconscious and when she does open her eyes it is such a shock for her to be where she is and usually Kevin or myself is comforting her until the paramedics arrive.

Her private Consultant always said,

"She was in danger of losing her life through the flashbacks."

You can imagine how hard it was to allow her to do normal things that could result in a fatal accident.

When she eventually acknowledges the flashback, she remembers her Uncle David pulling her ponytail as she had long hair when she was little.

I can recollect she asked her friend to cut it off. I was so angry at the time, it was just above the hairline, it looked dreadful I could not let her go to school looking like that so I rang our nearest hairdresser explained what had happened and could she do something to make it look better?

"All I can do is shave the back and blend it in." The hairdresser exclaimed; I was happy with that at least Emma would be able to walk around without looking like someone had gone at it with a pair of shears. Little did I know the actual reason why she had wanted it cut?

Reflection of one of these frightening experiences; when Emma was sat on the sofa which I made sure was made of a strong leather and very heavy, the second in twelve months. The first one we had; Emma had broken off all the legs. Although the new one was sturdy, she still managed to move it; the force of the flashbacks was incredible.

How did this beast of a man commit this despicable crime against my tiny, fragile, little girl?

Watching these flashbacks is heartbreaking. Emma my beautiful young daughter is being raped and sexually abused in front of my eyes. Seeing her facial features change, her lips nearly disappear; she frowns and whimpers as she is transported back in time to a place, she had desperately tried to forget all those years ago. It was all on tape and if you do not see it, you would never believe it.

First her head went backwards and forwards at an incredible speed then her head stopped suddenly and her body arches; her spine was bending backwards nearly double. Her feet are barely touching the ground, the settee is lifting off the floor with the force.

Watching and waiting for it all to stop as there is nothing anyone can do. In the beginning we tried gently tapping her cheeks to bring her out of it; but the psychologist at the time suggested it is better to leave her and let her continue,

"She needs to ride them out," he said, but it was easy for him to say this; when we had to witness her suffer repeatedly.

As soon as Emma opened her eyes, (In clinical terms she had been dissociated with reality) I was there; my hand gently rubbing her back as it began to slowly return to its normal position, every time I had to remind her to take deep breaths as her back always went into spasm.

I gazed in horror the first time her arms moved aggressively above her head and then her wrists cross over; it hurts so much to imagine my little girl going through all this pain, her father of all people.

It breaks my heart knowing that she was all alone and not allowed to tell anyone.

I remember Emma when she was so young, she stole some of my mum's jewellery and hid it in the garden. Looking back, I think she was trying to tell us something, because at the time my mum was gardening in her potato patch when she found a pair of Emma's-stained knickers, not realizing the consequence of her actions she just threw them away.

My mum only mentioned it years later when Emma was making her statement and that she had hidden them in her Nana's garden.

Eventually she disclosed that it was her father my ex-husband Steve who was holding her down from behind, with his hand covering her mouth to prevent her from screaming out; while her Uncle David, Steve's brother-in-law committed the rape.

On tape Emma is heard whimpering,

"Stop him dad,"

"He's hurting me dad."

While Emma's legs are being forced apart; she is seen to be trying to close them, then she stops and her body is being pushed and her stomach muscles are moving in and out, you can see it all happening in front of you but there is no one else there.

When she opens her eyes, she remembers what has just taken place. She is crying, the tears slowly run down her cheeks as she tells me what she heard her dad saying,

"Open your legs it will be over soon,"

Emma asks me to help get her arms down as they are so stiff, then she complains that she is sore in between her legs, slowly I manage to get her to sit up and when she stands her legs are like jelly, she needs a cigarette; that is something which brings her back to reality so much quicker.

The times she has fallen onto the floor, she always fell backwards, there was no warning she could be walking from one room to another, it has happened outside while on her way to the car parked in the driveway. In the Consultant's waiting room crowded with people. We have had all the medical tests done, but none of these are down to epilepsy she has had a brain scan to eliminate anything untoward.

It is all attributed to when she was a child, and her uncle pulled her hair. When she hits the ground, her back turns on its side and then starts to bend, I was always terrified that her neck was going to break, I tried to pull it forward, but the force was so strong.

Kevin and I tried to make sure that she always had someone with her, especially when she was ascending and descending the stairs. There were occasions when we have not always been on hand, we have found her unconscious.

Paramedics have witnessed this behaviour; they understood when we told them this happens on a regular basis. They waited for her to experience another one before they could move her to the ambulance, they had listened to what I was saying and as soon as the episode subsided, they quickly helped her to her feet.

Some paramedics were not as compassionate as others and did not realize what was happening when I had to explain they were intensity flashbacks from her past child abuse. Most of the ambulance staff were magnificent, allowing me to help with Emma in the ambulance when she experienced one while she was strapped to a bed. Kevin and I found that smelling salts helped to bring her back to reality; if she was having a flashback while she was in a vulnerable position.

I could never understand why these flashbacks continued intermittently over the years until I realized that her father was also responsible for the rape and abuse as well as her Uncle David.

Although Emma and her sister Katherine had gone to the police regarding their Uncle David and that he was charged for rape, attempted rape, and indecent assault; Emma kept quiet about her father knowing that he had committed the same crime and a lot more she never disclosed anything, she could not he was her father!

I remember when Emma first disclosed the rape and the sexual abuse from her Uncle David; I had left Emma upstairs in her bedroom while I went downstairs and explained everything to her dad I did not know where to start, it was so hard to put it into words what Emma had told me the previous night.

I thought he was understanding until he told me to fetch Emma downstairs, I will never forget the words he used when Emma slowly walked through the lounge door, her eyes were still red, and her cheeks tear stained I felt so much empathy for her.

I was shocked, before my husband told me to go upstairs. He said to Emma, in a very controlling manner without any compassion,

"Sit down there," he pointed to the sofa, I watched as Emma did what her father told her to do. She sat in the middle clutching her hands together, while he pointed his finger at her and spoke in a harsh tone,

"Now you convince me, like you have convinced your mother."

I went upstairs thinking how unpleasant he was, then a thought came into my head, ***maybe he is thinking in advance for when we get the police involved and Emma being strong enough to answer their questions.***

I let it go at that thought, but Emma would never speak to her father about anything regarding the abuse she suffered at the hands of her Uncle David.

When she revealed the ghastly memories of what her Uncle David did to her, listening to all the sordid details, I must have had an inner strength. After all, this was my daughter I could not help her at the time when she was a child; I tried my best to help her through that present trauma.

I did try to talk to my husband, as I needed to offload some of my feelings of anger and frustration, he could not support me and when I mentioned some details of the abuse, not specific ones, but when and where it took place. He cut me off by saying,

"I'm a man, and I know how a man thinks."

After that comment I never spoke to him again about the situation.

Emma and I wanted so much to let the authorities know. My husband was totally against it, I tried to convince him it was the right thing to do.

After disclosing everything she could remember, there was still bits of information coming out all the time.

Emma repeatedly said,

"There's more Mum, there is more but it won't come, I know there's more."

At the time I did not realize what that signified, it was only since Emma has disclosed the abuse and rape by her father; that those words now make sense.

Looking back, Steve did not want anything to do with the police when Emma and Katherine both made statements. He always said,

"I will be the one they see in court."

Not realizing that he was also guarding the fact if Emma was about to tell the truth about him being an accomplice, then his presence was enough to stop her from disclosing any information against him.

The power he had over her as a child and then as an adult was unforgiveable.

I am also hurt and so disheartened in the way Emma's siblings Katherine and Liam have behaved towards her. I understand it must be the most horrifying truth to believe what your father may be capable of.

To acknowledge that there is any possibility that their father could do what Emma is accusing him of takes an enormous amount of mental energy to discard any thought of it. So, it is understandable that Katherine and Liam support their father 100% it is unthinkable to believe Emma and so they make it hard for anybody else to believe her.

The love they all shared for each other seemed to change to hate which is a strong word, the attitude towards their sister was indescribable. Liam wanted nothing at all to do with Emma or her children except Zak and Jodie; they were Carl's children; who was a good friend and has been accepted into that side of the family for a considerable amount of time.

Liam's wife Emma also had an opinion regarding Emma, it was all based on what Liam had told her in the beginning, so she had an extremely negative response to her sister-in-law.

Then there is Katherine convincing Jodie that her granddad is innocent till proven guilty; but Emma never got the chance to prove it in court, mainly because her sister would not support her.

In fact, Katherine would say anything to protect her father. "I will do everything in my power to show Emma is lying."

There is only two people know the truth and that is Emma and her father. Unless there was any other part of her family present at the time of the abuse, they have no right judging her.

The whole situation is appalling; Katherine, Jodie's Aunty should be encouraging Jodie to communicate with her mother not allowing her to verbally attack her down the phone while Katherine and Paul are present.

Emma asked Jodie to come home on many occasions; then the last straw came when Emma had to physically face her father on the car park at the Theatre.

Since then, there has been an atmosphere between them, how can Emma possibly trust her daughter again?

She apologized to Jodie for not being able to watch her dance.

The constant rejection from her family made her more determined to prove her father is guilty of the crimes he committed against her.

She desperately wants her children's love and respect and there is only one way to show them that she is not telling lies about their granddad.

She has tried countless times to find a solicitor to take her case to a private prosecution but each time they have explained.

"It is a criminal case, and it would have to go to a Crown Court, the CPS could take over and stop the case from going any further."

No one legally is available to fight her corner.

CHAPTER 18

Moving On

E mma never felt safe or comfortable in her own home; always aware of a certain person knocking on her door.

She could not walk into the village to the shops or the bank. Whenever she needed to make an appointment at the doctors, she was terrified that she might bump into her father or see any of her family. It may have been a bit of paranoia, but there was always that possibility; as they all used the same surgery including her father.

She would love to have gone to Darren's Sport's Day, but Zak attended the same school, she was frightened she might see Carl or even worse her father.

Kevin did most of the shopping, unless they had driven into the city, then Emma was comfortable to walk around the shops, retail therapy always helped her feel better especially when she was away from the village.

Kevin always took Ginny with him when he walked Darren to School. I stayed with Emma as she could not be on her own; she felt so vulnerable.

Katherine had a friend at the top of Emma's Avenue; Cindy was playing outside with her friend's children, this made it difficult for Emma when she saw Cindy, but she could not go and speak to her. One time she had done, and Katherine had shouted her back.

This reaction from her sister upset Emma at the time, so then she felt if Katherine's car was in view, she could not step foot outside her front door.

One day she realized there was nothing to keep her in the village, Jodie was happy living with Katherine and Paul. Zak was content with his life with his father and his girlfriend whom he had stayed with for the past two years; Emma was happy Zak had some normal stability.

She spoke to Kevin about moving, selling the house, and getting out of the village, she wanted to live a normal life, to take Darren to school and Ginny to Nursery to do things a mother would do.

Walk comfortably into a shop without looking over her shoulder. Take her children for a walk or to the park.

It would mean Darren would have to leave his school, but when they mentioned it to him, he was happy to move to another school and live somewhere else. He was getting older and realized that his Mum was different than other Mums. She had tried so much to hide her feelings of depression, but Darren was clever and very observant, he showed his Mum how much he loved her in so many ways. This helped Emma to look at the future and that was her family, she had to be well for Darren and Ginny.

Kevin's niece Jade lived in another suburb of the city about five miles away from Little Beddington, for the past twelve months Emma and Kevin had been visiting her on a regular basis.

Jade and her husband Neil had two children Sophie just six months younger than Darren and Jake a couple of months older than Ginny, so it was nice that the children played together.

Emma was always happy to be in Jade's company and when she mentioned that they were contemplating a move, Jade told Emma there was a house for sale close to them.

A couple of days later Emma and Kevin were on their way to meet the estate agent and look round the house which Jade had pointed out to them. They both liked it.

When they returned home Emma immediately rang her solicitor who was also her deputy and looked after all her finances.

She told him of her plans, and he agreed.

Within a week their house was on the market, Emma's life was beginning to change. Little Beddington had been Emma's hometown for as long as she could remember, but it held so many bad memories.

This was a positive move, she asked Jodie if she would like to come with her and Kevin; her negative answer upset Emma. Every time Emma tried to contact her, she was verbally attacked with a load of abuse. Katherine and Paul were present while Jodie was allowed to swear at her mother down the phone, they did not take any responsibility in stopping her. It is so sad to see Jodie is still angry with her mum, I think she blames her mum for leaving her when she was little; unfortunately, she does not know the truth of how her mum fought for her children through the courts.

Katherine does not know about the devastation Emma underwent as she was in hospital at the time and when she was discharged, she never asked what had happened. When Carl tells people including Emma's family that she walked out on her children they believe him.

Emma put all her energy into selling their property and preparing to move. She had to think about herself and her husband, she also had two young children who were innocent in all this conflict, and they needed her to be well so she could care for them.

Emma's guilt nearly tore her apart but Richard her psychotherapist helped her to deal with it. We were all kept busy by decorating the old house and doing the few odd jobs which would help to sell.

Luckily Emma had enough left in her account to buy the house they had seen, it was perfect close to a good school for Darren and the shops; they did not want to lose it, so she asked her solicitor if she could use some of her finances until her house was sold.

He was a bit reluctant at first, but Emma's new house proved to be a lot more economical, it was his job to look after her, he saw it as a beneficial project and agreed to it.

Soon they were packing and moving into their new home, Kevin was happy as the town they were moving to was close to where he grew up and most of his family lived there. Emma was excited at the prospect of a life changing decision, sad that she was leaving her other two children who by that time had stopped speaking to her.

She was also apprehensive, she would have to be more independent; I would not be available as easy, as I would have to travel the five miles if they needed me. So, it was a good move for them to be a family instead of leaning on my support. I say this with a positive attitude.

During the next six months, after they had settled into their new home, Emma had gradually changed, she was happy, she had started venturing out on her own in the car and slowly she gained the confidence to come back to the village to visit me and my mum.

Peter and I had gone our separate ways, he was busy with his job, and I was completely occupied with things in my life. It was an amicable split; we have stayed good friends.

One day I received a phone call,

"Mum have you heard the news, they have found out Jimmy Saville was a paedophile and there's loads of victims coming forward."

"Yes, I have already seen it," I answered.

I was quite surprised that Emma had taken notice of this news; anything to do with paedophiles and child abuse cases she shied away from. She had been let down so badly by the police and the CPS.

Many times, I had mentioned that her father should not be allowed to get away with what he has done and might do again if the opportunity arose.

This upset Emma to the point where she told me in no uncertain terms,

"Leave it Mum, there's nothing we can do, I have to move on with my life."

I got the message; I knew I had gone too far mentioning it again, but I had to let Emma know if ever there came a time when there may be the smallest chance of her getting some justice then I will be there for her and give her one hundred percent support.

I have never let go of the anger I feel towards my ex-husband, and I will never rest until I have done everything in my power to see Emma get her justice and her father admit to himself and our family the pain and torture he has caused.

Week after week more victims were coming forward each time the news came on the television it was constantly about adults, some disabled, others' mentally ill complaining that Jimmy Saville had sexually abused them when they were children, some of them were inpatients in a children's hospital at the time.

Then other celebrities were being arrested for historic child sexual abuse, it was on the front pages of most of the newspapers.

Because the media were naming these paedophiles, I think other victims felt safe that they were now able to disclose to the authorities; what had happened to them as children.

I have waited so long for this day to come for the public to recognize the danger of these people who abuse children and how it affects the lifetime of their victims and splits families apart however close they may have been at one time.

On 6th March 2013, a day I will always remember when the Director of Public Prosecutions stated: There will be changes on how the Police and the CPS handle cases of Child Sexual Abuse.

17th October 2013 DPP Keir Stammer QC Announces new guidelines on prosecuting cases of Child Sex Abuse and investigate reviewing past cases of Historic Child Sexual Abuse.

Emma was still in contact with her psychotherapist Richard; her following appointment she mentioned how she was frightened of being thwarted again by the police and the CPS. She had invited me to attend her meeting with Richard, we spoke at length about the situation in the media regarding the changes towards historic child sexual abuse; Richard also agreed that the atmosphere was now different and that it was the right time to ask for a review of both cases; her Uncle David and her father.

Richard asked me my opinion and I was extremely positive about my answer,

"This is what I have been waiting for, for so long, the chance to prove that Emma is telling the truth and maybe her family might believe her and possibly reunite, if only her father could be charged with the crimes he has committed against my daughter; that would be acceptable. It would be a bonus if the cases went to court and then people would see my ex-husband for what he truly is."

I became quite upset while I was explaining my feelings and how much I wanted Emma to trust in the authorities again; she then exclaimed,

"Mum, I never said never, I'm just so frightened that if I go through all this again, if he walks free again it will put me six feet under."

I understand she feels like that with what she has had to endure her whole lifetime, but this is different she must do this, one more chance to see if she can get justice and her family back, including her own children.

I feel so positive this time; after we had finished the session with Richard, said our goodbyes he wished us luck with our next step.

I was constantly watching the news. Listening for any information which was relevant towards the correct way in which to proceed, making sure that I was using the right channels to request a review into both child sexual abuse cases.

The Chief Prosecutor for the CPS in our local city was being interviewed by a news reporter, he was making a statement regarding people abusing children.

I thought, y*es, that is the person I need to speak to.*

I rang Emma asking for her permission to contact Mr. Bensign on her behalf.

"Yes Mum, can I read the letter first before you post it."

I was pleased she was taking notice and allowing me to do this for her and myself.

"Of course, you need to sign it."

I sat down and carefully put a letter together explaining in short what had happened in the past and how the CPS had not been able to take the cases forward and would it be possible to review or reinvestigate them both.

We waited apprehensively for a response; we were fortunate as we did not have to wait long. Within a week we received a nice letter explaining that we need to go back to the original police station that first dealt with the cases. Mr. Bensign was sorry to hear about what Emma had experienced and sent his best wishes for the future.

Again, we put another letter together, only this time I had Emma helping with what and how to word it.

There was no acknowledgement that this police station had received a letter; we had sent it recorded delivery so we knew it would have been delivered to the correct address.

This waiting game was not helping Emma, her anxiety levels were at a high, Kevin was having to step on eggshells around her, she was so impatient at times; her short-tempered attitude affected everyone around her.

Emma was still seeing her therapist on a weekly basis she described to him how she felt, there was only one person who could help Emma at this time and that was Richard. She explained how she was finding it hard to accept that it was her father that did all these despicable things to her.

Emma had enlightened us that she did not have a dad and that her irrational thinking caused her to believe that Mark a friend of the family from years ago was her real Dad. She said she was not ready to talk to the police while she had these thoughts.

Richard had suggested she tries to remember some happy times of her childhood, hoping that would be a start into realizing that Steve was her father who badly let her down and abuse her like he did.

She desperately tried to find some happy memories. She had gone to this air show with her dad when she was around eight years old and she remembered they had sold most of the stock, her dad was really pleased so they had gone to a Little Chef, and he had bought her an ice cream sundae; but that memory soon faded away when she realized that she had to earn it and it was not through hard work.

The fantasy of Mark being her father was becoming quite serious; we had lost touch with him when he got married and emigrated to New Zealand. She was now trying to find him on an internet site, she asked me if I would have a DNA test to prove Steve was not her real Dad.

I remember Emma liked Mark she seemed to get on well with him, it was not very often that Emma laughed when she was a child, but Mark could always make her smile. I am surprised she can still remember him, let alone hoped I had an affair with him and that he was Emma's biological father. She asked me,

"Is there any way it could have happened." I had to apologise to her,

"I'm sorry love, I wish I could say what you want to hear, but I never had an affair with anyone."

On the way home from Richard's, she began to reminisce about things we did as a family, it was so important that Emma accepted that Steve my ex-husband was her father.

If the CPS hopefully decide to take these cases to court, she will be able to speak about what her father did and not fantasize that Mark was her father and that he was a good man.

A couple of weeks passed, Emma was distraught with worry and apprehension, I was also beginning to feel down hearted we had not heard anything from the police.

There were so many questions I needed to know. Have the police decided if there is enough evidence to re-investigate?

Are the police sending it on to the review panel?

I did not give any evidence as Emma's mother when the police first questioned my ex-husband. I feel I have an immense amount of information towards the case, and I want to be asked to make a statement as I was the first-person Emma disclosed that her father raped and abused her when she was a child.

I did not dare give Emma any positive feelings in case the police decided that there was not enough evidence to get a conviction, they will not charge her father unless they feel they can take it to court.

Emma asked me to ring and find out if there was any information?

I was shaking as I dialed the number,

"Hello, this is the PPU can I help you?"

"Yes please." I explained in short about the letter and the lady on the other end politely asked me if I would wait while she investigated the matter.

"Hello, it's DS McIntyre here, I have received your letter, and unfortunately we have been extremely busy as we are moving premises, so I haven't had the time to spend on it. I will be in touch as soon as I have all the relevant details, I have requested the past records from another department, and I will ring your number when I have some more information."

"Thank you," that is all I could say as he seemed very efficient. At least he acknowledged that he had received the letter; he seemed to know what he was doing about it and now we have got a name, someone we can ask for in person, it is so much better than having to explain everything each time we ring for an update.

Months later, Katherine had come to visit, we both got into a deep conversation about what Emma had said about her father.

"Do you believe Emma is telling the truth?" she said bluntly.

I was so pleased Katherine asked me that question.

"Yes, I do, there are lots of things you do not know about your dad, I know through what he has done to me in the past that he is capable of what Emma has said he has done to her."

Katherine seemed like she had something on her mind. I questioned her,

"Why do you want to know," I was hoping this conversation would lead to something positive.

"It was me I told Miss Rylands that Emma was telling lies, that she had a personality disorder I found the information on the internet and printed it off and gave it to her."

I explained to Katherine that Miss Rylands gave that information to the police before Emma could speak to them, so they already had false details about Emma, that should not have made any difference to the case, but I feel that it did from the very beginning.

"I am so sorry Mum," Katherine seemed remorseful I told her,

"I think you should be apologizing to Emma not me."

I arranged a meeting at my house that night for Emma to come round and Katherine to apologize to her.

At first, they seemed to be communicating but then Emma felt it was time to put Katherine straight and tell her everything, the whole truth and nothing but the truth.

Unfortunately, Katherine did not want to know, she tried everything she could to avoid the subject she just would not accept her father was capable of what Emma was saying about him.

This is where I have realized the extensive difference in personalities. I imagined people would empathize towards child sexual abuse. Especially Katherine already experiencing the trauma of what happened to her.

Unless you have personally been affected by incestuous rape and abuse or been near the victim it is extremely hard to put one's feet into another person's shoes.

I found that some people point fingers saying,

"The mother should have known or at least seen the signs."

To tell the truth there are no signs, I should know being a mother, I have racked my brains trying to see if I missed something, looking back for any visible signs, but there is nothing I can think of; except one time when Emma was fourteen years old, and she wanted to stay at her friend's house for a few days.

I did not mind as it was the summer term break.

The days went into a week and the weeks went into a month, I had to be firm with her and ground her just so I could make her stay at home for a little while; all the time believing that she was wanting to stay with her best friend Ollie short for Olivia. Her mum was working, and Ollie was left alone at home, so Emma wanted to keep her company. Also, she enjoyed the independence, helping Ollie cook meals for when her mum returned home from work. It was only when Emma disclosed the abuse by her father that she admitted the time she stayed away at her friend's was because she was terrified of her father and also becoming too close to me, she explained that she was frightened of having a loving relationship with me in case she was tempted to tell me what her father had done to her as a child, *I will never forget mentioning to my mother in law, that Emma wouldn't let me give her a hug.*

She remembered the threats.

"Your Mummy won't believe you and you will be sent away and never see her or your sister again."

That must have been horrendous for a child to bear and not allowed to tell her own mother, who would have certainly believed her and never disowned her; also, been able to give her the love she so desperately needed.

CHAPTER 19

Re-Living The Past

One morning I received a phone call from Emma,

"Mum did you feel an earthquake last night?" I replied,

"No."

Emma sounded so adamant that there was one and it happened while she was in bed.

"I have asked Kevin if he felt it, we have looked on the news to see if there was any information about the earthquake." I enquired,

"What happened?" Emma answered in a worried tone of voice.

"The bed was shaking badly, and the covers were moving, I turned over on my side to see if it would stop."

I knew it was psychological and that Emma was physically feeling a flashback; I explained,

"You know what it is don't you, did you manage to get back to sleep."

"I must have done because when I woke up this morning it was still vivid in my mind. I had hoped that it had been an earthquake, but I realize now what was happening to me. It was so frightening Mum."

Kevin and I decided that we need to keep a watchful eye on Emma.

We had gone for a day out and suggested we take two cars so my Mum could also come with us. Emma was driving her car. We were on a stretch of a 50mph road when Emma automatically put on her left indicator, swerved to the side, and stopped the car. She had a sudden flashback of when her Uncle David had picked her up from her paternal Grandmother's. With her father's permission he had raped her in a lay-by which was like the one, we had just passed.

I automatically pulled up in front of her, in my rear-view mirror I could see Kevin desperately trying to bring Emma out of a dissociated state.

I put on my hazard lights, told my mum to stay in the car with Darren; I did not want to alarm any of them. I jumped out and said,

"I won't be long."

I quickly ran back towards Emma's car. We needed to get Emma out and round to the passenger side. I put my hand up and stopped the traffic while I opened the driver's door, we managed to get her out and then her legs gave way and she slumped to ground.

People were getting out of their cars and offering to help; we thanked them and asked if they could wait until we got Emma to safety.

The traffic was now beginning to queue behind us as it was only two lanes, and we were not supposed to stop.

Kevin drove back he followed me whilst I kept a vigil in my rear mirror, terrified she may have another episode.

A few days later Emma had got herself a glass of water to take her medication she was walking back into the living room from the kitchen when she collapsed onto the tiled floor.

The glass smashed into hundreds of small splinters; there was blood everywhere, Kevin quickly rang for me to come and help, it was lucky that the children were in bed. When I arrived approximately twenty minutes later Kevin had managed to get Emma to her feet, but her arms and hands were bleeding, they were superficial injuries, so we did not need to go to the hospital. I helped clean Emma up while Kevin swept the floor making sure there was no broken glass left anywhere. From then on Emma used plastic cups.

The waiting was not easy for Emma, she was becoming anxious about how the police would come to a decision whether they were going to reinvestigate the cases.

It would be a bonus if they could reinvestigate her father's case and bring her Uncle David in as an accomplice, but we realize there is no concrete evidence to say it happened; it is Emma's word against her father.

However, there are camcorder tapes showing the intensity flashbacks of what happened when her Uncle David raped her, and her father was holding her down.

Watching these tapes; it is extremely emotional, I cannot put into words how I feel, staring at the screen knowing that Emma my little girl went through this horrific abuse and her father was there helping the abuser rape his daughter.

You can see the pain in her face as she flinches each time it happens. It is difficult to say what the imagination is conjuring up. Her face was all contorted as she came round desperately trying to breathe.

The jury must see this, I believe it should be enough evidence to convict them both. Emma has not seen these tapes and it is only recently she was told they exist.

I could not bear for her to consciously witness what it was like for her as a child; I do not think it would be beneficial for her.

I have contacted DS McIntyre and mentioned these tapes; I needed for him to see them himself and for me to make a full statement. Her Uncle David was charged and bailed on the statements Emma, Katherine and I made twelve years earlier.

I had no information then that her father was actively involved, so I would have appreciated being allowed to add to the previous statement with what I have learned in the last four years.

I have also a letter dated a few months before her contacting the police in 2009 regarding her father.

It was addressed to a local Consultant explaining the medical history of Emma, from the private Consultant she had been under for the past three years.

At the time Emma was experiencing bad intensity flashbacks, we were constantly getting the Emergency Services to send an ambulance to take her to the A&E department at the Hospital on the outskirts of the city.

Kevin and I realized it would be much easier if Emma was under the NHS so we would be entitled to some help by having a community psychiatric nurse to support us when Emma was experiencing these flashbacks.

I found it so hard each time I had to explain to a doctor what was happening and to ask for the medication which I knew would help her at that moment in time.

There was constantly a long waiting time to see an on-call Psychiatrist who eventually agreed to administer a muscle relaxant injection to allow Emma some relief.

Most of the on-call psychiatric Consultants were obliging others were reluctant to give her the intravenous medication.

Emma was not keen on the idea of leaving her private Consultant; he had helped her when she most desperately needed his intervention. The medication he prescribed enabled her to cope through many a crisis. He was understanding when Emma explained how she felt, he was apprehensive for her future, but also agreed that it would be better for her to have a Psychiatric Consultant close by; so the letter he wrote was a strong piece of evidence saying that Emma had experienced horrendous child abuse and that he had actually witnessed Emma having an intensity flashback of which he was adamant that it was not Dystonia (a neurological movement disorder).

Approximately a month after being transferred to a local Consultant with the NHS she disclosed the abuse by her father, which resulted in Emma experiencing bad intensity flashbacks.

That was where Miss Rylands caused so many problems in relation to the family and the criminal investigation as she had only recently met Emma and did not know all the relevant details of her history.

Emma was desperate to have a chance at making another statement with all the true facts.

For years it has been impossible for Emma to speak to anybody about the abuse her father inflicted on her, she was so terrified when she was a child. She had the strength to completely block it from her mind so she would always have a father, I suppose she was fantasizing from such an early age. It was so much easier to do that than accept what he did to her and how much he hurt her.

Now, years later she needs to unblock this truth, accept it so she can tell the police everything that happened and then perhaps move on from all the trauma, upset and unhappiness he has caused Emma and her family.

It is impossible to believe that her own father performed those despicable sexual acts of abuse on his daughter and then years later, deny it ever took place.

Emma has tried so hard in her therapy sessions with Richard to unblock everything that happened; but it just did not happen.

The date is getting closer for when the police want to decide whether they are going to reinvestigate or close the case. Emma desperately needs everything out in the open and in the forefront of her mind.

To enable Emma to do this, Richard suggested going back to the place where it all happened.

We had arranged for Ginny to be looked after by Kevin's cousin and Darren was staying with my Mum.

We decided to meet on the car park behind the shop where Steve and I first started our married life. If only those were happy memories, they used to be until I found out what kind of person he truly is.

Because of Emma's past experiences with flashbacks both Kevin and I were frightened of putting Richard into an uncomfortable position, so Kevin asked if we could come into the shop with them. Emma seemed pleased when we offered to do that.

I had not stepped foot in the place for twenty-five years, until I arranged with the proprietor if we could use her property for a purpose; I did not need to go into detail, the lady who remembered me from when we sold them the shop was kind as soon as I mentioned it might help my daughter.

The memory of how it used to be was vivid in my mind, the shop itself had changed, the layout was different, and the living quarters had the same wallpaper I had chosen all that time ago. It was still as nice; except it had been painted over, but you could still see the design. Emma was shaking, the tears were welling up in her eyes; her memories began to surface as she climbed the stairs one by one. Richard was slowly following behind; I had already warned him of the risk of Emma having a flashback. (Richard had never witnessed one of her flashbacks). He was more concerned for Emma, also conscious of how she can physically and mentally react in this situation. None of us knew what to expect, especially Emma.

Hesitantly she stepped into what used to be the bathroom, she knelt on her knees and spoke as she was a little girl in front of what would have been the bath; she sat staring for a while, the tears streaming down her face as the memories came flooding back.

She watched as the bubbles half covered her tiny frame; her daddy kneeling, one hand touching her naked body, the other beneath the water; then back to reality, she began to twitch as she felt that little girl's pain.

Slowly she got to her feet and walked along the landing towards the lounge, Emma could tell me exactly where the furniture was placed, what colour the suite was and the unit that was in the alcove, she pointed to where the television was. I nodded not knowing whether I should speak as she was in the present time and in the past.

Then she entered the bedroom, which she had shared with her sister Katherine. With a hand movement Richard suggested I go back to the top of the stairs where I stood with Kevin.

Richard then came over to us leaving Emma alone with her thoughts, he warned us,

"If you hear any screams or shouting don't worry."

We were prepared when we heard Emma shouting,

"Stop! Stop! Stop!"

Her voice became louder as she was telling her dad to stop hurting her, something she could never do as a child. A few moments passed, then Richard called,

"Mum come in now,"

I ran towards the bedroom, Emma was on the floor quietly sobbing; I crouched down and put my arms around her trembling body and said in a gentle voice,

"Mummy's here, you are safe now, Mummy's here."

I cuddled her for about five minutes. Then I helped her to her feet, Richard followed as we made our way to the top of the stairs.

She stopped; everyone stood back, Richard bent down as Emma went down onto her knees, he was holding on to her coat just in case she fell forward. She spoke saying,

"This is where I wanted to fly."

She sat there for a while, then she seemed to come back to the present time and decided she had seen enough.

We all went downstairs and thanked the proprietor and her tenant for allowing us to borrow her flat.

It was difficult for me to explain why we needed to use her facilities.

Barbara the landlord had been very understanding when I partly explained the reason; that a criminal act had taken place all those years ago. I had left her to speak to the lady who was residing in the flat above; she soon got back to me and said her tenant was happy for us to enter her home. Although we would be intruding on her privacy. Barbara and her husband lived just around the corner; they had modernized the upstairs of the property and converted it into a self-contained flat. I cannot thank them enough for being so kind and understanding.

Hopefully, it was enough to unblock Emma's reluctance at being able to see her father for what he was and not what she fantasized him to be.

Maybe now she can complete a full statement for the police.

She is now ready to speak truthfully about how her father abused her and the trust she put in him.

The following week was difficult to understand Emma; the child was still present in her psyche. She still felt small and frightened of completing adult chores, like making meals; she really could not remember how to use her cooker. Kevin was driving the car and she was watching; she knew she was not capable of being able to drive herself; yet only a few days earlier it had been automatic to her.

Emma was confused; she said her body feels small when she looked down, she expected to see little hands; she found it hard to accept the size of her adult ones.

The same night after she had visited the shop, I had taken her back to my house.

My Mum was not feeling well, she was in bed in her room that I had transformed into a small bed-sitter.

Emma wanted to see her Nan; while she sat in conversation with my mum, I made a drink in the next room which I had converted into a kitchen except for a sink. The bathroom was only across from there so there was no need for any major alteration.

When I entered with the cups, I noticed Emma looking confused, as she thought she still lived around the corner from us. I had to explain that she had moved to another village about five miles away.

She also thought her Nan was recuperating from a hip operation that had happened five years earlier. We tried to persuade her what year it was, but she was adamant that it was not the present time.

Then she decided that she wanted to go home and be with her husband and her children. She got in my car; I proceeded to turn left onto the main road and out of the village; she then asked,

"Where are we going?" Smiling I replied,

"I'm taking you home," we started to laugh. I was so glad she saw the funny side to the situation. As we got closer to her house I enquired,

"Do you know where we are?" She replied,

"No, I have not got a clue." And we laughed again.

During the rest of the week, she slowly came back to normal, except for her suite.

When Kevin and Emma had moved into their new home nearly twelve months earlier, they had chosen a new suite. Emma was adamant that her experience of recliner chairs was not going to spoil the fact that she wanted to purchase two large black leather sofas both with recliners.

She entered her front room on the night I had taken her back after the visit and immediately saw the sofas, Darren was already stretched out on one of the recliners. She went mad,

"Are they both recliners?"

She asked Kevin who had just walked into the room oblivious to the shock and horror that Emma felt when she noticed the sofas. He did not realize how her mind was acting at first when he answered,

"Yes." Abruptly she said,

"They will have to go, I did not choose them, why would I buy recliners when I have so many problems with them from my past?" Both Kevin and I explained,

"You wanted them, we tried to discourage you from buying them."

We pointed out the reason at the time why she should not get them, as we both knew how they affected her from the memories of the past abuse when her Uncle David and her father had used her Aunty Anne's for their own sexual gratification.

She had asked me to go up to her bedroom with her while she changed into her pyjamas and dressing gown.

As she walked into her room, she noticed herself in the mirror,

"Oh! My hair, where's my blonde hair?"

I told her that she had decided the week before she did not want to be blonde anymore; we had gone to see her hairdresser Lillian as she fancied being a brunette with red highlights. She had no recollections of it, and she certainly did not accept it, so much so that she phoned her hairdresser the following morning to change her colour back to blonde.

This action had also affected her mental health when she was little her hair was brown. Lillian was also a friend who she had known for quite some time so when Emma explained she did not like her new colour she just laughed.

As for the suite, Kevin's niece Jade had come round to see them, Emma mentioned that she was having trouble adjusting to the sofas. Jade said,

"Neil has been after recliners for ages, do you want to swop?"

Before Kevin and Neil had been asked their opinions; Emma jumped at the idea, they decided they would move them the same weekend.

Kevin was happy for a quiet life and was pleased to accept Jade's offer.

It was fortunate that Jade had a sister April who was expecting a baby around the same time as Liam's wife was due.

Coincidently April was taken into hospital to be induced as she was over a week late according to her due date.

Jade and Neil went to visit April the same day her baby girl had been born. As they were waiting to enter the maternity ward, Liam my son was in the queue. Neil recognized him from previous family occasions, he enquired,

"Has your wife had the baby yet?" His answer was, "Yes." Jade asked,

"Was it a boy or a girl?" Hesitantly he replied,

"A boy." Of course, I was told the news, apparently my grandson was born on Tuesday evening; it was now Saturday afternoon. It was obvious that Liam and his wife did not want me or my eighty-year-old Mum to know.

This upset me so much that me and my Mum, who was now living with me; decided to move away from the village where I had lived for the past forty years.

Some memories were not so happy, but most of them were as it was our family home. My children had been brought up there, so many wonderful times were spent with them.

Kevin had helped me build a raised decking in front of the dining room; leading down to a pond at the bottom of the garden; which I have tended over the past few years, cleaning and changing the water, especially when I was looking after Emma's friend's dog while they went on holiday.

Their huge boisterous German Shepard decided to bounce into the pond and his sharp claws went through the strong lining, thus causing the water to seep slowly through the holes.

I was so frightened of losing any fish as they also had babies from the year before and they were all surviving well. It was, 'Quick all hands to the deck,' Darren and Emma had fishing nets catching the large fish first and the babies; while Kevin and I tried desperately to save as much of the pond water as possible and transfer it into a large swimming pool. Eventually I managed to patch up the holes and the fish were happily swimming about in their own surroundings.

Thinking to myself, *I will miss walking down the steps watching them swim to the surface when I fed them and the summer nights sat listening to the calming gentle trickling of the waterfall, the colourful lilies floating on the surface; it looked like wonderland with a backdrop of tall conifers standing proud behind the stone water feature, the fountain reflecting from the lights that Kevin had painstakingly erected around the stone flags.*

I reminisce the memories of Peter digging out the large figure eight, sweating from the constant times that he had hit some clay which proved to be extremely hard to break up.

Kevin who was determined to complete the whole project; including the decking and made it beautiful; but now I feel it is the right time to move on, as it is difficult to imagine how I would feel if I were to bump into Liam or his wife as they had bought a nice three-bedroom cottage on the main road through the centre of the village.

Apart from receiving a lovely bouquet of flowers for my birthday Katherine had not been in touch with me or my Mum for nearly twelve months.

Mum and I chose a little stone cottage in another village about eight miles away from Little Beddington.

It is perfect for my Mum, as there is a Community Centre close by where the elderly people from the village spend their spare time having coffee in the company of others.

She is already looking forward to meeting the villagers and joining the local groups.

There is also a church where she can visit regularly without needing to use transport.

For me, it is close to where we keep Monty so I can easily visit him. Emma is also happy now that she does not have to risk seeing any of her family; when she came to visit me, she was always aware that anyone of them could be visiting Paul's parents of whom she had to pass to get to my house.

I have written each of my children a letter explaining my feelings and how I hope they will understand why I have got to leave my home, which I told them both that I have some wonderful memories from when they were growing up.

Congratulating Liam on the birth of his son and letting him know there is a place in my heart for my new baby grandson, all my grandchildren and my daughter and son. I asked them not to be sad or angry with me as I explained that I was trying to prevent embarrassment on both sides. Maybe in time we all might be able to forgive and forget.

Till then we must move on with our lives and hopefully reunite in the future.

It was imperative that none of my family knew that Emma was again seeking justice for the abuse her father inflicted on her and the involvement of her Uncle David.

Hopefully, the police will provide a positive outcome and charge Emma's father, concluding with a court appearance. It has now been months since we first contacted DS McIntyre and still have not heard anything except that the case was progressing. Emma and I are holding on to the fact that it is taking time which could be seen as positive.

Christmas was a lovely time, our little stone cottage looked like a Christmas card from the outside. We had bought a garland of holly for the front door and the lights from the

Christmas tree lit up the leaded bay window.

Emma and Kevin had invited both my mum and me to spend Christmas day with them.

What a lovely feeling watching Ginny's excitement at showing us what Santa had brought her. Darren was pleased with all his presents, quietly putting together one of his Lego trucks, he was so good with his hands and his brain was quick to understand the instructions.

Emma made a lovely Christmas dinner, I offered to help but she was adamant to do it herself she allowed Kevin to help her put it all out.

Emma then carved the Turkey after we all sat round the table including Kevin's Dad and his partner who had travelled down from Scotland.

Jodie had arrived the day before to see her Mum and Kevin, they had a lovely day with her. Darren and Ginny were pleased to see their big sister. My Mum and I called in to see her and gave her the present we had bought her for Christmas, also asking her to pass Zak's present on to him.

I could see Emma was pleased that Jodie made the effort to see her, but I could also see the hurt she felt that Zak her son did not want to get in touch with her.

My Mum and I sent some presents for Cindy and Liam's little boy we had bought him a little set of pants and a matching top with a small toy appropriate for his age.

I received a nice text from Liam after I had sent both him and Katherine, one wishing them both a Happy New Year. He was asking to see me and talk to me, but I found it difficult to agree to this as he was still in close contact with his father.

I would love to see Liam, Emma my daughter in law and Andrew my grandson but I ask myself?

How can I knowing I am supporting Emma his sister in trying to seek justice against their father? I would feel so bad like a smiling assassin behind his back and if the case against Emma's Dad does go to court? I would not feel like I betrayed Liam or Katherine.

It hurts like hell stopping myself from getting in touch with either of my other children and I know that many people would not be able to understand my actions.

When the whole sorry mess is over and hopefully my ex-husband has been convicted for the sins he committed against his young daughter; then maybe I can contact my son Liam and my other daughter Katherine with a clear conscience and God willing they will forgive me for the unintentional heartache that unfortunately I could not forestall.

CHAPTER 20

Lucky

I t has been several months since we heard something positive from DS McIntyre; I have contacted him on a regular basis at least once a month, unfortunately he could not give us any more news as to whether the CPS will agree to the case against Emma's father going to court.

His last statement,

"The case is progressing," which was better than hearing DS McIntyre saying an outright,

"No."

This waiting game was not helping Emma, she was becoming anxious; she needed to find something to take her mind off everything that was out of her control.

I was still spending time at the stables, looking after Monty, and riding him on a regular basis; this helped me take my mind off the whole sordid affair of which I felt so helpless and there was nothing I could do about it.

Since moving to our little village of Brierham my Mum has a new lease of life she helps me with Monty; she loves doing jobs such as preparing the hay nets and filling his water bucket.

Each morning I wake up looking forward to taking Tess our chocolate Labrador for a walk, she loves being off the lead and running across the fields, always making sure that the sheep are not around.

We respect the laws of the countryside and the farmers; there are some dog walkers that still allow their dogs to chase the sheep which can cause the females to abort their lambs.

Justine is still on the yard, she told me that a friend of hers had a pony that needed someone to look after her; she was a beautiful chestnut welsh section C, her owner did not have time to take care of her and give her some TLC.

I casually mentioned this to Emma in conversation, as lately we had to be careful what we said, she was very quick to respond in a negative way.

I was pleasantly surprised as she showed an interest in what I was saying, she wanted to see the pony herself. Immediately I contacted Justine; she rang her friend and decided for Emma to see her and the pony the same evening.

Emma and I arrived just after 6.00pm. Lucky was still in the field along with many other horses. Caroline pointed her out, shouted her name and she came cantering over towards the gate where we were standing. Emma's face lit up,

"She is gorgeous." I was so pleased with her response. Caroline put on her head collar and asked Emma if she would like to lead her back to the yard.

I was watching Emma and looking for some positive body language, Caroline asked her if she could brush Lucky while she got her tack. Emma then rode her down a quiet lane. She was coping well; the pain in her back was not too bad. Lucky had such a broad back Emma felt comfortable riding her. It did not take long for her to decide what do about this pony. Within three days we had borrowed a horse trailer and collected her from Caroline and took her to our yard.

Over the next few weeks Monty and Lucky became inseparable, although she was used to being in a field with a large herd of horses, she settled much sooner than we expected. The partition between them both had a small opening where the horses could groom each other. Spring was in the air, Jim the owner of the stable yard prepared the fields for all the horses to graze. Eventually it had dried out enough for them to enjoy the fresh air on a permanent basis, until the autumn came. It was such a wonderful experience to watch them all cantering round together; they also stood around grooming each other in the sunshine.

Caroline was so happy Lucky had gone to a good home; she asked Emma if she wanted to buy her for a small sum. It would also save Caroline the expense and the responsibility as she and her boyfriend were saving up to get married and they had just bought a house. Emma was pleased to accept the invitation to own Lucky.

Unfortunately, the winter weather caused health problems for Emma. I managed to help as much as I could, but the rain and the strong winds made it impossible to ride Lucky regularly. She needed to be in a field, Monty was not too bad accepting that he had to stay in his stable, but Lucky was finding it hard as she had always been used to permanent turn- out. The work which entailed in looking after a pony is hard and strenuous. Mucking out every day and lunging in the paddock proved to be too much for Emma; although she tried so hard to achieve this, the damage to her back from her traumatic past caused her to contact Caroline, she was understanding when Emma explained her dilemma, between them they decided to find someone who could offer Lucky what she needed.

Emma set to on her computer to advertise Lucky for full loan with a beautiful photograph of her pony. There were quite a few responses, but each one did not match up to what Emma and Caroline were looking for; until Sarah a nice lady in her thirties rang and she sounded perfect. She came to see Lucky and immediately fell in love with her. She ticked all the right boxes.

Sarah invited Emma, Caroline, and me to see where Lucky would be stabled, and the yard also offered some turnout for the winter months. It was lovely she would be able to go hacking at the side of a river.

There would be no need to ride on the road, although Lucky was good on the roads. She just came out of the gate and onto bridle path through some fields where she can have a canter and then down to the river. It was perfect. Emma found it hard to let her go but she knew she had to.

She was upset for a while and missed going up to the stables which at the time was also therapeutic and kept her mind occupied.

Emma is now under a pain Consultant; she will always suffer with nerve pain in her back. The treatment is ongoing, and she will have to have injections on a regular basis, but it will give her some relief from the pain and allow her to live a reasonably normal life with her family. Regrettably, the Consultant said,

"No horse-riding or strenuous activities."

She had always put her energy into her children's wellbeing; she decided to take Ginny swimming with Kevin; at first it was hard because of the association she had with water; but she managed to overcome her thoughts and enjoy watching Ginny, although she was only young, she took to the pool like a duck to water.

She also got more involved with Darren and went to watch him do his archery, something his dad did with him while Emma was at the stables with Ginny. She enjoyed that experience and was so proud of him.

Then when all her children were tucked up in bed, she began her counselling coursework. Receiving excellent results and getting good feedback helped her self-esteem. She was still seeing Richard; but not for therapeutic reasons, he had offered to supervise her with her counselling. He was so proud of how brave she had been and how far she has come.

CHAPTER 21

My Feelings

I t is now over twelve months since I first spoke to DS McIntyre. I was beginning to feel disheartened, thinking the whole system is against Emma from getting any justice. Until I received a phone call from him asking if he could come and see us with his Detective Inspector. I would also be introducing Emma to him for the first time.

I was feeling quite positive about the meeting; however, Emma had reservations, she was frightened to think positive and prepared herself for a negative outcome.

I tried to convince her that the reason the investigation has took so long must be positive and hoped that since Kier Starmer the Director of Public Prosecutions, had changed the way the police and the Crown Prosecution Service looked at the method in which the victims of historic child sexual abuse were treated.

I was dreadfully wrong to make that decision as the DS explained that the reasons why the case against her Uncle David was dropped would still stand and he would not be brought in for questioning regarding her father's case.

Also, the reason for not charging her father would stand as Katherine had not changed her mind and would still undermine the case against him. I tried to convince the DS and his Inspector that Katherine was not there at the time her father was abusing Emma; so how can she say it did not happen?

The DS explained that every single person on the jury had to find the defendant guilty without reasonable doubt. He said,

"There is not enough evidence to convict him and without a possible conviction the Crown Prosecution Service will not allow the police to charge your father."

Emma had heard enough, she apologized as she had to go outside for a cigarette; she could not accept what they were saying any longer. She needed some air and time to think. While I was alone with them, I mentioned the tapes which showed Emma having her flashbacks, it was also on the tape Emma enlightening me as to what had just taken place and who had done those despicable things to her as a child.

The DS explained that was just a small amount of evidence that the prosecution could use.

I said,

"What about all the reports from her private Psychiatrist who had actually witnessed the horrific flashback?" Again, he replied,

"Yes, but it is not enough, unless Emma had told anyone at the time such as a professional person, her teacher, or a Doctor the CPS have nothing to prove it happened so they can get a conviction."

I mentioned that her father had allegedly raped his sister when she was only nine years old. The DS began to ask questions,

"How old was he at the time?" I said,

"Sixteen," he wrote something down, I explained that she told me just after I split up with my ex-husband and that I had to live with that information for years; she denied it soon after I told my daughter Katherine as I was worried for my Granddaughter Cindy. He said,

"Unless Anne was to come forward herself and make the complaint against her brother there was nothing they could do."

Then I too made my apologies and went outside to join Emma, I needed to know whether she was alright? She came back into the living room with tears in her eyes and exclaimed,

"That's it I have had enough, close the case."

I understood and had to reluctantly go along with Emma's wishes. She had no fight left in her; she did not want to be a victim any longer.

After I had seen the DS and the Inspector out Emma told me,

"Mum I have to get on with my life, I will channel all my anger, frustration and sadness into something positive."

I was proud of the way she was coping with the devastating news that they were not pursuing the case.

However, I was not, it is now 3.40am I feel sick to the stomach, angry with the police but also, I am disappointed with myself. I should have spoken up, told them that I can discredit all the evidence that her fathers' defence would bring up against Emma.

I should not have allowed myself to give in and obey Emma's wishes.

For the first time since my life turned upside down, I am feeling sorry for myself. I still have plenty of fight in me, I cannot just let it go, and for the past sixteen years of my life I have supported and looked after Emma. She does not know; she has no memory of how I put my life on hold.

I remember when I learned of the rape and abuse concerning my two daughters, I was so outraged; I channelled all my anger into my counselling career.

I had already started my Level One before Steve and I separated. I blame the assertiveness course which I had taken alongside of the counselling course. It encouraged me to look at myself, my strengths, and weaknesses. Through the work I was accomplishing I found out then that I had an inner strength and when our Tutor asked us all on a Monday morning what positive thing we had achieved over the weekend? I was able to announce in front of all my fellow students,

"I kicked my husband out." They were all flabbergasted at my statement especially the Tutor she said in a shocked manner,

"I didn't expect you to go that far with your positivity." We all laughed, and I was proud of myself.

I will never forget how things lead up to that weekend. Steve had never wanted me to work unless it was in any of our businesses. When I asked for permission to go to college, I had to be very diplomatic as he was so controlling.

It was towards the end of my first counselling course. He allowed me to attend on the assumption that it would only be the one course but while I was achieving good feedback and receiving results of which I did not think I was capable, I decided to carry on into my Level Two Counselling when my Tutor thought I should. She gave me the confidence to go for it. Things were a lot different when I arrived home, feeling pleased with myself only to find my husband drunk again. Katherine was still in hospital almost ready for being discharged.

Liam was occupied with studying and doing his Football.

The atmosphere at home was unbearable, Steve was drinking whiskey from about 10.30am to bedtime. He was in a bad mood most of the time, swearing and full of self-pity. I had tried many times to get him some help but his attitude towards me was disgusting.

After I had asked him to leave so Katherine could come home. I carried on with my Courses, eventually enrolling for the Level Three which would have enabled me to have the privilege of calling myself a Counsellor and make a career of it.

Alas, three months into the course; I could not afford the expenses of having to pay for supervision. I was at the position of starting to work with clients.

I had found a Medical Centre that was willing to take me on as a student and set me up with three clients a week; this meant I had to have regular supervision depending on the number of clients I was working with.

I was disappointed and upset that I could not afford to carry on with the course, so I decided to put it on hold, get a job and save up enough money to enable me to afford to complete it in the next twelve months.

I was lucky with my Counselling Certificates behind me I was able to get a job in our local hospital on the mental health wards.

I loved my work, and the money was beginning to mount up so I could eventually go back to college and complete my Level Three.

That was my intention, it was the year 2004.

Emma had been married for almost a year when she started with those terrible involuntary movements which were clinically known to be psychotic intensity flashbacks.

Kevin was still working, fortunately she only had Darren at home, my mum cared for him while I gave up my job as a Nursing Assistant to look after Emma.

My counselling career was now a figment of my imagination, Emma was my priority and has been for the last ten years.

Getting back to the present time of 2014. I look back to see what I have lost. I do not have any regrets at having to support Emma but at the same time I have always wanted justice, with her Uncle David and now with her father.

In my dreams I expected Emma's father to be found guilty in front of a jury. He and his brother-in-law to be given a custodial sentence.

I put a great deal of trust into the police and the CPS. Depending so much on a positive verdict so I could see my son and my grandson. Have a relationship with Katherine and the other four of my grandchildren. Beg their forgiveness at not being able to tell anyone that I was seeking justice against their father, hoping, and praying they would understand when I explain why I could not see them all this time as I did not want anything to jeopardize the case.

I am feeling quite selfish, I am pleased that Emma is strong enough to move on, she has plenty of support from Kevin's family and new friends. Ginny, Darren, and her husband are her most important priorities, she is putting her energy into them and her counselling career. She would love to involve her other children in her future, unfortunately she has not heard from Jodie for quite some time, although every effort has been made on Emma's part. Zak, she hopes to see him when he gets in touch later in life. Till then she has let them both know she is always there for them if they need her.

However, I am left empty, angry that I have not got the justice, as a mother I feel I deserve.

I am trying to put all my energy into writing this book, Richard has encouraged me to finish it and tell Emma's story hoping that it will help someone who has experienced a similar situation. But at the same time, I cannot let go of the anger I feel. All I ever wanted was to keep my family together.

I had one more I idea. I thought if I write a letter to my ex-husband, maybe if he has got any feelings and morals the true words of what I say might make him look at himself and tell his family the truth of what sins he has committed against his daughter and take responsibility for the upset and devastation he has caused.

Dear Steve,

I feel it is time I did something to help our family be happy and move on with their lives.

Please find it in your heart to do the right thing and make things better.

Emma has suffered long enough, and our children need to be able to live a happy and normal life together. This is causing a lot of heartache for our grandchildren, Jodie, Zak, Darren, Cindy,

Virginia, and Andrew. They have all been victims in this situation.

Surely the love that you have for your children and grandchildren will help you choose the right path. You and I have lived our lives, please allow our children to be able to love one another and be happy. Each one of our children were born out of the love we once shared. Please find it in your heart to tell them the truth so that they can move on with the rest of their lives in peace and harmony. You owe this to yourself as you too must be feeling their pain. Having been so close in the past they are all heartbroken and suffering. Their future lies in your hands now.

Did he receive it? No, I never sent it!

There is one consolation my ex-husband will eventually meet his maker and then he will have to repent and admit his sins.

I had been awake for most of the night, tossing and turning; I think I must have fallen asleep around four o'clock only to be woken up at 6.30am by Tess. I decided to take her for a walk before breakfast.

It was warm, I was walking briskly up the hill with Tess trotting slowly by my feet. I needed to clear my head of all the trash that was spinning around.

Then I reached the top, stopped at a five barred gate, and stood for a while just taking in the most spectacular view.

I looked towards the east the sun had risen and its silvery tentacles spread across the land.

The early morning mist was gradually lifting to reveal the most beautiful scenery.

I was mesmerized watching a kestrel hovering over the freshly cut grass diving down for its prey. In the distance I could see deer as they were coming towards me and Tess. They must have picked up our scent as they seemed to change direction in an instant. I watched as they each jumped over the fence into another field, then disappeared out of view.

There was no one about, I was conscious of the silence, there was nothing moving except the birds chirping and flying in and out of the hedgerow.

It was so peaceful; my mind was full of conflicting thoughts.

I realized then that I had to release the anger inside of me that had built up over the last fifteen years.

A weight seemed to lift from my shoulders as I made that decision.

I just do not know how to end this story as there is no ending!

Suddenly, the church bells rang in the distance, a warm feeling swept through my body I smiled to myself as I turned around and headed for home, now I can live my life without the obsession of looking for justice which caused so much pain and anguish, the shadow of resentment which was always hovering above me. Now I can let go and move on.

The end.

Milton Keynes UK
Ingram Content Group UK Ltd.
UKHW030715041024
449263UK00001B/36